Crucibles of Crisis

THEATER: Theory/Text/Performance

Enoch Brater, Series Editor
University of Michigan

Crucibles of Crisis

PERFORMING SOCIAL CHANGE

Edited by
Janelle Reinelt

Ann Arbor

THE UNIVERSITY OF MICHIGAN PRESS

For My Mother, Jessie Bettencourt Gobby

Copyright © by the University of Michigan 1996
Published in the United States of America by
The University of Michigan Press
Manufactured in the United States of America
⊗ Printed on acid-free paper
1999   1998   1997   1996   4   3   2   1

A CIP catalogue record for this book is available from the British Library.

Library of Congress Cataloging-in-Publication Data

Crucibles of crisis : performing social change / edited by Janelle
  Reinelt.
        p.   cm.
    Includes bibliographical references.
    ISBN 0-472-09618-4 (hardcover : alk. paper). — ISBN 0-472-06618-8
  (paperback : alk. paper)
    1. Theater and society. 2. Drama—Social aspects.   I. Reinelt,
  Janelle G.
  PN2049.C78   1996   96-4110
                                                              CIP

"Subjectivity and Socialism: Feminist Discourses in East Germany" by Katrin Sieg was originally published in *Genders* 22 (1955), pp. 105–33. Reprinted by permission of New York University Press.

"Staging Whiteness: Beckett, Havel, Maponya" by Anthony O'Brien was originally published in *Theater Journal* (March 1994), pp. 45–62. Reprinted by permission of the Johns Hopkins University Press.

"Theater and Terrorism: Griselda Gambaro's *Information for Foreigners*" by Diana Taylor was originally published in *Theater Journal* (May 1990), pp. 165–82. Reprinted by permission of Johns Hopkins University Press.

Contents

Janelle Reinelt

Introduction

> If the cultural world for which one is fighting is a living and necessary fact, its expansiveness will be irresistible and it will find its artists.
> —Antonio Gramsci

> We have to emphasize that hegemony is not singular; indeed that its own internal structures are highly complex, and have continually to be renewed, recreated and defended; and by the same token, that they can be continually challenged and in certain respects modified....We have to think again about the sources of that which is not corporate; of those practices, experiences, meanings, values which are not part of the effective dominant culture.
> —Raymond Williams

What is the relationship of politics to culture? How does social change result in cultural change—or can various cultural practices initiate or precipitate change? If a simple base/superstructure model inadequately explains the dynamics of art and society, then how *do* they articulate? How does novelty emerge in representation? Looking back on this century, what has been the relationship between performance and social change?

This set of questions arises out of a desire to probe, in order to renew, the potential of the performing arts to participate in critique and social trans-formation.[1] The fin de siècle in the West seems marked by the gradual eclipse of the efficacy of live performance as an art form under the pressures of media saturation, the capitalization and commodification of all art, and the desiccated fragmentations of an obsolete opposition between high and popular culture. Many performance scholars and practitioners think the time is at hand when the live performance of staged texts may be seen as the quaint relic of a previous age; some of us, no doubt, think it is high time. This collection of essays is, in one sense, a rearguard action in that it makes an argument for the renewed viability and vitality of performance as a trans-formative social practice by examining certain twentieth-century nodal points at which theater and dance could and did contribute to the construction of new social formations. In another sense, however, reading through *Crucibles of Crisis* also reveals the limits on the performing arts' claim to any privileged role in the production of culture. Specific coordinates of space, time, and sociopolitical structures always circumscribe and partially determine the horizon of possibility. Thus, I make only modest claims here—born, perhaps, of the postmodern wariness of totalizing pronouncements about the nature of anything, coupled with my disappointment with much of contemporary Western performance practice, which seems too often empty and socially bankrupt.

This collection is also a part of the search for a post-Marxist theory that can illuminate the constitutive function of art in culture and its role in articulating a vision of a radically democratic sociality in the "age of Lenin in ruins."[2] For, while the interpretive framework of class conflict, Enlightenment progress, and revolution is indeed "ruined" definitively, there are many projects framed and understood through the discourses of Marxism that are not only not obsolete but more urgent now in a time of sociopolitical redefinition and flux. One such project is the capacity of cultural production to support or subvert the dominant social formation. Raymond Williams, writing in 1973, offered a detailed examination of the relationship of "superstructural" activities to the mode of production (base), theorizing the important spaces left open within hegemonic culture where novelty might emerge or contestations appear. This formulation still seems useful and empowering, even as we are poised on the brink of the year 2000:

> No mode of production, and therefore no dominant society or order of society, and therefore no dominant culture, in reality exhausts the full range of human practice, human energy, human intention (this range is not the inventory of some original "human nature" but, on the contrary, is that extraordinary range of variations, both practiced and imagined, of which human beings are and have shown themselves to be capable. . . . I am saying that in relation to the full range of human practice at any one time, the dominant mode is a conscious selection and organization. . . . But there are always sources of actual human practice which it neglects or excludes.[3]

Williams seems a precursor and "fellow traveler" of those contemporary theorists of color, women, and gay and lesbian critics who have fashioned a location on the margins and in the interstices of dominant cultural practices—a location that serves as a site of enunciation, empowerment, and pressure on the center. He observes that often the practices that are "neglected" are allowed to develop until they are recognized as dangerous, and then are attacked or repressed. However, not only is the dominant formation itself changed by what it absorbs, but also these disparate social practices may sometimes coalesce to challenge its dominance. The first two essays in this collection, Harry Elam's narrative of the performance of Amiri Baraka's *Slave Ship* during the height of the Civil Rights Movement in the United States, and Mary Trotter's description of the role of women in resisting English domination by helping construct an Irish national identity onstage provide specific historical coordinates of time and space for a full-fledged oppositional theater practice. They are positive first examples of contexts in which theater played a vital role in social struggle. Trotter's essay also demonstrates the coalescence of disparate groups in order to achieve the shared goal of political and cultural legitimacy. "Theater within the nationalist movement," she writes, "became a site of collaboration across religion, class, and ultimately, gender lines."

These essays are followed, in what at first may seem to be a deeply cynical placement on my part, by Adam Versényi's investigation of the relationship between the Mexican Revolution, religion, and theater. Demonstrating that the theater is not necessarily liberatory, Versényi shows how theater has served as an ideological tool of colonizing mendicants and also of the revolutionary, anticlerical government. "Where the mendicants insisted upon the salvific powers of Christianity, the revolutionary government preached a secular gospel that had to be followed to attain a state of grace. Both brands of millenarianism found it necessary to convert masses of people to avoid apocalypse, and in both cases those masses of people were of indigenous descent." Education and theater were the institutions that became crucibles of crisis in both historic moments. Reading Versényi after Elam and Trotter clarifies the *availability* of performance for many kinds of ideological work, radical and reactionary. Yet Versényi's essay also points to ways in which both the Cultural Mission Programme and the *teatro campesino* seem to have slipped the moorings of their sponsors to forge at least the possibility, as well as in numerous instances the actuality, of a transformative theater, one that does lead to positive social change. Performance can overrun ideology's containment.

Crucibles of Crisis images a vessel in which critical but nondeterminate transformations take place. The title also implies a test: one of the meanings of the word *crucible,* testing the limits and possibilities of crisis, provides a specific way to view each of the essays included here and also charts the larger concerns of the anthology. For *crisis* here is intended to be a positive possibility as well as a signifier of danger and extremity. Paul Ricoeur, writing about the circular space linking ideology and utopia in praxis, comments on the open and creative possibility poised in the transitional moment in all crises.

> What particularly interests me in the notion of utopia is that it is an imaginative variation on power. . . . The result of reading a utopia is that it puts into question what presently exists; it makes the actual world seem strange. Usually we are tempted to say that we cannot live in a way different from the way we presently do. The utopia, though, introduces a sense of doubt as it shatters the obvious. . . . There is an experience of the contingency of order.[4]

This indeterminate possibility arising in the heart of the given is the gap through which novelty enters discourse, through which agency is constructed and expressed—often randomly, always multiply, and occasionally fortuitously. Between rehearsing the new and contesting the old, there is a moment of productive confusion.

I do not mean to imply the total contingency of history. On the contrary, the accumulation of examples in these essays of specific historical instances when theater and dance performances played a shaping and constitutive role in an emerging social formation affirms the tension between causality and spontaneity in social change as something that can be grasped and understood, perhaps even modeled.[5] Certain forms of postmodern and poststructural critique, including its Marxist formulation (Althusser's anesthetizing theory of interpellation) have seemed to dematerialize agency and opposition, troubling feminists, postcolonial critics, and all those associated with "the new social movements," as they are sometimes called, although most are thirty years old by now.[6] The answer does not lie in reengaging what Chantal Mouffe and Ernesto Laclau have called the "Jacobin imaginary," with its images of unified subjectivity, homogeneous sociability, and a rational and teleological historical narrative. Rather, by emphasizing historical discontinuity and the confluence of heterogeneous and sometimes contradictory impulses that make up a given social formation, a space for resistance, novelty, or change appears—however unmarked—constantly available.

Materialist feminist, queer, and postcolonial critics have proved especially helpful in theorizing political possibility from within the productive confusions and contradictions of their location on the margins—without reinscribing essentialist notions of race, sex, gender, and nationality. Judith Butler, in insisting on the performative character not only of gender but of sex itself, has pointed to repetition and mimicry as forms of resistance that repeat but also contest the authority of sex and gender categories. Sometimes accused of voluntarism,[7] Butler actually negotiates the negative space between ideology and utopia—in this case between sexual identity and nonidentity.

Sex is both produced and destabilized in the course of this reiteration. As a sedimented effect of a reiterative or ritual practice, sex acquires its naturalized effect, and yet, it is also by virtue of this reiteration that gaps and fissures are opened up as the constitutive instabilities in such constructions, as that which escapes or exceeds the norm, as that which cannot be wholly defined or fixed by the repetitive labor of that norm. This instability is the *de*constituting possibility in the very process of repetition, the power that undoes the very effects by which "sex" is stabilized, the possibility to put the consolidation of the norms of "sex" into a potentially productive crisis.[8]

These constitutive instabilities, which accompany any reiteration of the hegemonic, offer a negative space, initially unmarked but potentially oppositional. Katrin Sieg's essay on "Subjectivity and Socialism" illustrates this specific process through her analysis of German Democratic Republic (GDR) "protocols," women's anonymous testimonies, arranged into collective oral histories: "The protocol volumes illuminate precisely those contradictions the accumulation and intensification of which precipitated the ideological collapse." Sieg treats the protocols as forms of performance, considering them alongside two "traditional" plays as social practices that illuminate the role of representation in, first, the demise of GDR socialist ideology, and, more recently, the critique of the mode of representation of the protocols themselves and the consequences for a problematic postwar relationship between feminists of the East and West.

Several of the essays point to the marshaling of latent instabilities in performances, which helped to form constellations of opposition in times of crisis. Patricia Schroeder's essay on women playwrights during the Harlem Renaissance highlights the new space for representation of African American women created by women playwrights in the 1920s as part of the general struggle to define African American culture. Although these plays could be seen as supplementing both a hegemonic white theater culture and a black male-dominated debate over aesthetic strategies appropriate for representing African Americans, Schroeder stresses their important legacy to contemporary writers: "Through their attention to representations of blackness and to the various dramatic forms appropriate to that task, the theater artists of the Harlem Renaissance reconfigured the field of performance inherited by African American playwrights, forever transforming images of blackness." Schroeder makes an important point about the present-day consolidation of past strategies that enables new work. *Rachel,* a play intentionally addressed to mothers, about a protagonist who refuses to mother children who will only be persecuted and oppressed, catches in its controversy the "extraordinary tensions" of motherhood for African American women, staging contradictions that have now accumulated a history of representation in the works of other black women such as Shirley Graham, Lorraine Hansberry, Ntozake Shange, and Adrienne Kennedy.

What I have been describing is a process of retroactive opposition: as history overtakes itself, to gloss Brecht, it is subject to criticism from and revision of the immediately following period's point of view.[9] Both Sieg and Schroeder document this process—the reworking of the possible meanings of past performances for novel formulations available only from the vantage point of the present context. Important in their own times, these "texts" are revalued from a different vantage point in the wake of post-1970s feminism, the demise of GDR socialism, and the interventions of African American feminists in critiques of white feminist and black male writing.

Retroactive opposition also appears within the context of postcolonial discourse. The necessity to theorize a space for the postcolonial subject that does not simply repeat the colonizer/colonized dyad has yielded an imaginative and powerful body of work, rich in insights for this inquiry. Stuart Hall, Paul Gilroy, Homi Bhabha, Gayatri Spivak, and many others have begun to decenter the white male European subject and to rethink the relationship between colonial and native cultures.

The middle section of the book focuses on South Africa and provides examples of retroactive oppositional readings of performances and also an example of a culture in the midst of a current and urgent crisis, where the moment between ideology and utopia is suspended in the negative space of possibility and danger and where performance dances and writes but is not yet legible. Loren Kruger examines the New African movement of the 1930s and in particular Herbert Dhlomo's contribution to the recognition and celebration of "the fundamentally international character of African national consciousness." With an emphasis on African appropriation of European civilization for its own purposes and a belief in the positive benefits of "modernization," the New Africans created theater in the 1930s that "highlight[ed] the critical limits of familiar oppositions between elite and popular, imported and indigenous, literary and oral culture." Within the New African formation, of course, were various contradictions based on the tension between European concepts of parliamentary democracy and civil rights and the concomitant exclusion of African blacks from participation in governing. With the repression of apartheid and the virtual closing down of African society, a more militant protest drama replaced the somewhat genteel drama of the New Africans. Kruger charts the relationship of 1970s protest drama (e.g., that of Shezi, Manaka, and Maponya) to Dhlomo's late play, *The Pass*. She also raises questions about the usefulness of a reappraisal of New African drama for the purposes of contemporary attempts to fashion a new theater for the new, postapartheid, multiracial South Africa.

South Africa, at the beginning of its transition to postapartheid status, offers a historic space between ideology and utopia in which the crisis of representation is visible. As Albie Sachs once wrote, "Can we say we have begun to grasp the full dimensions of the new country and the new people that are struggling to give birth to themselves, or are we still trapped in the multiple ghettos of the apartheid imagination?" South Africa's theater has had a very clear social and cultural function, and yet now it is also a theater suspended in nonbeing before the formation of new social practice. It is not clear what kind of theater will follow apartheid—it is in the making, indeterminate, full of possibility and danger. The possibility is that it may aid in the formation of a new imagination appropriate to a postapartheid, multiracial, multicultural society. The danger is that it will only reinscribe or reverse the categories and power relations of the previous social formation. One of the frustrations inherent in the poststructural critique is the knowledge that such moments will unfold with a logic that cannot be controlled or managed by a master narrative or a determinate shape. Instead, emergent enunciation empowers and shapes a future the materiality of which is temporarily deferred. Describing the project of postcolonial culture, Homi Bhabha writes:

To reconstitute the discourse of cultural difference demands not simply a change of cultural contents and symbols; a replacement within the same time-frame of representation is never adequate. It requires a radical revision of the social temporality in which emergent histories may be written, the rearticulation of the "sign" in which cultural identities may be inscribed. And contingency as the signifying time of counter-hegemonic strategies is not a celebration of "lack" or "excess" or a self-perpetuating series of negative ontologies. Such "indeterminism" is the mark of the conflictual yet productive space in which the arbitrariness of the sign of cultural signification emerges within the regulated boundaries of social discourse.[10]

These emergent enunciations are the site of performance as social change. South African theater offers a glimpse of this elusive yet critical practice.

One of the most powerful side effects of postcolonial theater has been the refiguration of received Western theatrical tradition in light of this critique. Anthony O'Brien and W. B. Worthen demonstrate another aspect of retroactive opposition in reconfiguring high modernist playwrights such as Samuel Beckett and in exposing the ideological substructure of supposedly metaphysical movements such as poor theater or the theater of the absurd. In short, the availability of cross-reading between cultures and theater performances allows the hegemonic to be interrogated, exposed, or even subverted. O'Brien reads Samuel Beckett's *Catastrophe* and Václav Havel's *The Mistake* through Maishe Maponya's *Gangsters* to reveal the first-world presumptions of authority, gender, and race in Beckett and the second-world revision of authority but not gender or race in Havel, while simultaneously infecting those texts with the possibility of foregrounding their myopia, of making it the subject of performance. O'Brien calls this intervention "staging whiteness," and writes, "To uncenter the whiteness of the white supremacist theater means, in the first instance, to *stage* that whiteness, to normalize it within a different set of rules. But that cannot be done without bringing in its wake an effect of retrospect on the white theater that has been decentered, the whiteness of its writing made newly legible."

Similarly, W. B. Worthen is able to consider the staging of the usually invisible ideology of the theater of the absurd as an effect of Fugard's use of it in staging *The Island*: "To see the absurdist texture of *The Island* as a decoy, a means of enabling the subversive reading of the obscene, is to suggest not so much that prison is an instance of the metaphysics of the absurd nor that the politics of apartheid are absurd. It is to suggest instead that the ideology of the absurd is invisible to the apparatus of the apartheid state. . . . In *The Island,* the metaphysic of the absurd is the ideology of the state." These insights into the working of the theatrical apparatus in theatrical representation show its usual complicity in hegemonic repetition while also marking an occasion for rupturing the seamless function of period, genre, and style.

The possibilities for novelty in theatrical representation during times of crisis also unleash an understandable anxiety in the face of the absence of familiar practices. In writing about Poland after the revolutions of 1989, Gregg Dion is able to describe the state of artists who, once part of a solidified oppositional identity—although rife with contradictions—find themselves after the revolution without a clear sense of purpose or social identity: "Although the Theatre of the 8th Day had survived twenty years of attack by devoting itself to a common purpose, in the new capitalist society a single purpose might not sustain it." The East-West conflict afforded fixed positions of hegemony and contestation, which have been upset by the seeming collapse of antagonisms. In fact, this is another moment of potentially creative possibility for the representation of new forms of sociability. As a consequence of the collapse of communism, a renegotiation of the meanings of democracy is inevitable but still unformed. As Chantal Mouffe has pointed out, "With the demise of Marxism, the illusion that we can finally dispense with the notion of antagonism has become widespread. This belief is fraught with danger, since it leaves us unprepared in the face of unrecognized manifestations of antagonism."[11] Convinced that distinctive political identities are necessary for a democratic politics that depends on recognizing articulated and contending differences, she sees the "blurring of political frontiers between left and right" as harmful because it makes establishing political identities difficult. For a company like Theatre of the 8th Day, the present "identity crisis" opens up the opportunity to participate in representing possibilities for new modes of sociability and subjectivity and beyond that even a new meaning for theater within that society. It could, however, also easily foreclose such opportunities through a dispersal of energy and purpose, leaving theater to the capitalist model of market-financed entertainments.

The issue of spectatorship and its role in the construction of meaning serves, in Diana Taylor's essay about Argentina, as a kind of counterpoint to Dion's emphasis on the identity of a theater company in a moment of crisis. In Taylor's discussion of Griselda Gambaro's *Information for Foreigners,* she points out the dangers of an oppositional theater falling prey to an economy of violence that turns critique into spectacle almost as quickly as Gambaro can dislocate its central perspective as a voyeur apparatus. Stressing the specificity of Argentina and the necessity for local audiences for her work, Gambaro unmasks the "vital role a population plays in a system of terror."

Lynn Conner's study of the socialist agendas of modern dance in the United States during the 1930s concludes on a note that might be characterized as elegiac (though not necessarily by Conner). She writes about the modern dance field in New York City during a brief period of radicalism when the Left found itself in a position of influence. In this case, "social change in the culture at large brought about a short-lived but significant reconfiguration of the modern dance." While Martha Graham and Doris Humphrey initially rejected involvement in any social agenda, insisting on a pure aestheticism, each came in time to associate herself with the Popular Front and to experiment with dances that were thematic (concerning the Spanish Civil War, for instance). Of course, after 1939, the American Left fell apart as a new world war took shape and the Soviet Union signed the nonaggression pact with Germany. Modern dance moved away from engaged mimesis. In Conner's narrative of those years, the double bind of "radical movements gone mainstream" is made visible. The early 1930s were the most radical years. The Popular Front was an expansive movement that by the mid-1930s was spreading itself thin as a radical social agenda even as it attracted the support of moderates and liberals. This dilution of purpose increased the mass following of the movement, but the new energy eventually dispersed as the period changed from one in which, in the wake of the Depression, there was a concrete need for imagining an alternative social order to one in which consolidation and conservation became expedient in the wake of the world at war. Economic necessity shifted, too, driven by the war industry, and the "radical moment" passed. The United States has never really had another, in my view, although the civil rights struggles (with which I began this book) and the antiwar movement of the 1960s also held some unrealized promise for widespread social change. In fact, each of the subsequent movements, feminist, ecological, and gay and lesbian, have opened up tremendous challenges to theatrical representation as they opened up potentials for social change. In the absence of true coalition, these have not yet come to fruition.

The essays in this collection document a wide variety of instances when the performing arts participated vigorously in social struggle, contributing to new social formations and/or leaving rich legacies for future artists and scholars. Spread across the century, touching on seven countries, moving from the "high art" of modern dance to the popular culture of the *teatro campesino,* they demonstrate and embody some answers to the questions with which I began this essay. Tightly circumscribed by their own temporality and local geography, these narratives from 1930s New York to the 1960s in the American South, from Johannesburg, to Prague, to Paris, call attention to historically situated specificity as the best analytic tool for grasping the relationship of performance(s) to social change. In many cases, these essays have centered on issues of Western nationalism, its definition and contestation. They do also, however, suggest some general insights into the workings of culture. As a social practice, performance is both constrained and free. The freedom is often elusive, chimerical, short-lived. It appears when many diverse aspects of a situation or context coalesce to produce a crucible of crisis in which performances can play a central role. That this process is a little mysterious, or, rather, part determined and part accident, makes a promise to the future. In his prison notebooks, Gramsci tried to think through the effort to create a vital, engaged art.

To fight for a new art would mean to fight to create new individual artists, which is absurd since artists cannot be created artificially. One must speak of a struggle for a new culture, that is, for a new moral life that cannot but be intimately connected to a new intuition of life, until it becomes a new way of feeling and seeing reality and, therefore, a world intimately ingrained in "possible artists" and "possible works of art."[12]

NOTES

1. In this book, "performing arts" refers to theater and dance. The newer meanings of *performance,* having to do with other social practices taken from everyday life and culture, also arise in some of the essays. Here I mean formal, traditional, staged performances of plays or dances.

2. This is a gloss on Arthur and Marilouise Kroker's stimulating discussion, *Ideology and Power in the Age of Lenin in Ruins* (New York: St. Martin's, 1991). Apropos of this post-Marxist moment, they write: "When the Berlin Wall finally came tumbling down, all of the old comfortable markers of political debate suddenly shattered, revealing in its wake a desperate urgency to rethink the meaning of ideology and power in a world dominated by the eclipse of the political legitimation of state socialism and by the seeming triumph everywhere now of the rituals of primitive capitalism" (ix).

3. Raymond Williams, "Base and Superstructure in Marxist Cultural Theory," in *Problems in Materialism and Culture* (London: Verso, 1980), 43.

4. Paul Ricoeur, *Lectures on Ideology and Utopia,* ed. George H. Taylor (New York: Columbia University Press, 1986), 299–300.

5. Chantal Mouffe and Ernesto Laclau, interpreting Rosa Luxemburg's "spontaneism," write: "In a revolutionary situation, it is impossible *to fix the literal sense* of each isolated struggle, because each struggle overflows its own literality and comes to represent . . . a simple moment of a more global struggle against the system" (*Hegemony and Socialist Strategy: Toward a Radical Democratic Politics* [London: Verso, 1985], 10–11).

6. See, for example, bell hooks, "Postmodern Blackness," *Yearning: Race, Gender, and Cultural Politics* (Boston: South End, 1990), 23–32; Cornel West, "The Postmodern Crisis of Black Intellectuals," in *Prophetic Thought in Postmodern Times* (Monroe, Me.: Common Courage, 1993), 87–118; Christine Di Stefano, "Dilemmas of Difference: Feminism, Modernity, and Postmodernism," in *Feminism/Postmodernism,* ed. Linda J. Nicholoson (New York and London: Routledge, 1990), 76; and Janet Wolff, "Prospects and Problems for a Postmodern Feminism: An Introduction," in *Feminine Sentences: Essays on Women and Culture* (Cambridge: Polity, 1990), 1–11.

7. See Janelle Reinelt, "Staging the Invisible: The Crisis of Visibility in Theatrical Representation," *Text and Performance Quarterly* 14 (April 1994): 97–107.

8. Judith Butler, *Bodies That Matter* (London and New York: Routledge, 1993), 10.

9. Cf. Bertolt Brecht, *Brecht on Theater,* ed. John Willett (New York: Hill and Wang, 1964), 140.

10. Homi Bhabha, *The Location of Culture* (London and New York: Routledge, 1994), 171–72.

11. Chantal Mouffe, *The Return of the Political* (London and New York: Verso, 1993), 2.

12. Antonio Gramsci, *Selections from Cultural Writings,* ed. David Forgacs and Geoffrey Nowell-Smith, trans. William Boelhower (Cambridge: Harvard University Press, 1985), 98.

1.

Harry J. Elam, Jr.

Social Urgency, Audience Participation, and the Performance of *Slave Ship* by Amiri Baraka

In the spring of 1970, the Free Southern Theater[1] toured a production of the black social-protest play *Slave Ship*, by Amiri Baraka, to rural black communities in the Deep South. The production was directed by Gilbert Moses, who had previously mounted the play to controversy and acclaim at the Chelsea Theater Center in Brooklyn, New York, in November of 1969. Black audiences along the southern tour route, like those in New York, often responded vociferously to the production. At one performance of *Slave Ship* in Baton Rouge, Louisiana, an aroused audience bolstered by the militant participatory action of the production stood at the end of the performance ready to riot. If not for the fact that the doors of the theater remained bolted until the fervor had subsided somewhat, this audience certainly would have acted on its resolve.[2] At another performance of *Slave Ship*, in West Point, Mississippi, the entire audience rose to its feet and joined with the actors, waving fists and chanting, "We gonna rise up!"[3] According to some observers, these collective, participatory reactions inside the theater translated into social action outside of theater. Director Moses reported that in certain southern cities the numbers of black people participating in voter registration efforts dramatically increased immediately following performances of *Slave Ship*.[4]

Despite accounts of increased activity in voter registration drives in southern cities following performances of *Slave Ship*, establishing a direct correlation between social action and the social protest performance is problematic. The social efficacy of social protest theater remains extremely difficult to prove. Rarely are posttheatrical events documented. Further-more, attributing postperformance activism solely to theatrical attendance is impossible when a myriad of other social and psychological circumstances exist. However, through reviews, firsthand accounts and other qualitative and quantitative methodologies, it is possible to analyze how elements within a social protest production like *Slave Ship* function, in conjunction with external sociopolitical conditions, to produce collective, participatory responses from theater audiences. I believe that the evidence of such com-munal interaction and participation can provide significant insight into the efficacy of the social protest performance. Audience participation, I con-tend, not only alters conventional exchanges between audience and stage but testifies to the meaning of the play's action for that participant commu-nity. Hence, the purpose of this essay is to examine how the construction and structure of the production, the social and theatrical environments, and the cultural and social makeup of the audiences all contributed to making the performances of *Slave Ship* participatory experiences.

Slave Ship, through sparse dialogue, music, sound, and movement, chronicles African American history from its origins in Africa, through the oppressive experiences of Africans aboard slave ships during the Middle Pas-sage, up to the struggles for civil rights and black power in the 1960s. For the Chelsea Theater Center production of *Slave Ship,* director Moses attempted to transform the performance space into a slave ship, a critical his-torical site of black degradation. Set designer Eugene Lee, resident designer for the Trinity Square Repertory Theater in Providence, Rhode Island, designed a set, in consultation with Moses, that captured "the feeling of a slave ship that if cut in half the audience could see into. In fact, it actually rocked back and forth."[5] As a historical site of unconscionable oppression, the slave ship potently communicated to its spectators an African American heritage of struggle and survival.

Yet in the Moses production of the Baraka text, the slave ship symbol contained not only historical connotations but immediate relevance for its spectators as well. Moses and Baraka wanted the audience for *Slave Ship* to understand that "America in a lot of senses is just a replay or a continuation of that same slave ship, that it's not changed."[6] As the action of the Moses production shifted in geographical locale and historical period, the domi-nant, iconographic symbol of the slave ship remained. Kimberly Benston observed:

> Baraka [Moses] transforms the entire theater into the slave ship whose
> black passengers' historical journey is from first enslavement to con-

temporary revolution, and whose mythical journey is from African civilization through enslavement to spiritual resendency.[7]

By maintaining the slave ship as the setting for all of the play's action, Moses connected African American experiences of the past and present. Through this visual representation, Moses intended that the spectators should understand that African American existence in America remained slavelike, devoid of a sense of belonging or ownership.

Moses purposefully created the sensation, for the audience, that they were aboard a slave ship. He staged the play environmentally; the whole theater became a performance space "where action might erupt at any point. Action could happen in back of you or right beside you."[8] The spectators endured their own personal Middle Passage. The audience witnessed slaves in the ship's hold being pitched and tossed about. They heard the slaves scream, cough, and vomit. One slave woman was raped, another killed herself, a third gave birth, all as the audience watched. Moses eliminated any distance the audience members maintained from each other or from the performers. As Walter Kerr remarked, "black bodies seem to come straight through the floor of the slave ship."[9] The production disrupted the spectators' normal expectations of theatrical proxemics and aesthetic distance as they sat extremely close together on hard, uncomfortable, wooden benches. Don Isaacs observed that the positioning of the slave ship set and the benches "forced the audience to hunch over to see what was happening during the first half of the play."[10] The performance violated the audience's space and disrupted its comfort and safety within the theater. As a result, attendance at *Slave Ship* held actual physical consequences for the audience.

By reproducing the site of oppression and its accompanying sensations, Moses forced the spectators to become more active participants in the theatrical event. At one point in the performance, slaves were auctioned to members of the audience. Such confrontational events within the performance compelled the audience to participate. Jerry Tallmer of the *New York Post* reported that, on the night he attended the production, "A beautiful little black boy of about 10 was 'sold' to drama critic Edith Oliver of the *New Yorker*."[11] As the production bombarded their sensibilities, the spectators experienced firsthand the uncertainty of confinement. The treatment that they confronted represented the real crowding and discomfort that slaves encountered within the hold of a slave ship. By trespassing the normal barriers that separate audience and performers, Moses created an atmosphere of disorientation and even hysteria.[12] Moses believed that the discomfort and

FIG. 1. Auction block scene from *Slave Ship* by Amiri Baraka, Free South-
ern Theater production directed by Gilbert Moses, New Orleans,
Louisiana, 1970. (Photo by Larry Songy, courtesy Free Southern Theater
Collection, Amistad Research Center, Tilton Hall, Tulane University,
New Orleans.)

dislocation of the spectators would make them more susceptible to the
play's messages of militancy and revolution.

To encourage audience participation, Moses and his performers, in
their rehearsals, experimented with what he termed "emotional space."[13]
Emotional space connoted the distance between the notes of a song, two
lines of dialogue, or two bars of music. These moments of silence were
taut, filled with anticipation for the spectators. Effective orchestration of
emotional space, manipulating the silences and pauses, could create a feeling of anxiousness and tension. The idea of emotional space came from
Moses's training with Paul Sills and had much in common with the practices of the experimentalists Peter Brook and Richard Schechner. Moses,
however, appropriated this technique for the purpose of fomenting audi-

ence participation and militant outrage. In his experiments with emotional space, music played an integral role. Moses, who wrote significant portions of the music for the *Slave Ship* production himself, brought in five musicians to assist the actors in rehearsal in their attempts to activate and control emotional space. The rehearsals resulted in the creation of a rhythm that in performance, according to Moses, "produced a communal euphoria and a cognizance of a cultural commonality."[4] He intended his manipulation of emotional space to help stimulate collective, celebratory protest in the theater.

Moses believed that in order for the performance of *Slave Ship* to achieve communion with and elicit participation from its audiences, his performers needed to be committed to black activism. The performers in *Slave Ship,* however, were professional actors cast through an audition process. The level of social commitment varied among the cast members. Given the theatrical background of his cast, Moses, himself an experienced professional, could have chosen to draw principally on the performers' professional experience and focus his rehearsal process on conventional performance techniques such as blocking, movement, and motivation. Yet, because Moses wanted his audiences to accept the performers as authentic black activists, he initiated rehearsal practices intended to help the performers persuade their audiences of their authenticity. Moses attempted to develop the performers' commitment to black liberation through the rehearsal process. At the initial rehearsals, Moses had the cast read and study African and African American history and Yoruba language and culture. They read and discussed current philosophies of black power. Rehearsal rituals attempted to bring the performers together as a cohesive ensemble. The actors worked to develop a greater awareness of the social context of the performance and of the objectives of arousing the political consciousness and militant sentiments of their black audiences.

It would be naive to assume that the entire *Slave Ship* cast became politicized through the rituals of rehearsal. Still, by compelling the actors to engage in consciousness-raising activities, by emphasizing the importance of activism and of communing with the audience, Moses and the rehearsal process of *Slave Ship* did reorient the professional actors' thinking about the performance and their roles within it. The production required the actors to physically, spiritually, and emotionally interact with their audience. The prominence of this audience interaction, as well as Moses's focus on the signifying intentions of the performance, required the professional actors to employ different skills and even to conceive of themselves differently.

Accordingly, their training in black history, cultural nationalism, and social commitment constituted a prominent component in their preparation for performance. This training directed the performers to conceive of performing in *Slave Ship* as a means to the end of inciting audience participation and outrage. Moses's rehearsal process encouraged them to perceive of themselves as socially committed black artisans and to recognize "being an activist" as "exercising the highest form of art."[15] Moses believed that through his rehearsal process the cast became committed to "communing with the audience; to coming together and healing; to raising awareness to a new level."[16] Moses considered the ensemble bonding of the performers in rehearsal to be an important precursor to the desired communion of the performers with the audience.

However, attributing the achievements of the performance of *Slave Ship* solely to the cast's development of a greater cultural consciousness is overly simplistic and diminishes the aesthetic achievement of Moses and his actors. The rehearsals as well as the performances of *Slave Ship* required creativity, improvisational skills, and adaptability. Despite the performers' indoctrination into the black liberation cause, they still needed a high level of artistic skill and technical proficiency to effect Moses's directoral concept and to engage the audience.

In order to increase the signifying potential and emotional investment of his performers, Moses employed the techniques of white experimentalists Grotowski, Schechner, and Artaud in his rehearsal process.[17] Moses's slave ship and its inhabitants, to a significant degree, emulated Grotowski's representation of a Jewish concentration camp, its horrors, and its victims in his seminal work staged with the Polish Laboratory Theater, *Akropolis*. Grotowski trained his actors, in a theater of personal, psychological cruelty, to self-penetrate, to reveal their inner souls with primal intensity. Similarly, Moses explored the psychological and physical pain of the black pre- and post-slavery experience. The use of Grotowskian principles foregrounded the authentic emotions of the performer. Through sounds, grunts, groans, and internal and external pain, the performers not only recaptured but relived the horrors of the Middle Passage and their personal experiences with discrimination. The objective was to further the performers' ability to communicate emotional outrage and militant determination to the audience.

In his Performance Garage, Richard Schechner experimented with ensemble acting techniques and environmental theater. Schechner intended to reorient the actor-audience relationship. Moses also wanted to alter the audience-performer relationship. He sensitized his performers to the concept of working as an ensemble and drawing the audience into the theatrical environment. Moses also appropriated the Artaudian concept of a hypnotic, trancelike theater that bombards the senses of the audience. Following Artaud, Moses worked on the performers' gestural and nonverbal communication as a means of influencing audience behavior and directing its actions.

Moses's employment of the theories of Grotowski, Schechner, and Artaud furthered the performers' articulation of the signifying intentions of the performance. In so doing, he expanded and even subverted the objectives of his predecessors' performance theories. While Grotowski imagined his theater as a therapeutic experience and Artaud expected his bombardment of violent cruel images to purge the audience's propensity for violence, Moses intended to arouse his spectators' militancy and direct them to take action in their own lives. Moses sought to develop performers capable of provoking an audience's theatrical participation and political outrage. The experimental performance techniques appropriated by Moses helped his performers to formulate their performative behavior as a sign that indicated to the audience the need for revolutionary social action. These techniques, appropriated by Moses, worked in consort with educative training in black nationalism and social activism to support the subversive, oppositional agenda of Moses and his production of *Slave Ship*.

Because the plot and character delineation of *Slave Ship* were so sparse, the other elements of the production increased in significance. The performance of *Slave Ship* emphasized gestures, sounds, symbols, and movements over the spoken word. Through spectacle, music, sounds, and smells, *Slave Ship* directly confronted and engaged the spectators. Created by jazz musician Archie Shepp and director Moses, the music covered the historical spectrum of black music from African drums, to jazz, to rhythm and blues. This music suffused the entire production, intensifying the emotional impact of onstage moments. Critic John Lahr in the *Village Voice* called the production "genuine musical theater."[18] Kimberly Benston asserted that the music in *Slave Ship* "is thus the strength, memory, power, triumph, affirmation—the entire historical and mythical process of Afro-American being."[19] As suggested by both Benston's and Lahr's comments, music in *Slave Ship* acted as much more than background. The conjunction of historical and contemporary African and African American musical styles symbolized and reaffirmed the African presence in the African American cultural continuum. Through the use of music and other performative elements of sight and sound, the performance of *Slave Ship* attempted to engulf the spectators in a total sensory experience.

The action of *Slave Ship* compressed the horrors of the Middle Passage and the degradations of centuries under slavery into succinct stage moments. These moments conveyed to the audience the continued abuse of blacks under a racist American government. The images of abuse and exploitation of blacks by whites in *Slave Ship* was intended to raise the black spectators' outrage and stimulate attitudes of militancy. Playwright Baraka and director Moses also created images and action that infused the present African American historical moment with symbols of African cultural heritage.[20] Yoruba dialect was spoken throughout the first twenty minutes of the play. Then, as the action moved from the roots of black civilization in Africa, through slavery, to the present, the characters continued to chant and speak phrases in Yoruba and to pray to African deities. Symbolically, this visual portrayal of African cultural retention informed black spectators that, despite the pressures from white America to conform, African traditions continued to survive in African American culture and experience.

Slave Ship also contested the legitimacy of and the black spectators' faith in traditional black religion. Baraka visually associated the civil rights ministry, the legacy of Dr. Martin Luther King, Jr., with betrayal and complicity by having the Uncle Tom house slave of the early slavery scenes and the assimilationist black preacher in later scenes portrayed by the same actor. Audiences familiar with the achievements of the immensely popular Dr. King might have found such an association troubling. Yet the signs and symbols connected with the black preacher in *Slave Ship* transformed the meanings embodied in the image of the black preacher as civil rights crusader. The performative action of *Slave Ship* worked to make new meanings, new ways of knowing this established image. When the preacher first appeared, the stage directions read, "Now lights flash on, and preacher in modern business suit stands with hat in his hand. He is the same Tom as before."[21] The transformation of the Uncle Tom slave into the black preacher called into question the preacher's credibility within the black liberation struggle. The representation of the preacher in *Slave Ship* read not as a symbol of black pride and authority but as a caricature in the minstrel tradition, a stereotype of accommodation. According to the stage directions, "He [the preacher] tries to be, in fact, assumes he is, dignified, trying to hold his shoulders straight, but only succeeds in giving his body an odd slant like a diseased coal chute" (142). With the guidance of these stage directions, as well as the language that Baraka creates for this character, the actor who played the preacher presented him as a demeaned and deferential Steppin Fetchit–like character. Through its performative action and imagery, *Slave Ship* reformulated the position and meanings of the black preacher and the Civil Rights Movement. The play worked to portray the nonviolent preacher not as a freedom fighter but as an obstacle to the cause of black liberation.

As a result, with newly awakened political consciousness and militancy, the other black characters on stage rose en masse and murdered the black preacher. For audiences at the Chelsea Theater Center in 1969 and those in the rural South in 1970, who were still close historically to the 1968 assassination of Martin Luther King, Jr., such an execution could have been shocking. Yet the cumulative effect of the symbolic action of *Slave Ship* worked to make this death appear to be a necessary revolutionary action. The preacher's execution removed an element contributing to black subjugation and also symbolically relieved a degree of the spectators' physical unease in watching the production. Soon the black masses onstage would encourage the black spectators to stand, further relieving their discomfort and encouraging their participation in symbolic revolutionary acts. Significantly, the black masses executed the preacher on the same part of the stage previously used as the auction block. They transformed this space into a site of rebellion and exorcised the negative vestiges of slavery. The transformation of space and the conversion of the complacent black masses into militant activists symbolized for the audience the notion that oppressive circumstances could be overcome, "transformed" through collective revolutionary action. The killing of the preacher visually dramatized the need of the gathered black spectators to eliminate from their consciousness the tendency to accommodate oppression.

The now militant black masses onstage followed the killing of the preacher with the symbolic execution of an offstage White Voice. This offstage White Voice, an invisible but extremely tangible symbol of the powerful psychological and sociological effects of white oppression, hovered above the play inhibiting black interaction. Implicitly and explicitly, the representation of the White Voice critiqued and commented on the power of representation. Although not physically present, the White Voice was powerfully represented, and with it the play charged the oppressive, white, capitalist system with perpetuation of a spiritually bankrupt, Christian ethos that promotes and legitimizes racism. At one point the White Voice announced to the onstage black masses, "I'm God. You can't kill white Jesus God. I got long blond blow hair. I don't even wear a wig. You love the way

I look. You want to look like me!" (145). These words underline racist representations and assumptions that have not only conditioned the treatment
of blacks by whites but have constrained blacks's self-image. Through control of the representational apparatus, the values of the dominant culture
have been perpetuated by whites and internalized by blacks, causing many
blacks to covet and accept everything white, including the concept of a
white, blue-eyed, blond-haired God. The black masses literally destroyed
and disempowered the White Voice, symbolically deconstructing its representational authority. The black actors, after dispatching the accommoda-
tionist black minister, moved en masse in the direction of the offstage White
Voice and attacked him. Subdued by the oncoming black onslaught, the
White Voice changed from confident disdain to fearful pleading and finally
to screams of horror. Simultaneously, other cast members removed from the
upstage wall and then smashed an effigy of Uncle Sam with a cross around
his neck—a grotesque representation of the connection between the Christian ethic and American capitalism. By controling the representational apparatus of *Slave Ship,* Baraka thus empowered the black masses and black cultural expression. Through the execution of the White Voice the black
masses symbolically expunged the visible and invisible hegemony of the
dominant culture.

The destruction of the White Voice fashioned new meanings for the
black spectators to associate with Christianity and conventional Euro-
American systems of beauty. No longer would whiteness, blond hair, and
blue eyes connote goodness, godliness, and purity. *Slave Ship,* consistent
with the rhetoric of black cultural nationalism, insisted that faith in the traditional white Christian orthodoxy was antithetical to black cultural, spiritual, and social advancement. In addition, signs and symbols within the performance offered new models for a more "Afrocentric" cultural philosophy
and spirituality. The characters' African dress and Afro hairstyles emphasized
Afrocentric standards of beauty and the concept that "black is beautiful."
The onstage black masses, even as they represented black life in post–Civil
Rights Movement America, continued to pray to African deities instead of
the traditional representation of a white Jesus. The action of the play irre-
vocably connected their religious sensibility with their political consciousness and with their irreverent treatment of the White Voice, "white Jesus
God." Spiritual faith in *Slave Ship* interacted and united with cultural
awareness and revolutionary consciousness.

Slave Ship explicitly invited the black spectators to become participants
in the symbolic overthrow of the White Voice. Frustrated with their

oppressed circumstances, the onstage black masses, chanting "When we gonna rise. Rise, rise, rise, cut the ties, Black man rise" (143), crossed into the audience, shook hands with the black audience members, and challenged them to stand and join in the chant and the attack on the White Voice. Significantly, despite the segregated appeal of the cast, performances at the Chelsea Theater Center moved not only black audience members but whites as well to stand and chant. Critic Stan Machlin of the *New York Post* observed that "The powerful play hypnotizes like a religious ritual; a mass in secular times: This was so extreme that many whites attempted to stand up and join the singing chanting blacks—both audience and actors, even though it was their own destruction."[22] Machlin's observation that white as well as black spectators attempted to stand attests to the often infectious power of the performance event. The music, the action, the rhythm, and the symbolism of the production potentially induced participation and inculcated audience allegiance regardless of race. *Slave Ship* presented the radicalization of the black masses and their violent revolutionary assault on the white power structure as inevitable, the anticipated developmental step in black historical evolution. The sparse plot of *Slave Ship* flowed from slavery to civil rights, omitting any record of emancipation. This deliberate omission implied that oppressive conditions for blacks had been continuous and were in need of immediate redress. The inexorable pace of the performance of *Slave Ship*—moving without pause to revolutionary insurgency—created a feeling of urgency that encompassed both actors and spectators. The performance of *Slave Ship* purposefully swept the audience up in the action. As Paul Carter Harrison expressed it, "There was no way for us [the spectators] to step outside of Gil Moses's production of Imamu Baraka's *Slave Ship*."[23]

Despite the performance's potential appeal to nonblack audiences, Moses and Baraka aimed *Slave Ship* specifically at, and intended to incite participation from, their black audience members. In contrast to Machlin's view, Nobel Prize–winning playwright Wole Soyinka recounted the impressions of a white critic who felt isolated and rejected by the cast of *Slave Ship* and who, during the climactic moments of the play, only shook hands with the black audience members.

It was a shock to him [the white critic] to find literally that the play, and his ordeal, was not over, that he had to experience yet another level of his unsuspected rejection. He, in spite of these feelings of identification which had been fed into him from the universality of suffering, found that his emotive identification existed only for him and was not necessarily reciprocal in itself with the essential truths of the evening.[24]

Appealing to the "universality of suffering" was not an objective of *Slave Ship*. *Slave Ship* asserted black pride and black self-determination. The performance attempted to engage all the senses of its black audiences, to join the black spectators' sensory and emotional reception with their intellectual and philosophical understandings of the need for revolutionary action. Stefan Brecht wrote of the incendiary effect of *Slave Ship:*

> The final revolt is a genocidal call to arms to young Afro-American audiences—a call for killing of the white man. There is a symbolic overthrow of Uncle Sam. The play joins the present with clenched fists, hymns, new flags. . . . The play incites to violence.[25]

By presenting new symbols of violent revolutionary change and inviting the black spectators to participate in the symbolic defeat of oppression, *Slave Ship* sought to influence those spectators' actions outside of the theater. The performance encouraged black spectators' participation while predicting in simplistic, visual terms the actualization of the black liberation struggle.

In the final moment of *Slave Ship*, Baraka directed the onstage black masses to invite the black spectators onto the stage to dance with the performers to the jazz music of Archie Shepp. This action reinforced the celebratory and communal bond between spectators and performers. Just when the party had reached some level of loose improvisation, however, Baraka called for the head of the Uncle Tom preacher to be thrown into the center of the dance floor. This symbolic, antistructural act transformed the atmosphere of the theatrical event. By throwing the preacher's decapitated head onto the stage, Baraka exposed the audience, in vivid and horrific terms, to the costs and consequences of the black liberation effort. He reminded the audience through this powerful image of the unfulfilled legacy of the Civil Rights Movement. In a tactic similar to that employed by Antonin Artaud and his Theater of Cruelty,[26] Baraka bombarded his audience with violent, cruel images. Rather than purging spectators of the propensity to act—the expected response to violent images that Artaud articulated in *Theater and Its Double*—Baraka intended for this ending of *Slave Ship* to induce the spectators' participation and compel their activism. The shocking introduction of the preacher's head abruptly shifted the mood of the action and forced the spectators to confront the realities of revolutionary action.

Genevieve Fabre argues that revolutionary black theatrical productions must attempt to:

> simultaneously plunge the spectator into terror and reassure him. . . . In terrifying the spectator, the production brings back reality which is no longer doubted, for the performance must go beyond the domain of the "magic" to reveal an order that is not dominated by the forces of destiny but regulated by the laws of history where change is necessary.[27]

Following Fabre's formula, *Slave Ship,* in its finale, jolted the audience back into the uncertain present reality where victory over white oppression had yet to be achieved. The horrible revelation of the preacher's head further dispelled the theatrical illusion and the convention that the theater is a safe environment free of the exigencies and consequences of daily life. Instead of continuing to celebrate, the spectators had to confront this bloody image. At the same time, they were expected to recognize that the preacher's betrayal of his black brethren made his death inevitable. This knowledge was meant to reassure the spectators of the validity and righteousness of their struggle. Social protest performances such as that of *Slave Ship* created for their audiences dichotomous experiences. Their intention was not simply to entertain but to confront and provoke the audience to social action. These performances held immediate, concrete meanings and real social consequences for their black audiences as they engaged in and with the climate of social urgency. The ending of *Slave Ship* conflated the symbolic and the real, heightening the meanings of performative action. The intrusion of the preacher's head into the action was not simply a symbolic act. It was also a real event that compelled the spectators, who were dancing on stage, to respond.

Although nonblack spectators attended the 1969 production of *Slave Ship* at the Chelsea Theater Center, audiences for the southern touring production consisted almost entirely of black people. Because the Free Southern Theater chose to perform at churches and in high school auditoriums in impoverished black enclaves of the rural South, its audiences were, on the whole, self-selective and largely homogeneous constituencies. Most of the poor, rural, black people who witnessed the production had little previous experience with theater. Uninhibited by Western theatrical conventions, they came to the performances steeped in the rituals and traditions of the black church, where participation is not only encouraged but expected. Thomas Pawley, in a significant article on black theater audiences, details a history of black participatory response in the theater and relates this theatrical behavior to the tradition of call and response in the black church.[28] Other scholars have traced this participatory behavior to African ritual practices. In either case, the vocal and physical responsiveness of the black audience suggests a self-conscious willingness to engage more fully in the performance and a responsibility on the part of the audience to confirm what is happening in the performance. Black spectators' involvement provides both performers and church ministers with immediate feedback on aesthetic effectiveness and cultural, political, social, and spiritual relevance.

In addition to their cultural background, the southern blacks who came to see *Slave Ship* in 1970 brought with them recent and firsthand knowledge of discrimination, racism, and economic and political struggle. They had direct, personal knowledge of black unrest, resistance, and rebellion. Certainly not all, nor even the majority, of the black spectators at the Free Southern Theater's production of *Slave Ship* were revolutionaries or social activists. They were, on the whole, working people, farmers, and share-croppers with an awareness of their subservient position within a system of economic and cultural oppression. Still, they had been affected by the urgency of the black liberation struggle. Many had witnessed the events and aftermath of the Mississippi Freedom Summer of 1966, the civil rights marches, the sit-ins, boycotts, and freedom rides. Most had watched the rise of black political power and voter registration throughout the South and had seen the spread, locally and nationally, of the Black Power Movement and black nationalistic ideologies, including the radicalization of Stokely Carmichael and SNCC. The tumult and upheaval of the black liberation struggle had influenced their lives outside of the social protest theater, as well as their reception of the social protest performance, and even their decision to attend the performance. Urgent, insistent times create an atmosphere for social protest theater and the effects of those times on audience reception and efficacy cannot be overstated. As a result of their knowledge of and involvement with the tumultuous and volatile racial conflagration in the United States and dramatic racial changes in the South, these were audiences already sympathetic to the messages they would hear disseminated in *Slave Ship*.

Even before these rural, black, southern spectators entered the theater, they composed ideological and cultural communities of interest. They shared common bonds based on notions of culture, ethnicity, and social and political struggle. The black audiences for *Slave Ship* represented a community not simply because of their racial homogeneity but because of their geographical identification, their rural orientation, and experiences that imbued them with a particular set of values and norms in everyday life. Community, as Anthony Cohen articulates it, is "largely a mental construct, whose 'objective' manifestations in locality or ethnicity give it credibility. It is highly symbolized, with the consequence that its members can invest it with their selves."[29] The symbolic construction of communities outside the theater by the black patrons for *Slave Ship* influenced the willingness of these audiences to commune with the social protest performers and the performance inside the theater. The integrity of these ideological and cultural communities affected the spectators' responsiveness to and decoding of the performances.

The performances before these black audiences in the rural South could be said to represent what Marco De Marinis terms "closed performances," which require a "model spectator."[30] De Marinis's phrase specifically refers to marginalized, alternative productions that appeal to specific interest groups and particular audiences removed from the more commercial mainstream. In contrast, De Marinis would classify performances within the commercial mainstream or from Western culture's classical theatrical canon as "open." And yet, while the productions of the American commercial mainstream—on and off Broadway and in regional theaters across the country—operate under the premise of accessibility to a wide audience, they still require specialized knowledge and processes of indoctrination for audiences to accept their premises. They are not truly "open." These productions have a long history of being "closed" to the interests and perspectives of minorities. When *Slave Ship* toured the South in 1970, the American mainstream theater was still overtly and covertly, culturally and economically, excluding blacks from participation in its productions. The creation of theater by, for, and about blacks by groups like the Free Southern Theater was in part a response to their lack of access to "closed" mainstream performances.

Despite its decidedly Western bias, De Marinis's theory of closed performances and model spectators is useful to this discussion of *Slave Ship*. For De Marinis cautions that "If, however, a closed performance is performed for a spectator far removed from its model spectator, then things will be different."[31] Accordingly, the reception and conception of the meanings of *Slave Ship* changed when spectators who were outside of the "model" constituency attended the production. As earlier noted, Baraka and Moses directed *Slave Ship* at a closed black constituency. Their advocacy of closed performances subverted and inverted the exclusion of blacks from the dominant culture's theatrical performances. During the southern tour of *Slave Ship*, closed performances before "model" spectators often represented "an element in the co-production of the play's meaning."[32]

By tailoring *Slave Ship* for a specific constituency, Baraka and Moses explicitly intended to "preach to the converted." Certain critics have denounced the practice of "preaching to the converted" as detrimental and redundant.[33] Yet it must be understood that with sympathetic spectators the principle goal of *Slave Ship* was not conversion. This is not to suggest that conversion was impossible but rather that Moses and Baraka perceived a distinct purpose and advantage in addressing an audience of those already faithful to their cause. Situated within the urgent movement for social change, the immediate intention of the performance was to rededicate sympathetic black spectators to the struggle. *Slave Ship* sought to reaffirm the virtues of the revolutionary cause and heighten optimism by predicting revolutionary victory for an audience composed of the converted. In addition, I believe that an audience of the converted, which shared a sense of community, values, and beliefs, was predisposed to respond collectively and to commune with the actors as cocelebrants in the social protest event.

Herbert Blau and other theater scholars, however, have argued that the possibilities for achieving collective participation and communal ritualistic reception are inherently flawed. Blau maintains that the "participation mystique" is simply that, a mystique, since the response to any performance, in the end, is not participatory nor communal but solitary: "This is the last blight on the participatory illusion: the enduring gravity of the theater is not a collective one but solitary."[34] The common critical perception is that, regardless of the manner in which the performance encourages communal response, each individual audience member interprets the performance signs for himself or herself. Every spectator's reading must be different, reflective of his or her own individuality. Because of the primacy of individual experience, collective responses and readings are difficult if not impossible to achieve. According to Keir Elam, "every spectator's interpretation of the text is in effect a new construction of it according to the cultural and ideological disposition of the subject."[35] Correspondingly, Susan Bennett acknowledges that the collective contract is difficult to sustain and that conventional theatrical environs encourage personal rather than social perception and response.[36]

These critics, however, do not take into account the cultural differences in reception. While white Americans are, by and large, acculturated to think of themselves as individuals, black Americans are more often conditioned by internal and external sociocultural factors to think of themselves as representative of their particular group. My intention here is not to essentialize processes of black socialization nor to promote monolithic group identities. But I do want to point out the potential cultural differences that encourage black collective reception. The dominant culture has classified blacks collectively as Other, outside the cultural norm. It has imposed upon blacks negative stereotypes and enduring group labels that have often defined and delimited their existence in this society. As a consequence, some blacks have internalized these collective stereotypes of racial identification. Due to the external forces of racism and discrimination, as well as to the internal social and cultural insecurities of being a "minority," many blacks have been conditioned to believe that their individual actions or the public behavior of members of their ethnic group speak for the group and reflect upon the "race" as a whole. Jill Nelson, in her memoir *Volunteer Slavery*, notes how blacks have been socialized to believe in their own collective culpability: "[W]hen you're a Negro in America, it's usually not just you who's making the mistake, its y'all, the race, black folks in toto."[37] In addition, because blacks have faced persecution and repression simply because they are black, they have, at times, needed to identify themselves collectively, to protect themselves through solidarity with the group in order to increase their chances of survival in a racist culture.

In the 1960s and 1970s, black power and black cultural-nationalist movements valorized collective identities and cultural communality. Collective action was believed to be critical to black strategies of social and cultural rebellion. The development of community and communal modes of empowerment were, in turn, perceived as crucial to that collective action. Accordingly, because of their socialization, their cultural and political history, and their internalization of their position as Other, as well as their involvement with and knowledge of the more immediate politics of Black Power, members of black audiences in the 1960s and 1970s were predisposed to adopt a group identity and to respond communally to social protest performances of *Slave Ship*.

When audiences stood and chanted at performances of *Slave Ship* in Baton Rouge and West Point, it clearly constituted a collective, communal response. Such collective reactions did not dissipate nor negate the individual experience in the theater; rather, they served to connect the individual reaction to the wider community's experience in the theater and to the cultural and social developments outside of the theater.[38] As Baz Kershaw argues, the collective impact of and response to a performance intensifies the individual spectator's experience as well as the performance's possible efficacy.

> For if a whole audience, or even a whole community responds in this way to the symbolism of a "possible world," then the potential of performance efficacy is multiplied by more than the audience number. To the extent that the audience is part of a community, then the networks of the community will change, however infinitesimally, in response to changes in the audience members.[39]

When the spectators understood the meaning of the play's events within their own experience and carried this meaning with them out of the theater, theatrical participation could be transformed into social action.

Audience participation transformed the relationship between the spectator and the performance apparatus positing the spectator in the subject position. Hence, the black spectators who actively participated in *Slave Ship*'s symbolic overthrow of the White Voice recognized themselves, their struggle, as the subject of the performance. By participating, the spectators no longer functioned as passive audience members but as cocelebrants. As subjects, the spectators understood that the performance was not only for them but about them and involving them. Subjectivity empowered and was empowered by active participation. Participation in the social protest performance created new relationships and new discourses between spectators and performers. When the spectators participated, the social protest performance experienced a dynamic and immediate duality, wavering between harmony and disharmony, order and disorder, insurrection and reconciliation. The emotional, vociferous participation at the performances of *Slave Ship* in Baton Rouge and West Point evidenced this duality. The audience response demonstrated not spectatorship but participation and active involvement with the play's message. The audience's decision to participate can be perceived as both a practical and a symbolic act of rebellion and audience participation, a critical indicator of social efficacy.

Some critics, however, have argued that a vociferous response in the theater dissipates the potential for social action outside of the theater. Following Aristotelian theory, these critics have interpreted the participation of spectators in social protest performance as a cathartic release that is not indicative of active commitment. After viewing a performance of *Slave Ship* at the Chelsea Theater Center, critic Charles Reichenthal commented that he did not perceive a groundswell of black outrage or white fear in the theater.

> Instead one recalls the emotional catharsis brought about. And that emotional purging happens to both black and white audience members. In a very real sense, this blood letting in "Slave Ship" back fires if the play is supposed to leave the black man filled with hate and the white man filled with anxiety. I found oddly enough, that upon leaving the theater, there had been created a bond between white and black spectators that was strong and visible. . . . The theatrical catharsis had aided both to take clearer looks at their backgrounds and beliefs.[40]

Reichenthal interpreted the emotional outpouring from spectators as a purgation and release of emotion. He did not agree with Stefan Brecht that *Slave Ship* was a revolutionary call to arms for young black Americans. As evidenced by other reviews and critical commentaries on the performance of *Slave Ship,* Reichenthal's perception of the communion between black and white spectators was clearly a minority view. However, his discussion of the cathartic consequences of audience participation directly correlates with repeated criticisms of social protest theater. Morgan Himelstein, in his critique of the Workers' Theater Movement of the 1920s and 1930s, concurred that an emotional participatory response in the theater is a cathartic response. Himelstein maintained that this cathartic response dissipates the potential for agitational action outside of the theater.

> The emotional catharsis induced by the drama made the theater a less satisfactory weapon than the [Communist] Party theorists had imagined. Apparently they had never read Aristotle's *Poetics.*[41]

The inability to link postperformance social action directly to interperformance participation leaves audience participation and its role in social protest performance open to speculation.

Augusto Boal, in his important work on revolutionary theater, *Theatre of the Oppressed,* differentiates revolutionary theater and the participatory response it engenders from Aristotelian tragedy and its cathartic response.[42] In a section entitled "Catharsis and Responses, or Knowledge and Action," Boal foregrounds Brecht's concept of theater as a social process and uses

Brechtian theories to develop his own concept of a revolutionary "theater of the oppressed." Boal postulates that, while the orientation of the Greek tragic hero is toward the past, the revolutionary protagonist focuses on the future. In an Aristotelian tragedy, the hero gains knowledge of his or her own tragic flaws and loses the propensity to act. The revolutionary hero, on the other hand, recognizes the flaws in society that must be addressed and develops the willingness to fight for a remedy. Boal concludes that the nature of the revolutionary play is not Aristotelian, nor is the audience response to such performances cathartic.

Boal maintains that the revolutionary audience becomes increasingly radicalized as it participates in the radical transformation of the revolutionary hero. The spectators are not purged of the desire to act socially but empowered with the will to struggle in their own lives. Rather than cathartic release, therefore, the fervent participation of spectators is a sign of conscious empowerment. According to Boal, demonstrative action inside the theater does not preclude or dissipate social action outside of the theater. Rather, it fuels the revolutionary fires. Applying Boal's theories to the social protest performances of *Slave Ship,* the active, emotional responses of audiences to *Slave Ship* in Baton Rouge represent signs of conscious empowerment. As these spectators watched the black masses in *Slave Ship,* they became more empowered to act in their own lives. The participation of the spectators intensified the interplay of material and symbolic forces within the social protest performance. Audience participation attested to the effectiveness of *Slave Ship*'s messages and signified that the audience felt connected to and invested in the social protest performance.

As evidenced by this analysis, audience participation in performances of *Slave Ship* was critical to the social protest performance. It can be read as an act of symbolic rebellion. When an individual spontaneously participated, it testified to the meaning and the import of the performance for that individual. This is not to suggest that participation in the social protest performance implied social commitment or immediately translated into social action. Many factors contribute to audience participation. Research in advertising and persuasion theory has shown that a key step in persuading an individual to take action after an advertising appeal is to convince that individual to perform a simple action, during the persuasive appeal, such as signing his or her name on a piece of paper. This technique, known as the "foot-in-the-door technique for inducing compliance" was first identified by J. L. Freedman and S. C. Fraser in 1966.[43] Freedman and Fraser's work, as well as subsequent experiments in persuasion, have shown that there is a direct correlation between the initial act of complicity and the long-term efficacy of the persuasive appeal.[44] The participatory involvement of the audience in a social protest performance such as *Slave Ship* parallels this basic persuasive principle. The audience's decision to actively participate was, in effect, like signing one's name in the foot-in-the-door technique. It affected the spectators' self-image and signified agreement with the overall strategy of the social protest movement. Audience participation in *Slave Ship* served to indicate the effectiveness of its appeal.

In addition, the performance and reception of *Slave Ship* depended on the surrounding social conditions. Situated in times of social urgency, the political, cultural, and racial upheavals of the late 1960s and early 1970s, the production of *Slave Ship* explicitly and purposefully preached to the converted. For these sympathetic black audiences, *Slave Ship* sought to reaffirm the virtues of the revolutionary cause, to heighten their optimism and commitment by predicting black liberation, and to celebrate black revolutionary consciousness by involving them in a symbolic victory over their oppression.

NOTES

1. In 1963, John O'Neal and Doris Kirby were field directors for the Student Non-Violent Coordinating Committee (SNCC) in Jackson, Mississippi. Gilbert Moses, later the director of *Slave Ship*, was a writer for the *Mississippi Free Press* in Jackson at the same time. Convinced of the need for a "legitimate" theater in the black enclaves of the Deep South, the three met and drew up plans for the Free Southern Theater (FST). The FST was to be "a movement theater going into the black community. It challenged the ethos of America, of the south." The group's original philosophy and organization was integrational, in line with the tenets of the Civil Rights Movement. However, by the time of the production of *Slave Ship*, the FST had become an all-black theater that endorsed the platform of black nationalism, in *Free Southern Theater, By the Free Southern Theater* (Indianapolis: Bobbs-Merrill, Co., 1969), eds. Thomas Dent and Richard Schechner, 211–12.

2. Val Ferdinand, "A Report on Black Theater in America: New Orleans," *Negro Digest* (April 1970): 28–29.

3. Ferdinand, "Report on Black Theater," 29.

4. Gilbert Moses, telephone interview with the author, August 23, 1990.

5. Gilbert Moses, interview, August 23, 1990.

6. Amiri Baraka, quoted in Theodore Hudson, *From LeRoi Jones to Amiri Baraka: The Literary Works* (Durham N.C.: Duke University Press, 1973), 172.

7. Kimberly Benston, "Vision and Form in *Slave Ship*," in *Imamu Amiri Baraka (LeRoi Jones): A Collection of Essays,* ed. Kimberly Benston (Englewood Cliffs, N.J.: Prentice-Hall, 1978), 174.

8. Gilbert Moses, interview, August 23, 1990.

9. Walter Kerr, "Is This Their Dream?" *New York Times,* November 23, 1969, sec. 2, p. 3.

10. Don Isaacs, "The Death of the Proscenium Stage," *Antioch Review* 31, no. 2 (Summer 1971): 250.

11. Jerry Tallmer, "Across the Footlights," *New York Post,* November 21, 1969, 64.

12. Gilbert Moses, interview, August 23, 1990.

13. Ibid.

14. Ibid.

15. Ibid.

16. Ibid.

17. Ibid.

18. John Lahr, "On-Stage," *Village Voice,* December 4, 1969, 51.

19. Benston, "Vision and Form in *Slave Ship,*" 183.

20. Ibid., 178.

21. Amiri Baraka, "*Slave Ship,*" in *The Motion of History and Other Plays* (New York: William Morrow, 1978), 141. All subsequent quotes will be cited in the text.

22. Stan Machlin, "*Slave Ship* Succeeds as Theater," *New York Post,* November 6, 1969, Collected Papers of Amiri Baraka, Mooreland-Springarn Collection, Howard University, Washington, D.C.

23. Paul Carter Harrison, *The Drama of Nommo* (New York: Grove, 1972), 197.

24. Wole Soyinka, "Drama and the Revolutionary Ideal," in *In Person: Achebe, Awoonor, and Soyinka,* ed. Karen L. Morell (Seattle: Institute for Comparative and Foreign Area Studies, University of Washington, 1975), 80.

25. Stefan Brecht, "LeRoi Jones' *Slave Ship,*" *Drama Review* 14 (Winter 1970): 215, 218.

26. For a discussion of the relationship between Amiri Baraka's practice and theory and the theater of Antonin Artaud, see Mance Williams, *Black Theater in the 1960s and 1970s* (Westport, Conn.: Greenwood, 1985), 21–23; and Leslie Sanders, *The Development of Black Theater in America* (Baton Rouge: Louisiana State University Press, 1988), 126–30.

27. Genevieve Fabre, *Drumbeats, Masks, and Metaphor* (Cambridge, Mass.: Harvard University Press, 1983), 103.

28. Thomas Pawley, "Black Theatre Audiences," in *The Theatre of Black Americans,* ed. Errol Hill, vol. 2 (Englewood Cliffs, N.J.: Prentice-Hall, 1980), 109–19.

29. Anthony Cohen, quoted by Paul Gilroy, in *There Ain't No Black in the Union Jack* (Chicago: University of Chicago Press, 1987), 235.

30. Marco De Marinis, "The Dramaturgy of the Spectator," *Drama Review* 31, no. 2 (Summer 1987): 103.

31. De Marinis, "The Dramaturgy of the Spectator," 103.

32. Sue-Ellen Case, *Feminism and Theatre* (New York: Methuen, 1988), 116.

33. See Morgan Himelstein, *Drama Was a Weapon* (New Brunswick, N.J.: Rutgers University Press, 1963).

34. Herbert Blau, *The Audience* (Baltimore: Johns Hopkins University Press, 1990), 190.

35. Keir Elam, *The Semiotics of Theatre and Drama* (London: Methuen, 1980), 97.

36. Susan Bennett, *Theatre Audiences* (London: Routledge, 1990), 142.

37. Jill Nelson, *Volunteer Slavery* (New York: Noble, 1993), 149.

38. Baz Kershaw, *The Politics of Performance: Radical Theater as Cultural Intervention* (London: Routledge, 1992), 35.

39. Kershaw, *Politics of Performance,* 28.

40. Charles Reichenthal, "Underlites," *Flatbush Life,* December 6, 1969, 20.

41. Himelstein, *Drama Was a Weapon,* 228.

42. Augusto Boal, *Theatre of the Oppressed* (New York: Urizen, 1979), 1–50, 100–106.

43. See J. L. Freedman and S. C. Fraser, "Compliance without Pressure: The Foot-in-the-Door Technique," *Journal of Personality and Social Psychology* 4 (1966): 195–202.

44. See Richard E. Petty and John T. Cacioppo, *Attitudes and Persuasion: Classic and Contemporary Approaches* (Dubuque, Ia.: William C. Brown, 1981), 167–69.

2.

Mary Trotter

Women's Work: *Inghinidhe na hEireann* and the Irish Dramatic Movement

Inghinidhe na h'Eireann has promoted the first Irish entertainments we have had, and it has laid, with its plays in English and in Irish, and its Irish celidh, the foundation of an Irish national theatre. While others have been talking the women have been working.

—Article from the *United Irishman,* 1901

At the turn of the century, nationalist Ireland produced a cultural renaissance out of its political crisis. Although officially Ireland had been a part of the United Kingdom in an uneasy alliance since 1801, England's authority over its western neighbor continued to foster anticolonial sentiment among Irish nationalists. The task of the Irish nationalist was to set herself or himself apart culturally from both British identity and the British caricature of the Irish personality. Several nationalist groups employed performance to create a sense of cultural identity among the Irish people different from the colonial definition of Ireland that had been established on the English stage. Instead of the shiftless "Paddy" and the childlike "Colleen" of London's popular theaters, these groups provided counterhegemonic representations of an idealized Irish culture and its heroes.

Yet, while all Irish nationalists sought autonomy from England, there were significant divisions within the movement as well. Many Catholic nationalists pointed to their religion as a sign of Irish resistance to England's cultural and political colonization. Meanwhile, Protestant Anglo-Irish nationalists negotiated their historically privileged, oppressive position among the Catholic majority within the movement. Members of the Irish Parliamentary Party and its supporters continued to seek independence through legislation in the British Parliament, while other groups, like the

Irish Republican Brotherhood, chose military force. And class and gender difference often served as a barrier to unity within the nationalist movement. Thus, political performance in turn-of-the-century Ireland was not only a means of resisting English domination. It provided the field on which different nationalist ideologies—different ideas of what made up Irish nationhood and nationalist identity—vied for political and cultural legitimacy. Many nationalist groups, despite the political and cultural differences among them, shared an interest in the development of a counterhegemonic representation of Ireland on the stage and an anticolonial national identity among their audiences. And, since they often shared the same spaces, and even the same audiences, much of each group's dramatic work had to have been influenced by the theatrical practices and cultural and political representations of Irish identity occurring on the other nationalist stages. Theater within the nationalist movement, therefore, became a site of collaboration across religion, class, and, ultimately, gender lines.

On April 2, 1902, in St. Teresa's Hall, Dublin, several organizations, led by the women's nationalist group _Inghinidhe na hEireann_ (The Daughters of Erin), collaborated to produce two Irish plays before an enthusiastic, nationalist audience. W. G. Fay combined actors from _Inghinidhe,_ the Celtic Literary Society, and W. G. Fay's Comedy Combination into a group called the Irish National Dramatic Company. William Butler Yeats and George Russell (AE) wrote the plays. The band of the Workman's Club played Irish music at the intervals. The performance transgressed several boundaries within the nationalist movement, as Catholics and Anglo-Irish from all classes participated, and the women involved played important roles in both production and performance. Since the playwrights and most of the actors would go on to form the Irish National Theatre Society, which would eventually become the Abbey Theatre, one year later, the evening is often remembered as the originating moment for the Irish National Theatre.

The playwrights, Russell (AE) and Yeats, and the director, William G. Fay, have received almost all the credit for the evening's success, while the efforts of the organization that produced the evening, _Inghinidhe na hEireann,_ have been reinterpreted, devalued, or forgotten. Yet _Inghinidhe_ and its members contributed more practical and organizational work to the establishment of the Irish National Dramatic Company than did any other organization. This essay explores _Inghinidhe na hEireann_'s material and aesthetic contributions to the development of the Abbey Theatre, Ireland's national dramatic house, and to the modern Irish dramatic movement. But it also examines the ways in which *Inghinidhe* members expressed their sense of Irish national identity through other political activities. *Inghinidhe na hEireann* saw itself as a united body of women performing nationalist tasks in the public sphere in an autonomous manner. Its members considered their collaborative work with men in the theater as a partnership rather than a subordinate relationship. Placing *Inghinidhe's* dramatic work in the context of its other activities in the public sphere points out how its involvement was instrumental to the success of the Irish Dramatic Movement and exposes the ways in which its social influence was ultimately both nationalist and feminist in scope. Further, it reveals how religious and class identity, as well as gender, complicated the idea of Irish nationhood at the turn of the century.

A conservative, highly moralistic nation, Ireland in the nineteenth century contained carefully delineated male and female spheres. Women's identity hinged upon familial relationships to men—wives, daughters, sisters. A woman's work, likewise, was valued only as auxiliary to the male role, and her primary duty, regardless of whatever outside labor she performed, lay in her position within the family—maintaining the household, bearing children, and respecting the familial status quo. A woman gained respect by performing her function within the family well, but women's work was not considered equal to men's labor. Thus, women's participation in the public sphere was devalued in light of the nation's rigid gender roles. Cynthia Enloe has noted how typically female tasks, like sewing and the care of children, are deemed natural, or "unskilled," labor,[1] which causes a woman's talents in typically female jobs to go unrecognized. Women especially skillful at their work are deemed "accomplished": their talent exemplifies their success in the feminine role, without an acknowledgment of the work involved in achieving and maintaining that skill.

At best, a woman could enter the public realm in a complementary role to that of men. Such was the case for Anna and Fanny Parnell, sisters of the leader of the Irish Parliamentary Party, Charles Stewart Parnell. In the early 1880s, when the leaders of the radical land reform movement, the Land League, were imprisoned, women, many of whom were related to men in the movement, formed the Ladies Land League. Their work was applauded by the League when it seemed that they were bearing the torch for the absentee men. But ultimately the women became more radical than their brothers, stepping up the number of public demonstrations in the west of Ireland and generally increasing the visibility of the issue (and the women themselves) within Ireland. However, the male leaders of the Land League coerced the Ladies Land League to disband once they had been released from prison.

With the dissolution of the Ladies Land League, the only group in which women could take an equal role in nationalist activity was the Gaelic League—a nonpartisan organization for the promotion of Irish language and culture. Founded by Douglas Hyde in 1893, the Gaelic League had branches throughout Ireland. Some were organized geographically, but in Dublin branches were often organized according to political or professional affiliations. The Gaelic League sought to "de-Anglicize" Ireland and its people through study of and, more importantly, participation in Irish language and culture. They sponsored *feisianna* (festivals), *caelidhs* (dances), and other entertainments and organized outings to places of historic national interest. Participating in these activities allowed Irishwomen and Irishmen to construct and perform national identities—on the streets at rallies and outings and on the stage through the *feis* and *caelidh*. These events made the Gaelic League essential to the development of Irish Cultural Nationalism in the 1890s.

But the Gaelic League's universal success hinged upon its nonsectarianism and nonpartisanship. Overt political activity required joining another group such as the Irish Republican Brotherhood or the Irish Parliamentary Party. Since these political organizations had only auxiliary branches for women, or did not allow women at all, it was difficult for Irishwomen to make their voices heard within the nationalist movement in anything other than a social or cultural context. Even when a woman performed "men's work" on her own—manual labor, military activity, political organizing—her gender position tended to devalue this labor. In the political forum, a woman's work, regardless of its "feminine" or "masculine" nature, tended to be represented in the feminine terms of natural labor or feminine accomplishment, making it difficult for her to transgress her gender position in the public realm. Irish nationalist women needed a forum in which to display their political as well as their cultural convictions.

On Easter Sunday, 1900, fifteen women met in the Celtic Literary Society Rooms to discuss nationalist issues. The conversation ultimately turned to Queen Victoria's visit to Ireland to encourage Irish enlistment in the British Army, which was then fighting the Boer War. During her visit, Victoria sponsored a Children's Treat in Phoenix Park, which five thousand children attended.[2] The nationalist women decided to retaliate against this overt English propaganda by sponsoring an Irish Patriotic Children's Treat that summer on the Sunday following the commemoration of Wolfe Tone. The idea was enthusiastically supported by men and women throughout the nationalist movement. By summer more than fifty women were involved in organizing the event, and in the four days before the treat twenty thousand lunches were packed for the children by more than a hundred women and men.[3] Dozens of individuals made financial contributions, including Fanny Parnell. The Irish National and Hibernian Clubs collected money for the event[4] and the Phoenix Brewery Company donated a kilderkin of ale for the chaperones.[5]

The treat itself became a kind of nationalist rally for the children who attended, the stewards who supervised, and the adults who looked on. An hour before the children arrived, "23 vehicles [bearing food and drink for the treat], adorned with Irish, American, French and Boer flags, started for Clonturk an hour ahead of the children, and presented an imposing specta-cle."[6] The children gathered around Beresford Place to march in a kind of parade to the site of the treat at Clonturk Park. This procession of more than twenty thousand children lasted ninety minutes and was two miles long. Along the route, the children waved flags and sang patriotic songs. The *United Irishman* noted that when the children passed the Orange Hall in Rutland Square, "from which a Union Jack was flying, the youngsters threw redoubled vigour and energy into their admirable rendering of 'God Save Ireland,' which was followed by lusty cheering."[7]

But children were not the only parade participants. Members of nationalist organizations marshaled the children on the march to Clonturk Park, and "about half-a-dozen bands" also attended.[8] Also, "the footpaths were thronged with people all along the line of route, and spectators occu-pied windows commanding a view of the procession."[9] Arthur Griffith commented in the nationalist newspaper *United Irishman* that "Dublin never witnessed anything so marvelous as the procession through its streets . . . of the 30,000 schoolchildren who refused to be bribed into parading before the Queen of England."[10] Indeed, the Patriotic Children's Treat became an incredible spectacle of the strength and fervor of Irish nationalism in Dublin—the largest political rally in the city up to that time. Within the park, the children participated in games, the Gaelic Athletic Association played a demonstration game of hurling, and four speakers (including Maud Gonne) delivered speeches from platforms in different parts of the park. In her autobiography, Maud Gonne MacBride commented that years later "middle-aged men and women would come up to [me] in the streets and say: 'I was one of the patriotic children at your party when Queen Victoria was over.'"[11]

On one hand, the Irish Patriotic Children's Treat seems like unempowering "women's work," since it was geared toward children. Daphne Spain points out how women gain no real power in the public sphere when they are given contact and authority over typically disempowered groups like children, the sick, or the poor.[12] Additionally, such positions allow women to do only what is regarded as private, feminine work—healing and nurturing—even if these acts are performed in the public sphere.

However, the Patriotic Children's Treat was an empowering moment for nationalist women. The women who organized the treat had full control over the event and the nationalist message it carried. They educated thousands of children about the nationalist cause. Male volunteers (who took on "domestic" tasks like making sandwiches and marshaling children at the treat) were subordinate to the women leaders, giving women an opportunity to lead men as well as women. Organizing the treat allowed women to find a public voice by uniting with other concerned women, empowering both the nationalist women's community as a whole and the individual women in it.

Inspired by their success, and with some money left over from the Children's Treat, the women created a permanent organization—*Inghinidhe na hEireann. Inghinidhe* attracted "many brilliant young women—but more than brilliant—illuminated by an idea and devoted in support of it."[13] Most were middle-class Catholics (although there were some Protestant Anglo-Irish and wealthy women as well) who had gained a degree of personal autonomy through the receipt of a good education and work or participation in activities outside of the home. In this uncertain period, when the nationalist movement was torn between supporting radical or parliamentary measures as a means to independence, *Inghinidhe* was committed to achieving Irish nationhood by any means, including military force. Some, like Mary Walker (Maire Nic Shiubhlaigh), Hannah Sheehy, and Maire Killeen, were members of nationalist families who sought a vehicle for personal involvement in the movement. Others, like Jenny Wyse-Power, Sinead O'Flanagan, Ethna Carberry (Anna Johnson), Alice Milligan, and, of course, Maud Gonne, had established nationalist reputations as authors and editors but wished to increase the visibility of the women's community in the cause of Irish nationalism.

Political women had to struggle constantly for visibility in the nationalist movement. In 1898, the Local Government Act permitted women to vote for and be elected to political seats beneath the county level of government.[14] Although subsequently many women entered the political establishment, they were typically elected into "feminine" positions, as advocates

FIG. 1. Maire nic Shiubhlaigh (Mary Walker) in the Abbey Theatre's 1905 production of Lady Gregory's *Kincora*. After beginning her theatrical career with *Inghinide na hEireann*, Maire Nic Shiubhlaigh became one of the most influential actors in the early years of the Irish dramatic movement. (Courtesy of the Harvard Theatre Collection, the Houghton Library.)

for the poor, the sick, or children, and were not given a strong legislative voice.

Apparently women could not cross gender boundaries simply by "passing" as men, doing men's work in the public sphere. Rather, in order to perform male political tasks in the nationalist movement, like making political speeches, they had to transcend both the masculine and the feminine spheres by becoming "extraordinary" women. Represented as atypical of their sex, these women did not pose a threat to male authority in the public realm, nor did they set precedents for typical women's involvement.

Women who were deemed truly extraordinary, like Maud Gonne and the Sheehy sisters, created visible positions for themselves in the nationalist public eye but only by characterizing themselves in, or allowing themselves to be characterized by, feminine ideals of beauty, performative skill, and accomplishment over the male parallels of charisma, presence, and talent.

Throughout the 1890s, Gonne, an ardent political nationalist, used her beauty and economic privilege to gain position in the public sphere. Her charm gained her admittance as a visitor in nationalist men's organizations, and her friendship with nationalist leaders gained her opportunities to speak publicly on Irish issues. Strikingly beautiful, six feet tall, with a strong voice and a keen sense of performance, Gonne knew how to make her presence felt at the most disorganized meetings. Gonne fought for Irish independence in Ireland, England, and France, where she edited *L'Irlande Libre* and wrote for other French papers about the Irish cause. Her writing and speaking made her a famous and powerful figure in the movement, as she risked arrest to speak before audiences, some of which may have been as enthralled by her personality as by her political ideals.

Gonne was as committed, savvy, and talented as any male nationalist figure. Yet in the eyes of the men in the nationalist movement her encroachment into the male sphere, speaking publicly about such issues as recruiting Irish volunteers to fight against the English in the Boer War, was balanced somewhat by her characterization as an ideal of feminine beauty. Arthur Griffith, who published her politically potent articles in the *United Irishman*, "affectionately dubbed her, 'Queen.' "[15] Indeed, Gonne seemed to cultivate this regal persona for herself, as she walked the streets of Dublin in long flowing robes with her dog, Dagda, at her side. Considering the nationalists' affection for such images of Ireland as those evoked by Kathleen ni Houlihan, Hibernia, and Queen Maeve, Gonne's public presentation of herself was a shrewd one.

Other women, lacking Gonne's physical and economic advantages, performed as extraordinary women by displaying their feminine "accomplishments," or emphasizing family ties. When Margaret M. Sheehy performed in Sligo to raise money for the Dominican Fathers in 1902, she showed her skill at the art of recitation. "This talented lady," the *Freeman's Journal* recorded, "who is the daughter of Mr. David Sheehy, ex-member of Parliament . . . delighted the large and fashionable audience."[16] Yet her political commitment is evident in her elocutionary selection, "Robert Emmet's Speech from the Dock." Her performance may have been in a culturally devalued, "feminine" form, but the political resonance of the speech of the hero of the United Irishman military rebellion could not have been ignored by the audience. Her representation in the newspaper places her work in the feminine sphere, but her presentation—a woman publicly reciting a speech promoting military insurrection—may actually have carried significant political weight.

The personal commitment of women like Gonne and Sheehy caused them to enter the public sphere as speakers and activists, but the representation of their acts by their audiences, male colleagues, and the press forced them to negotiate the phenomenological tension of female bodies doing men's work. Women whose work involved writing avoided the gender complexities inherent in performing physically in the public sphere. Ethna Carberry (Anna Johnson) and Alice Milligan, for example, edited *Shan Van Vocht,* a nationalist literary journal, from 1896 to 1899. Contributing writers, besides the editors, included Katharine Tynan, William Butler Yeats, and the socialist leader James Connolly.[17] Apparently writing, even about and in the public sphere, was deemed to be a "private" enough task for women to perform it without appearing to cross into the public, male realm. But at the same time integrating as many women as possible into the public sphere of the nationalist movement loosened the boundaries between women's and men's nationalist work, degendering many tasks and increasing opportunities for women's influence.

Inghinidhe na hEireann significantly contributed to integration of the nationalist movement by challenging the boundaries between private and public, personal and political, and individual and communal in women's political activity. The objects of the society included the following:

- To encourage the study of Gaelic Irish Literature, Music, and Art, especially amongst the young, by the organising and teaching of classes for the above subjects.
- To discourage the reading and circulation of low English literature, the singing of English songs, the attending of vulgar English entertainments at theatres and music-halls, and to combat in every way English influence, which is doing so much injury to the artistic taste and refinement of the Irish people.[18]

These objects were corroborated in the rules, which read, "Each member must adapt a Gaelic name by which she shall be known in the Association," and "Each member shall pledge herself to aid in extending and popularising Gaelic as a spoken tongue and to advance the Irish language movement by every means in her power."[19] Thus, the political act of affirming and proliferating Irish culture over colonial English influence was confirmed by the personal imperatives placed in the rules.

Another of *Inghinidhe's* objects, "To support and popularise Irish manufactures," called for the public act of strengthening Ireland's economy and decreasing its dependence on England. This object reflected *Inghinidhe's* rule that "[e]ach member shall pledge herself to support Irish manufacture by using as far as possible Irish-made goods in her household and dress."[20] In other words, an *Inghinidhe* member's public economic choices about maintaining her private sphere (dress, food, household goods) were recognized as politically charged activities that carried economic weight.

Finally, *Inghinidhe* members' commitment to the women's community is confirmed in the organization's first rule: "The *Inghinidhe na h-Eireann,* remembering that they are all workers in the same holy cause, pledge themselves to mutual help and support, and to stand loyally by one another."[21] Not only do the members' talents support the organization, but the organization's strength supports the individual members, providing a place where women's nationalist work will not only be allowed but valued.

Inghinidhe na hEireann immediately began classes in Irish language, history, and music for children over the age of nine[22] and it planned a Christmas Children's Treat for January 1902.[23] Yet their work included adult classes and entertainments as well. *Inghinidhe* sponsored monthly *ceilidhs* and invited members of other nationalist organizations such as the Celtic Literary Society.[24] An *Inghinidhe* member would read a paper on a Celtic heroine or famous woman in Irish history at each of these events, providing female role models for the other members and a public platform for the speaker.

The women also began to perform *tableaux vivants* on Irish themes, enlisting the help of Alice Milligan,[25] by then an active member of *Inghinidhe,* and a noted playwright in nationalist circles. Her one-act play, *The Last Feast of the Fianna,* had been performed by the Irish Literary Theatre in 1900. Titles of these tableaux included "The Battle of Clontarf," "The Children of Lir," and "The Fairy Changeling."[26]

The Irish nationalist community warmly received these tableaux, which were performed by *Inghinidhe* members and male collaborators in the project, including Douglas Hyde, the leader of the Gaelic League and a playwright and actor in his own right.[27] When an April 1901 production was staged before a full house in the Antient Concert Rooms, the *Freeman's Journal* noted that:

> the whole production reflects the greatest credit on all concerned, not only for the faultless manner in which the several performers acquitted themselves, but for the evident attention that was given to historic accuracy by those who had the difficult task of arranging and grouping the figures conceived in accordance with the tradition or story represented.[28]

The content of these tableaux reflects a degree of tension between traditional women's representations in Irish culture and the more independent identities *Inghinidhe* members were cultivating in their own lives. "The Battle of Clontarf," for example, tells the story of King Brian's army driving the Danes out of Ireland. The *United Irishman* stated that the tableaux "brought vividly back to us the fateful Good Friday eight hundred years ago when the Irish warriors broke for ever the power of the Vikings, and changed the current of European history."[29] Rather than beginning with the story of the battle, however, the first tableau established the well-being of Irishpersons—most notably Irish women—under Brian's reign. It presented "the bejewelled lady who wandered through our island, protected only by her maiden smile," while a "bewildered knight—more than likely a Saxon knight-errant" looked on, puzzled that the woman needed no protection from harm during King Brian's reign.[30] This first image implies that the eleventh-century (and, correspondingly, the nineteenth-century) Irish followed loftier ethical and moral codes than did their English counterparts. It also creates an idealized image of the Irish woman as beautiful and pure. Yet at the same time this idealization of Irish womanhood is ultimately passive, unlike the politically engaged *Inghinidhe*. Other tableaux, however, portrayed women in more active roles, including "Maeve, greatest of Ireland's ancient heroines, [and] Grania Mhaol visiting Elizabeth and pulverising the virgin monarch, who strove to impress the splendid Irishwoman."[31]

Inghinidhe na hEireann was also active in the production of Irish plays, performing the works of playwrights such as Alice Milligan and Father Dinneen.[32] The actresses were members of *Inghinidhe*, while male actors were recruited from such nationalist groups as the Celtic Literary Society and the Gaelic League. *Inghinidhe* hired William G. Fay as a teacher and director. Fay, with his brother Frank, had been performing as the W. G. Fay Comedy Combination and directing the Ormond Dramatic Society, but he was unable to support himself solely through the theater. Along with teaching acting and directing plays for *Inghinidhe,* Fay attended some of the group's meetings, reflecting some interest on his part in the women's other nationalist activities. *Inghinidhe na hEireann*'s dramatic events quickly became popular throughout the nationalist community, and it even earned the distinction of being the first group in modern Dublin to perform a play completely in the Irish language—P. T. MacGinley's *Eilis agus Bhean Deirce* (*Ellis and the Beggarwoman*).[33]

By 1901, *Inghinidhe* performances were well recognized and attended throughout the nationalist community, but it was not the only group working toward creating an Irish drama. The commercial dramatic house, the Queen's Royal Theatre, produced popular Irish melodramas based on nationalist themes with patriotic titles like *Wolfe Tone* and *The Famine* to packed houses, and these performances influenced the development of an Irish identity among the working classes. Gaelic League chapters throughout Ireland continued to promote their national identity through performances at *feisianna* and *caelidhs*.

The best-remembered company of this period, however, is the Irish Literary Theatre. Headed by W. B. Yeats, George Moore, Edward Martyn, and Lady Augusta Gregory, the Irish Literary Theatre represented an intellectual and class elite among nationalist theaters of the time. Its leaders were Anglo-Irish or wealthy Catholics who strove to create a "high" art for Ireland. Its leaders wrote prolifically in the newspapers about their productions and their goals: they even published a yearly journal, which addressed their philosophy, progress, and goals and published the texts of their plays. Although they were generally well received in the nationalist movement, they often alienated other nationalist groups who preferred more clearly political appeals for Irish independence. One of the Irish Literary Theatre's main conflicts with the nationalist movement emerged from its preference for trained English actors rather than local talent in the production of its plays. These English actors often could not pronounce the names of the Irish characters they portrayed. In 1901, during their third season, the Irish Literary Theatre disbanded, having determined that using English actors in Irish plays was futile but believing that there were no Irish actors qualified to perform their plays.

When they saw *Inghinidhe na hEireann*'s performances in the summer of that year, however, Yeats and his comrades changed their minds. The production was staged during the Dublin Horse Show as a nationalist alternative to Anglo-Irish entertainments. Along with a series of tableaux *Inghinidhe* presented Alice Milligan's *The Deliverance of Red Hugh* and *The Harp That Once,* along with P. T. MacGinley's *Eilis agus Bhean Deirce.*[34] In his autobiography, Yeats remembered, "I came away with my head on fire. I wanted to hear my own unfinished *Baile's Strand,* to hear Greek tragedy spoken with a Dublin accent."[35] In 1902, the Irish Literary Theatre, Fay and the *Inghinidhe* actors (now known as W. G. Fay's Dramatic Company), and *Inghinidhe na hEireann* agreed to collaborate on a production in April 1902.

The groups decided to perform George Russell's *Deirdre,* but since it was too short for a full evening's entertainment Yeats (with the assistance of his collaborator, Lady Gregory) contributed *Kathleen ni Houlihan,* a one-act drama set around the United Irishman Rebellion of 1798. In this, the most blatantly nationalistic of Yeats's plays, the Gillane family is preparing for the marriage of their son, Michael, and looking forward to happier economic times to be brought by the bride's dowry, when an old woman enters the house. The "Poor Old Woman" turns out to be Kathleen ni Houlihan, a mythic folk figure who beckons Ireland's young men to defend the nation. Kathleen woos Michael away from the house, and the young man abandons his bride to die for his country. But his blood sacrifice renews the land, represented in the transformation of Kathleen. After Michael rushes out of the house, his younger brother, Patrick, reenters. His parents ask him if he has seen an old woman on the road. Patrick replies, "I did not, but I saw a young girl, and she had the walk of a queen."[36]

Yeats wrote the part of Kathleen with Maud Gonne in mind, and he asked her to play it. Gonne had refused to perform in Yeats's *The Countess Cathleen* with the Irish Literary Theatre a few years earlier, but, recognizing the political influence her presence would create on the stage and wishing to support the event, she agreed to perform the role. In her autobiography, *A Servant of the Queen,* Gonne remarked that she performed the role because "it would have great importance for the Nationalist Movement."[37]

Gonne's visibility in Irish nationalism at demonstrations, meetings, and other events, and as the founder of *Inghinidhe na hEireann,* made her a controversial and, some argued, unfeminine public figure whose work was already too "theatrical" to be taken seriously. Dudley Digges, an actor in the 1902 performances, commented on the danger implicit in her taking the stage: "[Gonne] hesitated to give the loyalists a chance to ridicule her and say: 'Ah . . . yes . . . of course . . . the stage, that's where she belongs.'"[38] Gonne was aware of the emotion her identity in the movement would generate when she played Kathleen ni Houlihan, the ghostly figure beckoning Irishmen to die for national independence. Theatrical performance potentially could have broken the balance Gonne constantly negotiated between her presentation of the nationalist cause and her representation as an "extraordinary woman." She hoped her reputation as a nationalist figure would make the play more political, but it could easily have made her political activity seem, in retrospect, pure theater. Perhaps that is why she served the Irish theater later as an administrator rather than as a performer and reserved her public presentations for strictly political events unmediated by the traditional stage.

But Gonne enthusiastically took the risk to show her support for the production and the groups involved in it, and the gamble with her reputation ultimately paid off. The actress Maire Nic Shiubhlaigh, who would later perform the same role at the Abbey Theatre, said of Gonne's performance that "in her, the youth of the country saw all that was magnificent in Ireland. She was the very personification of the figure she played on stage."[39] Gonne's ability to play upon her political identity in Irish nationalism in her portrayal of this mythic national figure made her performance one of the most remembered in Irish theatrical history. Likewise, the affiliation of the other actors with *Inghinidhe na hEireann* was also visible to the audience.

Kathleen ni Houlihan, despite its folkloric theme, is set at an actual moment in Irish history—the landing of the French at Kinsalla during the United Irishman revolt of 1798. Russell's *Deirdre,* however, is based upon a story from the Red Branch cycle of ancient Irish myth, making the political overtones of the play more oblique.[40] By using a mythological story, Russell sidestepped an overt discussion of contemporary issues of cultural identity or national history. Yet to tell a story from Ireland's ancient past was to mythopoeticize Ireland's ancient heroes, making them and their situations metaphors for the author's and performers' contemporary situation. The ways in which Russell manipulated his source story, and its performance by *Inghinidhe* members and nationalist actors with other affiliations, transformed the myth into a metaphor for the need for unity and inclusion among different groups within the nationalist movement.

In the source story, Deirdre, a beautiful woman promised to Concobar, High King of the Red Branch (an alliance of kings in Ireland), runs away with the warrior, Naoise, and they exile themselves in Scotland. Concobar, in his jealousy, convinces Fergus, another Red Branch king, to persuade them to return to Ireland, assuring Fergus that he has forgiven the lovers. Deirdre and Naoise return to Ireland, but Fergus stays behind to attend a feast, planning to join them later. Concobar betrays his word and kills Naoise. Deirdre later commits suicide.

Usually Deirdre is portrayed as an Irish Helen of Troy—a passive beauty whose treachery brings down the alliance of the Red Branch. In Russell's story, however, a divine vision rather than uncontrolable passion brings Deirdre and Naoise together. Their elopement is not so much selfish as it is inevitable—an admission of the predominance of Divine Will over earthly law. Russell also adds another strong female character, the Druidess, Lavarcam. Acknowledged as a wise woman by all the characters, Lavarcam foresees the ensuing tragedy and advises Naoise and Concobar to set aside their quarrels and maintain unity among the Red Branch at any cost. Deirdre, likewise, understands the political consequences of Naoise and her actions and urges him to avoid conflict with Concobar, knowing it will lead to the destruction of themselves and of their culture.

Deirdre and Lavarcam, thus, are not femmes fatales or benign beauties passively awaiting rescue but active and sympathetic figures. Russell's play gives them a high degree of agency, and both characters are respected for their wisdom and bravery by the men in the play. *Inghinidhe na hEireann* members who played these roles, therefore, portrayed these Irishwomen as brave, intelligent, willing to live or die for their ideals, and worthy of the respect of their male counterparts. This is the role for Irishwomen that *Inghinidhe na hEireann* cultivated on stage in their dramatic performances and offstage among the nationalist community.

Inghinidhe's involvement in that performance, on April 2 in the Hall of St. Teresa's Total Abstinence Association, was highly visible. The organization's name was listed first on the program cover, and it also received credit for sewing the costumes. The house, which was "too crowded for comfort," with "an audience vibrating with enthusiasm and quick to seize every point and to grasp every situation"[41] can also be credited to *Inghinidhe,* which publicized and sold tickets for the event.[42] Further, the actors in W. G. Fay's company were all either members of *Inghinidhe na hEireann* (Mary Walker, Maire Quinn, Maud Gonne) or members of the Celtic Literary Society who had performed in *Inghinidhe* performances: "[T]he large banner of the 'Inghinidhe na h-Eireann,' having a gold sunburst on a blue ground, hung near the stage."[43]

The *United Irishman* most clearly stated the significance of the event: "*Inghinidhe na hEireann,* aided by the Messrs. Fay, have made it possible to dispense with the English actor in the presentation of Irish drama."[44] But in

FIG. 2. Cover of the
program for *Deirdre* and
Kathleen ni Houlihan, April
2–4, 1902. (Courtesy of
the Special Collections
Department, Northwest-
ern University Library.)

the gendered language of the more mainstream presses (and ultimately historical memory) these signs of *Inghinidhe*'s involvement were practically
invisible. The tasks performed by the organization as a whole, which could
not be attributed to an individual, like sewing costumes, organizing, and
selling tickets, were deemed unimportant, anonymous, or simply "women's
work" by the press and in later recollections by participants in the event.
Thus, they were relegated to devalued labor and not worth notice.
Although *Inghinidhe* originally gathered the actors together and hired Fay to
direct them, Fay's position as director has caused him to be remembered as
the only developer of that company.

By the time of the performances' closing reviews, *Inghinidhe*'s involvement as an organization had disappeared from representations of the event
in most Irish newspapers. The *Freeman's Journal* review of April 7, 1902,
records the speeches delivered by Russell and Yeats, the playwrights, who
expressed their excitement over the future of Irish national theater. The

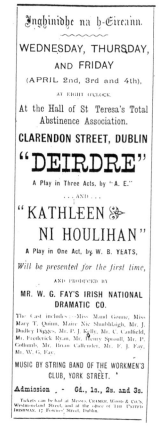

FIG. 3. Advertisement for the performance of *Deirdre* and *Kathleen ni Houlihan*, as it appeared in the nationalist paper, *The United Irishman*. (From the April 5, 1902 issue.) Courtesy of Dublin Corporation Public Libraries, Dublin and Irish Local Studies Collection.

only acknowledgment of the production itself recorded in the review was a comment by Yeats.

> He congratulated Mr. Fay upon the great success of his effort at the formation of an Irish National Dramatic company which in his opinion had already shown itself well fitted to carry on the work of the Irish Literary Theatre.[45]

Yeats's comment obliterates the Inghinidhe's involvement by crediting only Fay with gathering the actors when actually he had been hired by the Inghinidhe. Further, by implying that the company will carry on the work of the Irish Literary Theatre, he appropriates the successful history of Inghinidhe's dramatic efforts, aligning it to his own failed project.

Thus, the collaborative effort of this performance project by several groups was ultimately recorded as the work of a few individuals. *Inghinidhe* members who acted in the play were regarded as actresses but not as nationalists. Ultimately Gonne's performance would become the most remembered aspect of the performances, and it did provide added political resonance to Yeats's play. But with the disappearance of *Inghinidhe* in the history of the production her involvement is remembered mainly as a favor to Yeats.

Maire Nic Shuibhliagh, another *Inghinidhe* member who performed in *Deirdre* in 1902, continued to work with Fay and the Irish National Theatre and acquired a great reputation on the Irish stage. But just as the Inghinidhe has receded from the historical memory of the Irish Dramatic Movement, Nic Shuibhliagh's political activity has receded in light of her acting career. Not only was Nic Shuibhliagh active in the Inghinidhe but she fought as a senior member of the *Cumann na mBan,* another women's group, in the Easter Rising of 1916.

By the time the Irish National Theatre Society was established in 1903, *Inghinidhe* had discontinued its official dramatic activity, although some of its members were involved in both organizations.[46] In fact, *Inghinidhe* members would become visible everywhere in the Irish national movement. They were stars of the Abbey Stage, leaders of *Sinn Fein* and *Cumann na mBan,* union leaders, suffrage leaders, and, during the Easter Rising, soldiers. They were performing women's work not as auxiliary women in male-dominated groups, as they were in the 1890s, but as women in increasingly integrated political organizations. Yet the work of *Inghinidhe na hEireann,* ultimately caught in the gendered representation of Ireland's history, has remained more or less invisible.

To a large extent, the early history of the Irish Dramatic Movement is a gendered history, focusing on the work of men like William Butler Yeats, George Moore, and the Fays while until recently it devalued or ignored the group contributions of organizations like *Inghinidhe na hEireann* and the work of individual women like Alice Milligan, Maire Nic Shuibhliagh, Annie Horniman, Lady Gregory, Maud Gonne, and many others. Women are usually recounted in the history as they were perceived by the men in the movement. But recording the women's work in this way occludes the true diversity and complexity of the early Irish Dramatic Movement while denying the significant aesthetic, organizational, and political contributions women made both in the context of Irish theater and in the nationalist project of which that theater was a part. To deny these women their place in the history of Irish theater is to veil the true heterogeneity of Irish cultural identity within the Irish nationalist movement and the wide aesthetic and ideological scopes of performance practices at this volatile time in Irish national history.

NOTES

I wish to thank Tracy C. Davis of Northwestern University for her advice and guidance on the conception and research of this essay.

1. Cynthia Enloe, *Bananas, Beaches, and Bases: Making Feminist Sense of International Politics* (Berkeley: University of California Press, 1990), 162.

2. Margaret Ward, *Unmanageable Revolutionaries: Women and Irish Nationalism* (London: Pluto, 1983), 48–49.

3. Maud Gonne MacBride, *A Servant of the Queen* (London: Victor Gollancz, 1974), 294–95.

4. "Patriotic Children's Treat," *United Irishman,* June 9, 1900, 6.

5. "Patriotic Children's Treat," *United Irishman,* June 30, 1900, 8.

6. "Patriotic Children's Treat," *United Irishman,* July 7, 1900, 7.

7. Ibid.

8. Ibid.

9. Ibid.

10. Ibid.

11. Gonne MacBride, *Servant of the Queen,* 295.

12. Daphne Spain, *Gendered Spaces* (Chapel Hill: University of North Carolina Press, 1992).

13. Padraic Colum, "Early Days of the Irish Theatre," in *The Abbey Theatre: Interviews and Recollections,* ed. E. H. Mikhail (London: Macmillan, 1988), 61.

14. Rosemary Cullens Owens, *Smashing Times: A History of the Irish Women's Suffrage Movement, 1889–1922* (Dublin: Attic, 1984), 30.

15. Ward, *Unmanageable Revolutionaries,* 47.

16. "Miss Margaret M. Sheehy in the Provinces," *Freeman's Journal,* April 7, 1902, 2.

17. C. L. Innes, *Woman and Nation in Irish Literature and Society, 1880–1935* (Athens: University of Georgia Press, 1993), 135–36.

18. Printed on the back of the "Programme for *Deirdre* and *Kathleen ni Houlihan*" (Dublin: N.p., 1902), 4.

19. Ibid.

20. Ibid.

21. Ibid.

22. Ward, *Unmanageable Revolutionaries,* 52.

23. "Inghinidhe na h-Eireann: Christmas Treat to Children Learning Irish," *Freeman's Journal,* December 31, 1901, 2.

24. Ward, *Unmanageable Revolutionaries,* 52.

25. Robert Hogan and James Kilroy, *The Irish Literary Theatre, 1899–1901* (Dublin: Dolmen, 1975), 85–86.

26. John J. Reynolds, "The Daughters of Erin," *The Gael* (August 1902), 258.

27. Ibid.

28. "Inghinidhe na h-Eireann: Gaelic Tableaux Vivants," *Freeman's Journal*, April 10, 1901, 5.

29. "Inghinidhe na hEireann: The Gaelic Tableaux," *United Irishman*, April 13, 1901, 5.

30. Ibid.

31. Ibid.

32. Hogan and Kilroy, *Irish Literary Theatre*, 85.

33. Reynolds, "Daughters of Erin," 258.

34. Ward, *Unmanageable Revolutionaries*, 56.

35. William Butler Yeats, *Dramatis Personae* (New York: Macmillan, 1936), 72.

36. William Butler Yeats, "Cathleen ni Houlihan," in *The Collected Plays of W. B. Yeats*, 57 (New York: MacMillan, 1953).

37. Quoted in Robert Hogan and James Kilroy, *Laying the Foundations, 1902–1904* (Dublin: Dolmen), 76.

38. Dudley Digges, "A Theatre Was Made," in *The Abbey Theatre: Interviews and Recollections*, ed. E.H. Mikhail (London: Macmillan, 1988), 33.

39. Quoted in Ward, *Unmanageable Revolutionaries*, 56–57.

40. George Russell [AE], "Deirdre," in *Plays of the Irish Renaissance, 1880–1930*, ed. Curtis Canfield, 66–91 (New York: Ives Washburn, 1929).

41. "Two Irish Plays by Mr. W. B. Yeats and A.E.: The Performance Last Night," *Freeman's Journal*, April 3, 1902, 5.

42. "Inghinidhe na h'Eireann," *Freeman's Journal*, April 1, 1902, 7.

43. "Two Irish Plays," 5.

44. "All Ireland," *United Irishman*, March 29, 1902, 1.

45. "'Deirdre' and 'Kathleen ni Houlihan'," *Freeman's Journal*, April 7, 1902, 7.

46. Ward, *Unmanageable Revolutionaries*, 57.

3.

Adam Versényi

The Mexican Revolution:
Religion, Politics, and Theater

The 1994 New Year's rebellion by the Zapatista Liberation Front in Chiapas, Mexico, is only the most recent event involving marginalized populations in modern Mexican history. In its negotiations with the Mexican government, the guerrillas, members of a number of indigenous populations, have demanded significant reforms in landownership, education, and political structure. Above all, they have demanded respect for indigenous religion, rituals, and practices and assurances that those practices will continue unmolested. All of these demands, the performative nature of the timing of the uprising, and the combination of religious with political concerns, echo the mixture of politics, religion, and theater present in Latin America since the time of the Conquest. Rebellion, mixed with the coming of a new year, and the possibility of change inherent in the presidential political process of that year, together with the costumed presence of the rebels in their ski masks and the media savvy of Comandante Marcos, are all elements that signal the theatrical nature of the Zapatista rebellion and the potential impact certain aspects of performance can have upon politics. In capturing the imagination of the Mexican populace at a particular moment in time the Zapatistas enter the pantheon of political actors in Latin American history who have capitalized upon performance in order to effect social change. Throughout Latin America, theater has historically been seen as a catalyst for change in the existing social order. This was most evident in Mexico at the beginning of the twentieth century when the Mexican Revolution greatly affected the form and content of the theater and the course of Mexican education. As elsewhere in the region, theater and education were inextricably linked to political and religious concerns. In the emergence of the Zapatistas and their determination to redress the wrongs inflicted upon Emiliano Zapata's constituency by the Revolution, the repercussions of Cortés's greeting to the Twelve Franciscans at Tenochtitlán continue to reverberate throughout Mexico several hundred years after the Conquest.

Where the mendicants saw themselves as tilling the land in the New World in order to prepare the soil for salvation, Mexican history presents a picture of the revolutionary government approaching education with apostolic fervor. The mendicants' millenarianism led them to practice certain theater forms designed to support mass conversion and to undermine Aztec authority. The twentieth-century Mexican government also saw itself as living on the cusp of a new millennium. Where the mendicants insisted upon the salvific powers of Christianity, the revolutionary government preached a secular gospel that had to be followed to attain a state of grace. Both brands of millenarianism found it necessary to convert masses of people to avoid apocalypse, and in both cases those masses of people were of indigenous descent. With its educational policies, however, the revolutionary government unleashed its own Armageddon. Its fields of combat were the schools, the Cristero Rebellion, and the theater.

The Franciscans' highly successful combination of Christian symbolism with Aztec spectacle as an armament in their evangelical arsenal meant that Christian influence, whether welcomed or battled against, has been a nearly universal presence in Mexico ever since. During the Conquest and the War of Independence images of the Virgins of Guadalupe and the Remedies were carried into battle by both sides and were frequently awarded military rank after successful campaigns. The Mexican Fr. Miguel Hidalgo y Costilla started the fight for independence at his church in Dolores, Guanajuato, with the cry "Long live the Virgin of Guadalupe and death to bad government!" The Royalist army carried banners with the image of the Virgen de los Remedios, which had been brought with the Spaniards to Mexico during the Conquest. Both virgins attained the rank of general during the War of Independence.

> When either side got a banner away from the other with the "enemy" Virgin on it, it was shot like a traitor. During the ten years of fighting, the people did not dare to have an image of the Virgin of Guadalupe in a niche outside for fear of being shot by the Royalists. But after the Insurgents won, their Virgin had more influence than ever. Now her image is seen everywhere—in churches, chapels, in niches on bridges

and houses, even on liquor bottles; it is reproduced in paint, stone, metal, glass.[1]

The summary executions of religious symbols bears a marked resemblance to the ritual "Flowery Wars" engaged in by the Aztecs to propitiate the Sun God, which were appropriated by the Franciscans for use in mass theatrical spectacles for evangelical purposes.

While a combination of religious and military activity was a part of Mexican history throughout the first quarter of the twentieth century, religious spectacle of a theatrical nature persists to the present day in villages scattered throughout Mexico and the southwestern part of the United States that was once Mexican territory. These are plays of a religious character performed by villagers with no formal training who enact and improvise from a predetermined scenario. Such scenarios tend to fall into four categories: portrayals of biblical stories from the Old and New Testaments, dance-dramas (the most famous of which is probably the *Dance of the Moors and the Christians*), reenactments of the Crucifixion of Christ, and plays that depict religious events in the New World such as the miraculous appearance of the Virgin of Guadalupe.[2] Of all of these types the plays depicting Nativity and the Passion were the most popular. Barker describes the common Nativity play as follows.

In addition to their common theme of the pilgrimage of the shepherds to Bethlehem, most of these plays have one or more episodes in which the Devil attempts to break up the procession. In most of them, also, it is the Archangel Michael who finally vanquishes Lucifer and leads the shepherds safely to the Holy Manger. Although the plays vary in their recital of the events connected with the Nativity, almost all of them end with the adoration scene in which the shepherds present their humble gifts to the Christ child.

Similarity of plot in many of the shepherds' plays is paralleled by similarity of characters and lines. Besides the Devil and St. Michael, many of the plays feature a hermit, not too holy to be tempted, a gluttonous shepherd named Bato, and his coquettish wife, Gila, and a lazy and crusty old shepherd named Bartolo, who provides comic relief. The various episodes of the plays are introduced by quatrains sung by the *letra*, or chorus; the passage of time between episodes is indicated by the singing of the *caminatas*, or marching songs.[3]

In terms of the continuity of indigenous practice mixed with Christian forms, perhaps the most interesting of these religious dramas is the passion play *Las tres caídas de Jesucristo* (Jesus Christ's Three Falls) as performed in Ixtapalapa, D.F., Mexico. For the most part it is a fairly straightforward dramatization of the Passion beginning with Caiaphas and Herod's decision that Jesus' death is the only way to remove the threat to their rule, and ending with the Crucifixion and Resurrection of Christ. Unlike some other folk dramas, this play isn't a scenario but a full-fledged script. While the opening scenes are heavily expository and static, the dynamism of the events that it chronicles and the inherent conflict they contain gradually creates dramatic interest. The day after the play's performance is completed, Saturday of Holy Week, the Ascension is depicted in the San Lucas parish church by the simple recourse of raising Christ's image, superimposed over some white and gold cardboard clouds, above the altar in such a way that the strings that support it cannot be seen.

The most interesting aspect of this play, however, is the way in which the person portraying the part of Jesus is required to go into seclusion thirty days before Holy Thursday when the play begins. During that time the actor is to "dedicate himself to the practice of spiritual exercises, which will serve to prepare him, and to contemplate deeply, with all proper spiritual absorption and respect, the role he is about to play." The actors who portray the two thieves, Dimas and Gesta, are also kept in seclusion, but only during the fifteen days prior to Holy Thursday. During this time period all three actors receive simple, Spartan meals.[4] This ritual purification of the three actors is reminiscent of the ritual purification of the actor portraying the role of Quetzalcóatl in the annual Aztec festival for Quetzalcóatl. While *Las tres caídas de Jesucristo* presents us with nothing approaching the conflation of the matrix of actor/character/audience present in the Aztec festival—the actors playing Jesus Christ and the two thieves aren't actually crucified—there is an association of the actor with the character portrayed. In order to portray character the actor must be set apart so that he can attain a purified state distinct from that experienced in daily life. The play already deals with material from the holy scriptures, and by introducing the purification ritual it becomes a sacred rite. What we are seeing here is the end result of the early evangelical theater after it had adopted the spectacular and transformational aspects of ritual performance and wedded them to Christian theological and political concerns. As in the days of the Conquest, Christian and colonial ideology has been incorporated into indigenous ritual. The sacrificial aspects of the ritual have been removed, but the perfor-

mance still has a transformational character. As in the Aztec festival of Quetzalcoátl, the ultimate purpose of Las tres caídas de Jesucristo is convergence of
the community in worshiping the god.

Similar in conception and execution to Las tres caídas de Jesucristo is the
version of the Passion performed annually at Milpa Alta, D.F. The Milpa
Alta play dramatizes the events of the Passion as well, the differences being
the inclusion of scenes enacted within the church itself (rather than exclusively at sites in the open air scattered about the village), frequent interpola-
tions of various sermons appropriate to the scene being played, and substitution of an image of Christ for the actor-priest playing the role at a certain
point in the story. The text itself seems less dramatic and, as the interpola-
tions of sermons demonstrates, more didactic than that of other passion
plays. There are also numerous times when Falvio, servant to Pilate sent to
observe the events, speaks directly to the audience in anachronistic passages
drawn from the later scriptures describing what will happen to those who
denied the Messiah at the time.[5]

This play presents us with a further step in the evolution of Mexican
ritual performance. Here the actor portraying Christ is an actual priest, supposedly virtuous enough to dispense with purifying rites, but even the priest
is seen as an inadequate substitute for the god, who is more fully represented
by his iconographic image. The evolution from the sacrificial offering of the
actor-god Quetzalcoátl to the highly symbolic crucifixion of an iconographic representation of Christ demonstrates that ritual performance, in
this instance at least, has moved further and further away from a direct
impact upon the actors involved and reached the level of abstract theological representation. Although folk performances of religious dramas dealing
with biblical subjects can contain elements of indigenous forms and presentation, the majority of them seem to have more in common with medieval
European cycle plays. As in the medieval drama, content is drawn from the
scriptures and even the interpolation of comic characters appears to have
come about in a similar fashion. There is another Mexican theatrical presentation, however, that seems closer to both the indigenous spectacle and
the mendicant evangelical theater. This is the so-called theater of masses,
which takes the methods of religious folk drama and tries to reorient them
toward an understanding of Mexican history and the possibilities for
progress informed by the goals and ideals of the Mexican Revolution.

Official government interest in the teatro de masas was the natural outcome of the Mexican government's approach to education after the Revolution. At the beginning of the twentieth century more than 70 percent of

the Mexican population was illiterate, and the majority of schools were run by the Church, which was frequently more interested in religious instruction than comprehensive education. The Porfirio Díaz dictatorship, itself more interested in the economic and political strength of the nation than in its schools, did little to challenge the Church's hegemony over education. Allowing the Church free reign in educational matters was, in fact, a relatively painless way for Díaz to ensure Church support in other areas.

The Mexican Revolution permanently changed governmental attitudes toward education. The 1917 Constitution guaranteed the right to a free primary education, and in 1920 President Alvaro Obregón named José Vasconcelos, an idealist with a messianic approach to education, secretary of public education. Obregón's successor, Plutarco Elías Calles, a former schoolteacher, proclaimed the institution of universal public education. Calles's "socialist" schools were bitterly opposed by the Church and the Cristero rebels, who often left the public schools bathed in their teachers' blood. The populist presidency of Lázaro Cárdenas extended the reach of public education by requiring each industrial and agricultural firm in the nation to maintain a school for its workers' children. This edict increased the number of public schools to fifteen hundred, all under the control of the secretary of public education.

In 1921, the secretary of agriculture and economic development authorized the construction of a regional open-air theater by Rafael M. Saavedra in San Juan Teotihuacán. Using the traditional religious dramas as a springboard, Saavedra produced plays that were a combination of didactic scenes and popular diversions. The works presented included "a choreographic representation of native industries, a rhythmic pantomime of daily tasks in saddlery and blacksmithing," and a "mime about the life of slavery lived by the Indians on the cane plantations in the State of Morelos."[6] Saavedra's theater was soon taken over by the secretary of education and was abandoned when Saavedra himself moved on to other interests, but he had provided the model for the mass spectacles to come.

In 1929, a gigantic open-air theater with nine thousand seats was constructed at the Centro Social Deportivo para Trabajadores "Venustiano Carranza." One of the first pieces performed in this theater was *Liberación* (Liberation, 1929) by Efrén Orozco Rosales (1903–73). Orozco Rosales has said that his greatest concern in writing the play was "to make the Mexican people more conscious of their great tradition so that they would be able to identify themselves with that which was theirs and feel proud of the fact that they were Mexicans."[7] *Liberación* is nothing more nor less than a dramatization of Mexican history from the founding of Mexico City to the early twentieth century. The piece calls for a cast of 1,235 people who perform against a "schematic representation of the Valley of Mexico."[8] Largely a hieratic display with the occasional interpolation of phrases spoken in unison by the gigantic cast, *Liberación* attempts to focus on the most important moments of Mexican history. In its progression from the Conquest to the Cacicazgo (the period following the French intervention, which was ended by urban aristocrats and rural caciques, who, with clerical and military support, took advantage of the confused political situation to steal land and increase their economic and political power) the play presents the events leading up to the Mexican Revolution and the country's final liberation. In its use of spectacle, battles, and music, *Liberación* resembles the mendicant evangelical theater. While Orozco Rosales's play does not end with mass conversion through baptism, as do a number of the mendicant plays, the triumph of the Revolution is presented as a secular form of salvation for the Mexican people. This salvation is the result of a reorganization of society in which the meek and the humble are vindicated for all their years of suffering and afforded proper respect for their contribution to society. That reorganization is the direct result of the *mestizaje* (mixture) that has characterized Mexican history. The mixture of Spanish and indigenous bloodlines translates into the mixture of various classes necessary to create a revolutionary society. *Liberación* seeks to demonstrate the vitality of this new Latin American society and, in a symbolic display containing numerous ceremonial aspects similar to the Catholic Mass, to confirm the Revolution's viability in the eyes of the faithful.

Orozco Rosales wrote a series of these plays for the *teatro de masas,* including *Tierra y Libertad* (Land and Liberty, 1933), a gigantic pantomime about the Mexican Revolution that presents the innovation of short dialogues made possible by hidden microphones; *Creación del Quinto Sol* (Creation of the Fifth Sun, 1935); *Sacrificio gladitorio* (Gladiatorial Sacrifice, 1935), written in conjunction with Carlos González and first performed for the Twentieth Lions Club Convention in 1935; and *El mensajero del sol* (Messenger to the Sun), presented in 1941 in honor of the Second Inter-American Travel Congress and the Fourth Pan-American Highway Congress. *Creación del Quinto Sol* depicts the sacrifice of the Aztec gods Tecusitecatl and Nanaoatzin, who threw themselves into fire, creating a new sun and moon, in order to save the world from darkness. *Sacrificio gladitorio* presents a dramatization of the Aztec custom of permitting prisoners to engage in single combat with their warriors. In this case the prisoner wins and is given the hand of one of the court ladies. The performance, which ends with a lavishly costumed display of various aspects of Aztec life, required three thousand actors for the three sections.[9] *El mensajero del sol* was another massive open-air performance requiring fourteen hundred participants and depicting the annual Aztec ceremony in which a "Messenger to the Sun" was sacrificed in order to maintain the sun's light and heat.

Each of these plays rejects colonially imposed history and resuscitates Aztec nobility of spirit as the foundation upon which the nation's life after the Revolution should be based. Where the folk-religious drama moves closer to the forms imposed upon indigenous ritual practice by the evangelical church, the *teatro de masas* recaptures the indigenous rituals themselves, utilizing them as a moral foundation for the new regime. At the same time, however, these plays put forth the notion that the people must be guided by the Revolutionary government. Thus, the paternal authority of the Church is replaced by that of the regime, and the attitude toward its people exhibited to this day by the Institutional Revolutionary Party (PRI) in Mexico is already in place.

While the series of works described present the peculiar spectacle of supposedly consciousness-raising works for the Mexican populace being patronized by international business and trade organizations, in the 1940s the Mexican government determined that this sort of spectacle could have educational benefits, and the Department of Public Education began to produce performances of its own. In 1944, it produced an Orozco Rosales piece called *La bandera nacional* (The National Flag), which utilized close to four thousand actors and recounted the history of the national flag. In 1945, the department produced a piece called *Siembra* (Sowing Time) written by Orozco Rosales in collaboration with Waldeen and Julio Prieto. The play attacks illiteracy, showing the illiterate as dominated by personifications of evils such as poverty, hunger, alcoholism, witchcraft, and general misery. The schoolteachers in the play fight to free the people from these tyrannical oppressors by planting the "seed" of learning.

Obregón's appointment of the philosopher-educator José Vasconcelos to the post of secretary of public education completely transformed the face of Mexican education. Vasconcelos approached his new role with apostolic fervor and missionary zeal. His role, he said, was to "preach the gospel of the *mestizo* by trying to impress on the minds of the new race a consciousness of their mission as builders of entirely new concepts of life."[10] He saw his duty as "saving the children, educating the youth, and redeeming the Indians" by sending them "teachers who would imitate the action of the

Catholic missionaries of the colonies, sent among the Indians, who did not, as yet, know the Spanish language."[11] In order to carry out this ambitious task, Vasconcelos, exhorting his teachers to carry out a "holy crusade for civilization," fostered the creation of the Cultural Mission Program, which led to the notion that every school was a "house of the people." In all of this, as had been the case with the colonial missionaries, theater played a large role.

The Cultural Missions aimed to improve the economic well-being, health and sanitation, homes, nutrition, and cultural conditions of the rural communities. This task was accomplished, however, not by imposing solutions brought by the *misioneros* , but by stimulating the people themselves to take action and utilize their own intelligence and resources. The *misioneros* were the facilitators, not the dictators, of action. Unlike the mendicants, who utilized indigenous forms primarily for the parallels that could be drawn between them and Christianity, replacing Aztec authority with Christian authority, the *misioneros* encouraged the population to discover ways in which their own daily practices could provide solutions to the problems they confronted.

One of the most effective educational tools utilized by the *misioneros* was the theater. In 1930, a *misionero* conceived the idea of using theater to educate the people in his village about the dangers of the alcoholism that was widespread there. He wrote a one-act play and, together with his students, constructed a small open-air theater. Building the theater and rehearsing the play proved to be so successful in terms of providing the participants with recreational opportunities other than those afforded by the local bars that the idea of theater as a force for social change spread rapidly throughout the country. In the next two years, 3,500 to 4,000 open-air theaters were built in rural communities. Many of these theaters used a wall of the village church to form the back of the stage.

Consciously or not, these revolutionary missionaries were repeating many of the same methods used by evangelical theater after the Conquest. The Church in the New World created the new architectural form of the *capilla abierta*, or "open chapel." The open chapel gave out onto a large courtyard (*atrio*), modeled upon that of the Aztec temples, and provided an ideal setting for a theater audience. The Catholic missionaries, at first lacking the ability to converse with the indigenous population in their native tongue, employed theatrical technique and the preexisting artistic ability of the Indian population to convert that population to Christianity. Hundreds of years later the *misioneros*, lacking conventional educational resources in rural communities and frequently confronted by a population that spoke no Spanish, seized upon the artistic ability of the descendants of the colonial Indian population as a means of converting that population to the social doctrine of the new revolutionary government. While the methods the *misioneros* used were nearly identical to those of their religious forbears, the *misioneros* taught a totally secular doctrine that focused upon temporal, not spiritual, well-being.

An example of this new practice can be found in *Teatro y poemas infantiles,* by M. Concepción Concha de Becerra Celis, which gathers together fourteen pieces dealing with social injustice and the steps the revolutionary government was taking to rectify it. Her short, didactic plays address such subjects as an investigation of landlordism, a paean to May Day, and a dramatization of Lázaro Cárdenas's speech announcing the nationalization of the oil fields. Alongside the presentation of didactic dramas based upon the people's daily lives, the Cultural Missions also actively promoted the revival of indigenous music and dance as a means of encountering a national heritage uncorrupted by colonial influence. While the plays that Becerra Celis anthologizes, and those described in other sources, are of poor artistic quality, the Cultural Mission Program wasn't dedicated to the creation of a Mexican regional theater network but to the empowerment of rural communities. The theater, and the arts in general, are seen as a tool to be used in creating strong, healthy communities in the most marginalized sectors of Mexican society. It is the theatrical process, not the performative product, that is of ultimate importance.

The Cultural Mission Program, as Vasconcelos conceived it, was to be a force for eliminating the colonial structures and attitudes that led to repression of the rural communities. This would be done by incorporating these rural, largely indigenous populations into the social fabric of the larger nation, inculcating them with the ideals and goals of the revolutionary government. While such a program was well intentioned, it is clear that it could be seen as simply the substitution of one kind of authority for another. Instead of colonial administration and Christian doctrine, the Indian peasants were given revolutionary authority and socialist doctrine. As the Nicaraguan government discovered when it attempted to integrate the Miskito Indian population of the Atlantic Coast into the national sociopolitical system following the 1979 revolution, misinformation about the population's history and cultural attitudes, as well as the way in which government officials perceive those attitudes, greatly affects the success of any such program. Accustomed to autonomy over their lands and affairs, the Miskitos responded to government intrusion by forming their own *contra* military organizations.[12] The literature reflects a similar tendency to run roughshod over the indigenous populations it was ostensibly trying to aid on the part of the Mexican revolutionary government.

Hughes describes some of the problems encountered by the Cultural Mission Program among the Popolocas Indians in Veracruz. Isolated for centuries, used to their traditional ways, and speaking only their indigenous language, the Popolocas refused to accept the health-care advice of the Missions' nurses. The nurses complained that, in spite of the fact that gastrointestinal diseases, water-borne diseases, parasitosis, malaria, and tuberculosis were rampant among the Popolocas, Indian men forbade their wives and daughters to attend literacy classes taught by a male instructor even though no female literacy instructors were available.

> The solution of the problem depends, in the opinion of the supervisors of cultural missions in the Popoloca area, upon teaching the people Spanish and integrating them into the national life and culture. The success of a program of Spanish teaching among these peoples, however, depends on the solution of their socioeconomic problems, since their ignorance and antipathy result in large part from prolonged isolation. Before much headway can be made, therefore, roads and other means of communication must be extended into the Popoloca area. As a consequence of these factors, it has recently been agreed that the basis of all education among the Popolocas should be Spanish teaching, so that the process of assimilating the Indians can be accelerated. . . . The Popolocas are typical of isolated and retarded Indian peoples in many parts of the country. They are the peoples most in need of the services of the missioners [*sic*], but to-day because of language barriers peoples of this sort generally do not participate voluntarily in the cultural mission program.[13]

While the cultural insensitivity and racist language of the last paragraph cited conceivably reflects more closely the opinion of the UNESCO author than that of the Cultural Mission Program itself, the supervisor cited by Hughes displays a similar contempt for Popoloca culture and looks upon the rapid assimilation of these people into "national life and culture" as their only hope for salvation. Toor cites one rural population's response to an offer of federal help.

The Municipal President of Putla, Oaxaca, summed up their reasons for not wanting schools to a Federal School Inspector, as follows:

"I shall tell you why we do not want to learn to do the things you do and teach in your schools. In your cities the majority of the people have gone to school. What they learned there must be very bad, because many of them lie, take what belongs to others, betray their friends, stab a man in the back, and it is seldom they are ashamed of their acts.

You are well acquainted with our laws, so you will know that what I am saying is true. If we tell you that we are your friends, it means until death; the same is true when we hate you. But we are incapable of betraying friends as you do. Here we kill one another like men, face to face, and murders are never pardoned. . . .

This village is poor but healthy. Don't hurt it by making it like your places because it will lose its health, freedom and happiness. If you love our people, don't teach them anything; don't make them lose faith in their beliefs as I did when I served the priests of a large church."[14]

Intelligent and articulate, this man is clearly cognizant of his community's needs. His plea for allowing the villagers to retain their faith untarnished reflects the power of the rural Church in certain areas of the country. Vasconcelos's revolutionary educational crusade brought the Mexican government into direct conflict with the Catholic Church and its rural constituents.

Since the founding of the religious schools by the various mendicant orders after the Conquest, education had been one of the main pillars of Church power. The Church perceived secular education as an infringement of its own historical prerogatives and actively fought against it. Cultural missionaries and rural teachers were attacked, and some were killed, by parishioners whose impetus for action came from weekly sermons that railed against the state schools. The Church attacked public education primarily by threatening to excommunicate parents who sent their children to the public schools. At the same time the Church continued to operate and expand its own educational system.

Alongside Vasconcelos's new national, revolutionary schools, the Catholic clergy promoted Church schools as the basis for its work in the social sphere. For this reason the conflicting goals of the Church and the Mexican Revolution were most evident in education. The Church feared that state education would create a "revolutionary child" who would be free of all religious influence. To battle such an invidious creation, Catholic educational policy adopted a dual approach. Its immediate goal was the best possible education for Catholic children within the confines of the revolutionary government. Its second, and much more important, goal was complete clerical domination of all education in Mexico. The second goal represented the Church's ultimate aim and as such put it on a collision course with the Mexican government. The Revolution's demands for a completely secular, antireligious system of education were entirely antagonistic to and incompatible with the demands of the Church. The extreme nature of the policies of both sides left no room for compromise. The revolutionary government's attitude toward the Church's role in education and society was more than the application of idealistic battle cries. It was also a continuation of the historic state response to the Church in Mexico and can be interpreted as the result of the conflicting interests of the Church and the state.

All of this came to a head in 1926, when the Calles government, in addition to its offensive against religious education, ordered the deportation of foreign priests and compulsory registration of the native clergy in order to give it the power to decide which priests would be placed in which churches. The Mexican Episcopate responded by ordering the suspension of all religious services as long as the Calles decrees remained in effect. Tensions increased, leading to the beginning of guerrilla warfare between religious forces and the government in 1926.

As Meyer has observed, "It was a colonial war, carried on by a colonial army against its own people, and followed the course of all wars of this type: the harshness of the repression, the execution of prisoners, the systematic massacre of the civilian population, scorched earth, looting, and rape; all left in the wake of the Federal troops the germ of fresh uprisings."[15] The Mexican military displayed an almost rabid desire to defeat the Cristeros rebels, but misunderstanding of the degree of their popular support, geography, and numbers—the federal army never had numerical superiority of more than two to one—made a guerrilla war unwinnable in the field. It was only the indefatigable efforts of the U.S. ambassador to Mexico, Dwight W. Morrow, and the change of presidents from Calles to his former minister of government, Portes Gil, in 1928, that made a settlement possible.

With that settlement the Church entered into a modus vivendi with the government in which it agreed to register its priests if, in return, the government would allow it to carry out religious education on Church property and recognize its right to petition the government for the change of laws. Although Portes Gil promised amnesty for Cristero soldiers who voluntarily surrendered to federal troops, many of those who did so were summarily executed. While the settlement was bitterly denounced by militant Catholics as nothing more than surrender, since 1929 Church schools have operated openly under the convenient fiction that they are private and secular. What the long struggle has meant for the Mexican Catholic Church in general is that it is one of the least progressive in Latin America and will probably never again be a major player in the struggle for social change in Mexico.

The Mexican Revolution and the Cristero rebellion had strong repercussions for the nature of early-twentieth-century Mexican drama. We have seen how revolutionary ideals affected the Cultural Missions' open-air theaters and the *teatro de masas*. In addition, aristocratic antipathy for revolutionary principles can be seen in the upper-class commercial theater embodied by the Comedia Mexicana. In the sort of plays presented in the Comedia, however, political questions are largely secondary to the melodramatic investigation of the personal problems of these plays' characters. But another type of drama, more vibrant in its presence, which developed out of the Mexican "drama rural," was used by both sides in the conflict. This was a particularly Mexican form of revolutionary drama.

As Meyer has observed, when the government labeled the religious rebels Cristeros it went a long way toward defining the nature and significance of the conflict: "The persecution of the priest, a revered figure, loved as the dispenser of the Sacraments, who brought about the coming of Christ under the semblance of bread and wine, was resented as a diabolical war against Christ Himself; the persecutor was, therefore, the Devil himself."[16] The infernal nature of revolutionary policies is best reflected in the plays of Francisco González Franco, a fierce partisan of the Church.

The most fully realized of these works is the full-length play *La perfecta alegría* (Perfect Happiness, 1938). *La perfecta alegría* deals with the Cristero uprising against the Calles government, painting the Catholic forces as betrayed by an alliance of the White House, the Jewish Morgan Bank [*sic*], the Mexican government, and weak Catholic prelates and bishops swayed by Ambassador Morrow's diplomacy. The purpose of the betrayal is a peace that will be conducive to the ordered functioning of Yankee businesses in conjunction with their Americanized Mexican associates.

The play centers around the character of Lina, whose husband Manuel is an officer in the Cristero army. Leaving her son and daughter with relatives, she has gone to the mountains where she lives in a Cristero community that, like the early Christians, maintains a clandestine church in a cave.

An Americanized cousin of hers, whose offer of marriage she refused years ago, arrives. Predicting the imminent alliance of forces that will put an end to the uprising, he attempts to persuade her to join him in convincing Manuel that a mine in which he owns the controlling interest should be reopened. When she refuses the cousin proceeds to turn her husband against her with manufactured stories of infidelity and sends her son off to be educated in the United States where, Americanized, he turns against her, too. The daughter falls ill and dies.

When the peace accords are signed the cousin returns and tries to force Lina to marry him. She is protected by an orphaned Catholic boy, whom she has taken under her wing, and by some of the Cristero soldiers who, though wounded, refuse to surrender. One of them smashes his gun to bits and leaps off a cliff. The standard bearer is brought before a firing squad but not before he gives the orphan the Cristero flag. In the final scene Lina and the orphan carry the flag as a tremendous thunderstorm destroys the cave and she cries:

> Now, poor orphan, symbol of the Mexican people, sad and unprotected, let's go delight ourselves in the most perfect happiness: the poverty, nudity, hunger, disdain, incomprehension, revilement, desolation, oblivion, infamous betrayal, the full, dark night sung by those great disconsolates Catalina of Siena, Teresa of Avila, and John of the Cross. The horrible, divine solitude, the obscure infallibility of Him on Mt. Calvary . . . when he saw himself abandoned by all, even his Father in Heaven![17]

While the play is extremely verbose at times, it has portions of undeniable theatrical power. The characters of Lina and the cousin are well written, and the final image of a woman stripped of everything and everyone taking an orphaned child under her wing is a good one that would benefit from a less insistent hand. González Franco's plays have been treated with disdain by the few critics who know them and ignored by theatrical producers. Nevertheless, the fact that many of the plays have been printed several times attests to their power and their ability to remain a potent means of propaganda. Other playwrights such as Rodolfo Oneto Barenque and Ezequiel de la Isla mined the same territory, but none come close to González Franco's accomplishments.

As previously described, the kind of evangelical theater developed by the mendicants in the sixteenth century still exists in rural Mexico in the

form of the passion plays, biblical stories, and religious processions performed at Easter and on Catholic holidays in the indigenous languages of
Nahuatl, Maya, Zapotec, Mixtec, and Tarasca, among others. While the
Cultural Mission Program had largely abandoned the use of theater by 1950,
the 1960s and 1970s saw the creation of a *teatro campesino* (peasant's theater),
which links education and theater through a Freirean approach, an approach
whose process stresses empowerment of the marginalized sectors of the population, thereby pointing the way toward sociopolitical change.

Originally begun by students from the national drama school, the Instituto Nacional de Bellas Artes (INBA), a theater program called Arte
Escénico Popular toured plays in rural areas where the students would work
in the fields and perform plays in exchange for a small wage. Due to the
twin factors of a repertory that seemed irrelevant to the audience members'
lives and the difficulty of maintaining a stable company with students who
frequently left after short stints, INBA ultimately revised the program. Now
the plays are performed by the rural people themselves. As in the cultural
animation work undertaken by the Cultural Mission Program, amateur
artists or schoolteachers receive four months of theatrical training from
INBA and then are sent back to their communities to form theater groups.
These groups are often composed of indigenous persons who perform the
plays in both Spanish and indigenous languages. The plays focus upon the
need for communal organization in order to solve common problems. In
addition, INBA also supports puppet theater groups whose performance
style blends pre-Columbian puppetry techniques with those introduced by
the Spaniards. They perform a repertory that includes folklore pieces for
children and dramatized *corridos* (Mexican ballads) for adults.

In the late 1960s, students from the Prestaciones Culturales division of
the Bureau of Mexican Social Security formed a theater group called Transhumante, after the Transhumante Indians, a nomadic tribe from central
Mexico that disappeared after the Conquest. Transhumante took performances into the sprawling *barrios* of Mexico City and taught drama classes in
factories and church halls. In 1972, Transhumante obtained a trailer truck,
which it converted into a traveling theater. With the truck came expansion
of the group's work from theatrical performances to more wide-ranging
educational programs. A small library of elementary geography and history
texts kept on the truck was made available to the group's audiences before
and after each performance. Slide shows on basic hygiene and sanitation
were developed, and, since many of the *barrio* dwellers regularly returned to

family plots in the countryside, educational films addressing such topics as soil conservation and greater crop yields were shown.

In addition to Transhumante, the Proyecto de Animación Desarrollo (Cultural Animation Project), which centers its work around the Mexican indigenous population, also uses theater as a means of empowering its audience. PRADE has created a theater company called Nimayana in the village of San Miguel Tzinacapan, which creates plays through improvisations that focus upon the loss of indigenous identity as people leave the village for the city and the remaining population finds itself exploited by nonvillagers through commercialization, the health care system, and alcoholism. The conclusions of these plays generally deal with the need for collective action to address the problems confronting the community.

As well as Transhumante's work in Mexico City, the Mexican Institute for Community Development (IMDEC) has also used theater as a tool for social change in urban areas. In Guadalajara, another prominent Mexican urban center, IMDEC founded the Experimental Workshop on Popular Expression (TEEP). While the primary concern of IMDEC rests with improving health care, housing, and cooperatives, theater is employed as a means of raising the community's consciousness regarding such issues. A theater company was created out of the urban migrant youth population of the Santa Cecilia *barrio*. Its first collectively created piece was a play called *Thrown Out There and Kept Down Here,* which related the story of a rural migrant family that had moved to the city and the problems it confronted there. The play was based upon the company members' personal experiences and gave both the company and its audience a sense of historical awareness and a means of dealing with their present situation. The play demonstrated that there was no reason to be ashamed of the rural past and provided a stimulus for confronting the problems that both the performers and their audience members faced in common.

The work of another group of youngsters sponsored by IMDEC even more forcefully presents the interconnections of religion, politics, and theater traced here. Asked to perform the Stations of the Cross during Holy Week, the group chose to perform the Seventh Station and its depiction of Christ's second fall on his journey to Calvary. Rather than presenting the typical image common to such religious processions, the group adapted the image of the Seventh Station to contemporary reality by creating a performance that showed industrial workers repeatedly beaten down by injustice and oppression. This performance was so positively received that the group decided to concentrate its efforts upon theater as a means of *concientización*. The themes the performers chose were simple yet powerfully resonant in their community. For example, two of their subsequent plays, entitled *The Trial of a Mother* and *The Trial of a Father,* dealt with, respectively, Mother's Day and Father's Day. The first play treats a family's propensity to neglect and abuse the mother except for one day a year, and the second characterizes the father as a member of the working class, thereby introducing aspects of the class struggle. *The Trial of a Father* makes use of a public tribunal composed of audience members, which evaluates and passes judgment upon the characters' actions.[18]

In all of these cases the relationship between the state and the theater first established in the Cultural Mission Program has been extended and altered. While the initial impetus behind, and justification for, state support of these theater companies was the incorporation of marginalized sectors of the population into the social fabric in a way that would not threaten state hegemony, the theatrical process itself has tended to subvert the intentions of its sponsors, creating instead a space for social transformation and political empowerment. Perhaps the clearest example of how this has happened is found in the history of the Teatro Conasupo de Orientación Campesina (1971–76). In 1971, the National Popular Subsistence Company (Conasupo) established a theater company in order to forge a new form of contact between the peasantry and the state, one that would be less "formal and bureaucratic but more human and alive." [19] Teatro Conasupo was originally conceived as a part of Conasupo's agricultural extension work. The company would go into a community, perform medieval farces and Molière or Chekhov one-acts, and then provide the *campesinos* with information on how to sell their produce, build warehouses, best utilize fertilizer, and improve nutrition. Over time the theater company's orientation evolved until a cultural and political dimension was added to the agricultural work.

> These brigades have three tasks. The first could be called informative. It consists of teaching the indigenous *campesino* how to fight against violations of the law. For example, how to organize themselves for that purpose. Next comes orientation work. Say, how to overthrow the landowner or the exploitative enemy. Finally, the peasants are shown how to appreciate their own cultural heritage.[20]

To accomplish these new objectives, Teatro Conasupo's repertory also changed from international works to collectively created pieces performed by young people in a variety of indigenous languages (Tzeltal, Taotzil, and Tojolabal in Chiapas, Nahuatl in Tlaxcala, and Triqui in Oaxaca) with themes such as "The fight against venality, corruption, the lack of adequate resources. It is then that the theater becomes a weapon in the people's hands; a weapon against exploitative mechanisms and practices; a weapon to help transform the prevailing oppressive structures in the rural environment. Change is induced by means of theater."[21] All of the groups described pay particular attention to audience response in open forums after each performance, revising and refining the productions based upon that response. In each case the aim is to create theater that truthfully depicts the audience's own experience of injustice and oppression, and, more importantly, to provide a catalyst for action aimed at solving the problems faced by the community. In the case of Teatro Conasupo, these audience discussions resulted in significant reforms in Conasupo itself. Denounced for having colluded with the local power elite to force the peasants to sell their grain at a price below market value, Conasupo's analysts were dismissed and jailed. Twenty schools were established throughout the country to train *campesinos* as Conasupo analysts.

> The actor truly formed a loop for interchange and information in two ways, he brought information concerning all the corruption that existed within Conasupo; with the result that all but one of the grain quality technicians were fired for corruption. The one who stayed admitted his guilt and remained to help train new technicians.
>
> From that moment on technicians were appointed by popular election in the communities, totally changing the entire structure. Forms of payment to the peasants changed, the people who paid out the money certainly changed, and by means of the theater the structure of the relationship between the peasants and the State really changed in a radical way. It was a truly popular theater, one that truly carried out a beneficial function for the peasant classes.[22]

With the end of the Echeverría government in 1976, the Teatro Conasupo program came to an end, but the experiences and knowledge gained there led many participants into the Arte Escénico Popular and many other *teatro campesino* companies. The privileged position of indigenous language, sensibility, and thought in the *teatro campesino* continues to explore avenues opened by the Cultural Mission Program, yet it also creates a much more dialectical relationship between the state and the theater it supports. By recapturing and reinvigorating indigenous traditions the colonial imposition of Catholicism by the mendicant evangelical theater is exposed. Theater is the means by which religion and politics are put into the hands of those the Church and the government are supposed to serve but who, in actuality, are often ignored. Religious folk drama, the *teatro de masas,* the Cultural Mission Program's use of theater, González Franco's theatrical forays in support of the Cristero cause, and the *teatro campesino* all demonstrate the mixture of religion, politics, and theater still evident today in Mexican, and, indeed Latin American, theater.

NOTES

1. Frances Toor, *A Treasury of Mexican Folkways* (New York: Crown, 1947), 175–76.

2. *The Shepherds' Play of the Prodigal Son (Coloquio de pastores del hijo pródigo),* ed. George C. Barker (Berkeley: University of California Press, 1953), 3–4.

3. Ibid. The name Bato has passed into general Spanish usage to denote "a stupid man, a rustic without much sense" and by extension took on the meaning of "man" in Mexican slang. From there it has entered Chicano speech as *vato* with the colloquial meaning of "guy" or "homeboy."

4. *Drama de la Pasión que se representa en Ixtapalapa, D.F. llamado "Los tres caídos de Jesucristo"* (Mexico City: Imprenta Universitario, 1947), 7.

5. Adalberto Fuentes Cruz, *Drama de la pasión como se representa en Milpa Alta, D.F.* (Mexico City, 1949).

6. Rudolfo Usigli, *Mexico en el teatro* (Mexico City: Imprenta Mundial, 1932), 125.

7. John B. Nomland, *Teatro mexicano contemporáneo (1900–1950)* (Mexico City: Instituto Nacional de Bellas Artes, Departamento de Literatura, 1967), 90.

8. Efrén Orozco Rosales, *Liberación* (Mexico City: Departamento del Distrito Federal, Dirección General de Acción Civica, 1935), 2.

9. Nomland, *Teatro,* 91–92.

10. Robert E. Quirk, *The Mexican Revolution and the Catholic Church (1910–1929)* (Bloomington: Indiana University Press, 1973), 116.

11. Ibid., 117.

12. See *NACLA Reports on the Americas* 14, no. 6 (November–December 1980): 41–43; and 15, no. 3 (May–June 1981): 25–30. See also *Cultural Survival Quarterly* 4, no. 4, 8–9; and 6, no. 1 (Winter 1982): 20–26.

13. Lloyd H. Hughes, *The Mexican Cultural Mission Programme* (Paris: UNESCO, 1950), 67–68.

14. Toor, *Treasury,* 98–99.

15. Jean A. Meyer, *The Cristero Rebellion: The Mexican People Between Church and State, 1926–1929* (Cambridge: Cambridge University Press, 1976), 51.

16. Ibid., 198.

17. González Franco, *La perfecta alegría* (Mexico City: J. I. Muñoz, 1938), 57.

18. Kees P. Epskamp, *Theatre in Search of Social Change* (The Hague: Center for the Study of Education in Developing Countries, 1989) 93–104.

19. Germán Meyer Pape, *Memoria del Proyecto Arte Escénico Popular,* Proyecto de Arte Escénico Popular, Dirección General de Culturas Populares, Secretaría de Educatión Pública, manuscript, n.d.

20. Donald H. Frischmann, *El Nuevo Teatro Popular en México* (Mexico City: Instituto Nacional de Bellas Artes, 1990), 54.

21. Ibid., 58.

22. Ibid., 70.

4.

Katrin Sieg

Subjectivity and Socialism: Feminist Discourses in East Germany

Theater and revolution have been intertwined in German history, and the upheavals of 1989 are no exception. In the fall of that year, the stages, particularly in Berlin, became platforms for public confrontation and debate. In numerous cases, theater professionals intervened directly in the political process, subscribing to the Brechtian notion of Theaterarbeit when they announced that "we must step out of our roles."[1] Some plays and productions were able to shape the process of social change by channelling political energies, formulating progressive agendas, issuing warnings, and sounding alarms. More important, however, was the brief transformation of the street into a "tribunal of the people," as some East German critics observed.[2] On December 3, 1989, the East Berlin Volksbühne hosted the inauguration of the first autonomous women's movement in the German Democratic Republic (GDR) that viewed itself as part of the many forces working toward social and political renewal. In this, as in previous German revolutions, women played an important part in working toward radical change, first side by side with their male colleagues in the new democratic grass roots organizations, but soon at odds with a politics that threatened to bypass women. After such a theatrical beginning, the absence of East German feminists' voices from the stage has been glaring, in contrast to both West German feminists and East German men.[3] In the years following reunification, women on either side of the former border had to abandon the hopes for a unified and invigorated feminist movement and a more powerful negotiating position in the post-Wall patriarchy. On the contrary, the steep incline in female unemployment and the 1993 abortion ruling, which imposed one of the strictest laws in Western Europe, would seem to indicate a large-scale economic and ideological masculinization of Germany.

Rather than concluding that GDR feminists were bad or failed revolutionaries, I would suggest that the concept of revolution, no matter how often it was repeated in the media, is inadequate to account for the relationship between feminism and socialism, before, during, or after 1989. Feminism's orchestration of critical subjectivities within (but also at odds with) socialist state ideology offers crucial insights into the mechanics of social change, especially about the role of "personal" dispositions and practices in political transformation. The feminist critique of socialism that the GDR women's movement articulated also illuminates historical continuities between socialist and capitalist Germany.

Feminists now confront the questions of how high a degree of material equality between men and women had actually been achieved in the GDR; how the ostensible equality of GDR women relates to their resistance to large-scale and long-term feminist organizing, borne out by recent years; and how socialist feminism, which first emerged in that state during the mid-1970s and resurged in 1989, negotiated a patriarchal critique with a commitment to socialism. These troublesome questions revolve largely around the paradoxical structure of socialist femininities in political and personal discourses, which is summarized by the misnomer "double burden." Rather than describing one person working two jobs, it designates the practice of contradictory ideologies in public and in private: while the market and the law ostensibly recognize no difference between genders, the home is characterized by a sexual division of labor familiar from bourgeois societies. This contradiction has grave consequences for the articulation of socialist subjectivities in the performance genres discussed here, which include the public discourse of the theater as well as the private discourse of the so-called protocol.[4] The protocol arranges mostly anonymous testimonials into collective, oral histories, which differ considerably from official accounts. It has predominantly been used by women and highlights the discrepancies between dominant gender prescriptions and subjective experiences. Since the demise of the socialist state was arguably brought about by vast numbers of people sharing a dissatisfaction with the status quo that had never been publicly acknowledged or redressed, I believe that the personal documents collected in the protocol volumes illuminate precisely those contradictions the accumulation and intensification of which precipitated the ideological collapse. The first section of this essay, a reading of two plays, Doris Paschiller's *One Great Family* (1975) and Monika Maron's *Ada and Evald* (1981), shows the ways in which East German women experienced, addressed, or challenged the contradiction of the "double burden," especially in view of the strict control exerted by state agencies over public articulations of a political critique. The second section examines GDR women's representations of subjectivity in a collection of protocols for their interpellative and/or critical function vis-à-vis official constructions of a socialist subject. These two sections are situated within the nascent feminist critique in the GDR during the 1970s and early 1980s. The third section examines the female/feminist identities that emerged in the protocols published between 1990 and 1991 and revised the "private" mode of representation and address established by the earlier collections.

At present, the dialogue between feminists from both sides of the former border is stalled. While GDR feminists resent the admonitions of their capitalist "sisters," West German feminists accuse their eastern counterparts of complicity with a paternalistic state, thereby risking duplication of the hegemonic dynamic of condemnation that has fanned the sociopolitical tensions of recent years. The East-West strife among German women illustrates the entanglement of feminist critiques with nationalist imperatives and constraints. This might prove instructive to feminist movements elsewhere that are increasingly self-conscious about the multiple axes of power crisscrossing their heterogenous constituencies.

I.

During the 1970s, the contradiction between the promise of equality and the praxis of women's socioeconomic oppression sharpened. In 1971, the eighth congress of the ruling Socialist Unity Party (SED) confirmed the return to traditional role divisions by assigning reproductive work to women.[5] The government expected women to shoulder the "double burden" of productive and reproductive labor, granting them economic equality in the marketplace but failing to challenge domestic role divisions. A calcifying bureaucratic apparatus continued to dispense an egalitarian rhetoric that was no longer implemented through social policies (contrary to official claims) and not experienced at the subjective level. In the mid-1970s, the burgeoning GDR women's literature interpreted these contradictions as symptoms of patriarchal structures, even though the term *feminism* was used with great reluctance due to its western baggage. The socialist-feminist discourse that emerged in women's writing suggested that gender difference and "female" alternatives might yield remedies to the current crisis when imagined concomitantly and dialectically with the state's gender legislation and the principle of gender equality, both of which were supported by women's organizations.[6] The nascent feminist literature provided not only insights and impulses in regard to the vicissitudes of gender in the GDR; it also yielded a fresh perspective from which to invoke a socialist utopia. That project, however, was fraught with Cold War anxieties and taboos, and it was configured as adversarial to state socialism. Feminist literature, attempting to speak from a socialist perspective outside of "real existing socialism," was caught in a defensive posture, constantly forced to prove its loyalty to a state that suspected its authors of collaboration with the West German women's movement.[7]

Women writers and literary critics in the GDR were visibly uncomfortable with the task of defining and evaluating a "women's literature" whose western manifestation opposed its own patriarchal-capitalist society. As late as 1989, GDR critic Ilse Nagelschmidt insisted on the "integrative" aim of socialist women's literature, which advocates socialism rather than opposing it, illustrating feminists' efforts at legitimation if not apology.[8] Writers accepted the critique of the patriarchy as a peripheral contradiction and subordinated it to the utopia of communism, a goal shared by both genders. With this maneuver, GDR feminism reproduced some of the dominant culture's exclusions and blind spots.

Moreover, the innovative gesture of socialist-feminist literature, namely, the articulation of a radical critique of the patriarchy with the goal of fundamental social change, was not accompanied or sustained by any social movement. Women's fiction relegated the missing base in the displacement of emancipatory impulses to the level of fantasy, the surreal, and the grotesque. Women's plays that executed similar moves, such as *Ada and Evald*, never reached the GDR stage. The ones that did, like *One Great Family*, were caught in the shackles of socialist realism. The decreasing number of plays written by women during the 1970s and 1980s demonstrates a shift from public discourse toward more personal modes of expression. The dramas attest to women's desires, wishes, and utopian longings, but they also register the policing and suppression of those impulses. GDR women's literature, including drama, functioned not only as a counterdiscourse to the socialist patriarchy but also as a dominant discourse vis-à-vis those who refused the politics of integration. This mechanism can be most clearly observed in the arena of sexuality, in which female noncompliance threatened the socialist subject's national allegiance. Here, difference from the sexual-socialist order is invoked only to be crossed out: alternatives are either deplored as an absence, marked as fantasy, or negated. Since the relation of the socialist subject to state ideology was cast in the terms of compulsory heterosexuality, the exploration of political or sexual alternatives fell off the dramatic horizon.

Doris Paschiller's play *One Great Family* retains the realist style but turns the genre against the ideology it was meant to sustain. With depressing accuracy, the play traces the development of its protagonist, Conny Rosen, who throws off the shackles of her marriage with much enthusiasm only to settle for relationships that represent no great improvement. The once obligatory happy ending of socialist-realist drama, its sense of purpose, and its confidence in achieving utopian goals are missing completely from Paschiller's play. Instead, it exhibits an unprecedented sobriety in the face of obstacles and time spans looming ahead and acknowledges the sluggish pace of historical processes.

Sexual desire in women's literature of the 1970s and 1980s measured the gap between individual happiness and social progress. Marriage as a symbol of calcified social structures and women's desire for self-determination could no longer be forced into harmony. The critique of marriage prompted the search for alternatives. In *One Great Family,* Conny, who leaves her husband shortly after her thirteenth wedding anniversary, joins a group of students who spend most of their time in a bar. Her initial illusions about a fun life at the side of one of them, Victor, are shattered when she becomes pregnant and Victor demands that she have an abortion. The "great family," which offers Conny a place but little sympathy, does not fulfill her hopes for a good future but represents at best a first step away from a bad past. When Victor asks Conny in the final scene why she still comes to the bar, she answers ". . . where else should I go? We are one great family, and we will run into each other wherever we go. And we'll have to learn how to get along."[9] The traditional roles that the nuclear family reproduces are not superseded by a socialist model of gender relations. Instead of providing ready-made utopias, the play offers a rough sketch of the possibility of *Menschwerdung* (becoming human), a frequent term in GDR women's literature.

Conny's journey from the privacy of her living room into the public space of the bar suggests that a loose network of friendships and acquaintances may pose one social alternative to the nuclear family. Among these relations, female friendships, such as the bond between Conny and the singer Batseba, a single, independent woman, occupy a privileged position.

Dependency and domination are replaced by the principle of support according to individual need, which requires a greater degree of maturity and sensitivity. In the GDR, where alternative life-styles were not encouraged and rarely practiced, Paschiller's insistence on finding alternatives to marriage challenged patriarchal role divisions in the private sphere.[10] However, the single woman who searches for an autonomous identity is always embedded in the context of the "great family" so as to preempt possible separatist or antisocialist interpretations. Thus, the critique of the patriarchy remains within the bounds of reformist suggestions for improvement; gender roles continue to be securely locked within the rhetoric of the family.

Monika Maron's drama *Ada and Evald*, which was published in a book of short stories by a West German press in 1981, uses fantastic and surreal elements in a style that aligns it with GDR women's fiction of the time. Similar to *One Great Family*, the play juxtaposes a stale affair between Ada, a "liberated" woman who nevertheless dreams of romantic love and fulfillment, and Evald, a married man and a writer, with the fragile community of outcasts in a bar. Among the customers are Clairchen, a giant fat woman; Suizi, a suicidal man who walks around with a rope around his neck; and a preacher who prophesies the impending end of the world. What all of these characters share is a sense of stasis, passivity, and paralysis. In contrast to Paschiller's gloomy realism, Maron's recourse to surrealist images and metaphors enable her to weave her characters' utopian wishes and fervent longings into the representation of gendered power structures.[11] The play's fantastic images of desire explode realist constraints, and allow Ada and Clairchen to exit the frozen rituals of their daily lives. While Ada learns to overcome her dependence on Evald and ends up leaving him, Clairchen unites herself with a tree. In the final scene, Evald's unanswered calls for Ada are juxtaposed with the miraculous image of Clairchen's merging with the tree trunk until she becomes invisible. While the GDR state defined historical progress as the advancement of "techno-scientific socialism," Maron offers a critique of the conquest of nature and the victory of instrumental reason, a critique that was advanced by prominent GDR feminists at the time.[12] Clairchen's fantastic wedding signals her move outside of official history and her rejection of its philosophical underpinnings; however, it also risks duplicating the dominant equation of femininity with nature that has sustained women's exclusion from political power and historical agency.

Intimacy among women gained importance in female (self-) representations of that decade, but it also marks the limits of the socialist-feminist critique. The women writers' subscription to an ideology to be realized together with the men is inscribed in their texts' commitment to heterosexuality, even though its social institution, marriage, became the target of criticism. In literary representations, heterosexuality became the arena of gender contestations in which ideological constraints became the most visible.

Paschiller marks heterosexuality as the site of women's exploitation and oppression where patriarchal property relations prevail. With Batseba's dystopic demand for paid sexual intercourse—exempting those "capable of love"—Paschiller takes the idea of socializing reproductive services to the extreme and thus foregrounds the limits of the egalitarian paradigm for feminist politics.[13] The principle of economic equality as a model for interpersonal relations is thrown into question, suggesting instead that the utopia of "love," modeled not on equality but on the "wish for fulfillment and self-determination," provide the grounds for change in the socioeconomic realm as well.[14]

Maron characterizes heterosexual frustration as a fundamental law—sexual desire fosters the eroticization of passivity and stasis.

> Clairchen: You're always babbling about love, sadly enough you don't know what you're talking about. You don't see the logic. Which is this: Ada waits for Evald because he doesn't love her. (To Ada) Why don't you wait for Suizi who loves you.
> Ada: Because I don't love him.
> Clairchen: Wrong. Because you'd have to stop waiting. And what would you do then.[15]

This recognition mobilizes the women's sexual and political imagination so that they can break out of the loop of eroticized passivity, traditional femininity, and political stagnation. By marrying a tree, Clairchen leaves the level of human relationships, which can be read as a sign for unimaginable, unrepresentable sexualities. Her "love" emphatically marks a blank, utopian space in patriarchal discourse. In a dream scene, Ada rehearses liberation through role-play in which she plays Evald and Clairchen plays Ada. In this way, she comprehends and distances herself from ritualized behavior patterns and becomes capable of overcoming them. That step empowers her to reclaim the language that Evald and the patriarchal "word thieves" have stolen from her. *Freedom, longing, hope, happiness*—terms that have been appropriated and instrumentalized by a stale political rhetoric, are recuperated from an imaginary position outside of socialist reality. Maron stages that wish but marks it as unrealistic within extant gender and ideological structures, twice removed through the role reversal within the dream. The breaking away from oppressive roles is here dramatized in the interaction of two women, and Evald's cry for Ada at the end remains unanswered. Ada and Clairchen exemplify two alternatives to heterosexual constraints: while the former signals the refusal of traditional role expectations, the latter marks the leap into the unknown. Within the androcentric parameters of Maron's drama, the women's sexual or political desire cannot be represented realistically. When Clairchen and Ada vanish from the dramatic horizon, women's exclusion from cultural production is reinscribed into the text.

The production statistics show that feminist plays by women were rarely seen on GDR stages.[16] The orchestration of "political" discourses by state agencies into public spectacles of consent, and the rising stakes of engaging in a public, political debate, effected a change in sites of political articulation. The wave of expulsions of dissident artists after 1976 rendered public dissent all but impossible. In the absence of countercultural spaces, the theater became so ideologically charged as a potential site of dissent that it was subjected to a high degree of censorship. The representation of contradictions between party rhetoric and individual, lived experience could no longer occur in public but was displaced to the "personal" genre of the testimonial. Protocol collections such as Maxie Wander's *Guten Morgen, Du Schöne (Good Morning, Beautiful,* 1978) became one construction site for a critical-socialist subject.[17] The other locus, of course, was the prison and the insane asylum, where the drama of dissent and dissidence was staged covertly.

2.

The protocol functioned as a particularly East German genre by carving out a voice situated in and speaking from the realm of subjective experience that challenged official, monolithic formulations of a socialist subject. It lent itself to the articulation of gender contradictions that had been confined to the personal arena, barred from public visibility and political import. Wander's landmark collection of women's testimonials made an important contribution to identity politics in the GDR, carving out a female subject position that challenged the ostensibly gender-neutral concept of the socialist New Man, embodied by the worker-hero. As a document of women's consciousness-raising in the GDR, it called attention to the tensions and discrepancies between public and private acts and experiences of gender, but most importantly it questioned the egalitarian paradigm as a valid political goal for the future of socialism. Couched in the terms and language of personal experience, Wander's critique of real existing socialism was better equipped to address the shortcomings of dominant gender ideology than was the public discourse of the drama. The book's ostensibly apolitical, often lyrical tone exemplifies the "cunning of slave language, the outsmarting of the censor," which Andreas Huyssen notes in regard to subjective, literary discourses in the GDR.[18] The collection deployed a "private" style and mode of address that endeavored to recover and mobilize precisely those energies and impulses that had been excluded from political discourses. Christa Wolf, one of the GDR's most visible authors, whose introduction to the volume became a manifesto of GDR feminism of sorts, regarded those energies as essential for the improvement, even survival, of a socialist society.[19] Central to this enterprise, as in much socialist women's fiction at the time, are dreams, visions, and fantasies. They mark what has been suppressed, censored, and rendered impossible. "When I am continually prevented from deviating from the prescribed path, at home, at school, at work, in politics, even in love, it makes me angry and drives me back into the dream," says one of them.[20] But the dream also points to the hopes, to the longing for alternatives to a flawed reality, which these women imagine and which suggest a politics of "love." That term, partially evacuated from its patriarchal, romantic meanings and operating as a utopian notion in socialist-feminist discourse, marks the potential for solidarity and community that was lost in the progress of "techno-scientific socialism." Christa Wolf calls it "sisterliness."

The intimate explorations of socialist subjectivity, while purporting to "speak privately," actually created a performative, quasi-dramatic genre built on dialogue, diversity, and collective enunciation. In her preface Wander emphasizes the collection's function of rendering audible what had gone unheard, but she also wants to provoke resistance, asking her readership to engage in a productive reception of the texts (7). Women created the protocol as an alternative to the censored authorial voice on the legitimate stage; it privileged anonymity over one writer's originality; it was based on dialogue (between author and subjects, texts and readers, stage and spectators) rather than the presentation of a unified point of view; and it valued disagreement over persuasion. The disappearance of feminist concerns from GDR theater by women does not mean that feminists relinquished dramatic expression; it means that critics must look for it elsewhere in the culture. Just as women artists responded to the gender-specific polarization of public and private spheres in earlier centuries by creating the "personal theater" of the salon, feminist writers in socialist Germany published their personal conversations with friends and strangers as a way of stretching the boundaries of the private to include political, collective acts.[21]

The seventeen protocols collected by Wander chart a feminist departure from socialist gender ideology. The volume begins with the voices of exemplary socialist women whom the GDR's gender policies and programs have turned into successful, self-assured, and unquestioning party members. Lena K.'s biography, the first piece in the anthology, provides a point of departure for Wander's critical project. As an academic, party functionary, and mother of three, Lena epitomizes the successful GDR woman, yet her report throws the accomplishments of socialist femininity into doubt. Lena describes her life as highly instrumentalized: "All of that [her professional, political, and sexual success] is only possible if I can organize and discipline myself, yes, if I become as functional as a machine" (32). In conforming to patriarchal standards of effectiveness, she duplicates the most stereotypically derogatory evaluations of her own gender. While Lena K. never questions her gender identification, the reader is led to ask if male standards guarantee a fulfilled life. Her story marks the limit of the egalitarian ideology and signals the longing and the search for alternatives that run through the following pieces.

The largest group of protocols concerns women whose lives deviate from the norm and who raise criticism of real existing socialism as a stagnant set of rules rather than a system inspiring its citizens with the spirit of collectivity. Students protest the all-too-orderly process of socialization in the schools. Women who have achieved all the system has to offer, like the physicist Margot W., who has turned to painting, question and reject it. Rosi S., a secretary, questions the decreed historical optimism and sense of accomplishment touted by the party when she describes socialism as a house with red wallpaper: "When you scratch the red color, all the old crap comes to light, one layer beneath the other, back to the times of the empire" (70). Rosi views the current ideology as a thin veneer that has replaced previous belief systems in name only. She asserts that socialist society has failed to cope with its fascist past, encouraging conformism and dogmatism instead of curiosity, risk taking, and the courage to change. Yet her criticism is founded on a communist sense of solidarity and commitment. Change, she contends, must be motivated by love, whether for oneself, one's partner, or society.

A sizable number of protocols exhibit the damage extant conditions have done to women, in effect turning them into subjects incapable of socialism and precariously close to bourgeois gender ideology. Several women inhabit the newly constructed sleeper cities of the industrialized southeast. In critical GDR literature, these so-called newtowns had come to represent techno-scientific socialism at its worst, turning the promise of a new beginning, affordable comfort, and communality into concrete nightmares reflecting the bureaucratic response to economic exigencies. While Ruth B. responds to her alienated existence with despair, others, like Doris L., demonstrate the commodity-oriented mentality fostered by such an environment. Doris associates happiness with a pair of expensive boots, illustrating the loss of utopia on the subjective level of imagination and desire.

Sexuality operates as a differentiating factor between the "true" and the "real existing" socialists: while Rosi and Margot are erotically voracious, Doris is frigid. Overall, the book displays a range of sexual experiences, expressions, and desires extending from same-sex attraction to promiscuity and open relationships. Such sexual pluralism challenges the sanctioned, monogamous norm. Wander renders the ideological crisis of the GDR in the mid-1970s in the language of sexuality, offering a specifically socialist version of the feminist tenet that the personal is political. *Good Morning, Beautiful* reveals the sexual hierarchy in socialist Germany, topped by the privileged practice of heterosexual monogamy, as a collective collusion not unlike the petrified dogmas sustaining the political hierarchy and its party functionaries. The protocols suggest that a sexual ideology that ensures the division of erotic practices into correct and incorrect, moral and immoral ones through surveillance and self-censorship prevents rather than facilitates the identification of individuals with the larger social order. The student Susanne T., who is taught in school to parrot party rhetoric but watches western television at home, parallels Angela N., who lies to her parents about her sexual activity. Both young women feel contempt for the authorities that solicit such hypocrisy, and regard the lack of openness as a weakness. The perpetuation of oppressive morals is not ascribed to state repression but rather to the individual, quotidian reproduction of outdated values and inhibitions.

Wander deflects the danger of autonomous, female sexualities or bonds between women by focusing on the compensatory effects of friendships between women. The girlfriend, albeit the object of erotic desire at times, as Lena K. and Barbara F. report, is often the only source of solidarity, help, and care in a life otherwise devoid of love, as is the case with Doris L. The most noteworthy document in this respect is certainly the piece "The Grandmother," in which the seventy-four-year-old Berta H., who otherwise does not think highly of her fellow females, speaks of her intimate connection with the women of her large family. On the one hand, this protocol highlights the regenerative effects of bonds that benefit hard-working women but ultimately sustain the system that oppresses them. On the other hand, Berta H.'s long life exemplifies real changes in women's living conditions, which is probably why the piece was accorded the place of honor at the end of the book. The improvements that socialism brought to women are illustrated by Berta's daughter-in-law, Anna, who "participated in the progress of the village" and, despite continual pregnancies, worked for the establishment of a school, a kindergarten, and a community laundry. "I raised eight of her children; one died when it was only a few weeks old. Anna started out in the cow barn, then she worked in the fields. Now she drives the new harvester-threshers. She could only do all of those things because of me, the grandmother" (192). Berta's sacrifices have contributed to eradicate the circumstances that made them necessary: her grandchildren already have "real jobs and don't understand what hardships we went through" (193).

Berta H.'s biography, which crosses ideological divides, testifies to the accomplishments of the GDR. Her personal knowledge of the past places the socialist state, despite all its flaws and shortcomings, in historical perspective as the most beneficial, egalitarian, and just model of human organization. Overall, however, Wander's collection pays remarkably little attention to the past, focusing instead on the present and the future. References to West Germans are uniformly negative, assuaging the fear that a feminist critique implies an outside perspective and a conspiracy with capitalist women.

Wander turned personal narratives into poetic literature while maintaining the fiction of authenticity. By means of that technique she was able to sidestep censorship, since overtly political references are missing from the text, yet as a whole the collection throws into doubt the patriarchal assumptions underlying socialist gender legislation. It stresses the necessity to break the silence concealing individual differences, doubts, questions, experiments, errors, and variations in the process of becoming socialist. The book issued a call to replace egalitarianism, as the foundational paradigm of socialism, with the acknowledgment and celebration of diversity. Wander's collection stresses the need to mobilize individual fantasies and efforts for a shared ideological goal, if the socialist state did not want to put that very goal at risk. While criticizing real existing structures and practices, feminist literature like Wander's collection took over the task of ideological interpellation, which the state and its apparatuses performed with increasing difficulty.

Good Morning, Beautiful applied categories of "private" experience to public discourse when it suggested a politics proceeding from love and "sisterliness." It also politicized the private as the realm of emotions and energies the state couldn't afford not to tap as a powerful national resource. Endeavoring to do just that, Wander's book, while expanding the parameters of gender performance, duplicated certain silences and invisibilities within dominant discourse. Only with hindsight do the omissions become apparent. Despite the many erotic moments between women, representations of lesbian sexualities or life-styles are missing from this book along with dissident voices that did not share in the unspoken consensus of Wander's interviewees that socialism, despite its many flaws, was preferable to capitalism.[22] Like the drama, the protocol refrained from depicting nonheterosexual desires or intergenerational bonds among women, which took center stage in the western feminist discourse of the 1970s. Feminist literature in the GDR never contested the homophobic casting of the female subject's commitment to an ideology administered by men in the terms of heterosexuality. Women writers challenged the dominant conflation of criticism with sabotage, yet they implicitly agreed that a sexuality not oriented toward men was treason. Ursula Sillge's book *In-Visible Women,* published in 1991, excavates a history of lesbian persecution in the GDR that is based on that assumption.[23]

Good Morning, Beautiful created a space for the discussion of questions and conflicts concerning gender—a space the theater denied to women. Many small and studio theaters recognized the dramatic potential of this genre. They used it by putting Wander's women onstage, thereby creating further opportunities for a dialogue between women and enabling them to touch across biographies and experiences. In her introduction, Wolf called attention to the polylogous aspect of the collection. She could not foresee the extent of cross talk initiated by Wander, which would span the decades. Twelve years after the publication of *Good Morning, Beautiful,* GDR women authors responded with the book *Good Night, Beautiful* (1990), continuing the dialogue among and about women in socialism. The genre's subjective and collective mode of communication carved out a cultural space that Wolf described as "more spontaneous, also more sociable than the structures of the novel or the drama."[24] Wander's protocols created an alternative performance site to the state theater, not only in terms of content but especially in terms of a communicative structure based on a multiplicity of voices, on contradiction during and across moments of enunciation, and on the informal articulation of individual and collective utopias. Collections like Wander's stimulated and participated in the informal but highly reliable networks of communication located in the private sphere. In 1989, Nagelschmidt noted the difficulties and pleasures involved in buying feminist books and discussing them with friends.[25] They attest to the transformation of the private sphere into a growing site of civic consciousness and responsibility.[26] The 1980s witnessed the emergence of semipublic, quasi-political spaces and relations. Although feminism, or any of the other oppositional practices that emerged during the 1980s, was not formally recognized for the political alternatives it suggested, women's consciousness-raising was no longer restricted to the family or the home.

3.

In the turbulent years around reunification, the protocol as a genre based on collective memory, and by virtue of its collage-like, fragmentary shape, proved congenial to addressing a society in transition. It accommodated the need to rethink the past and come to terms with it, often in painful processes of confrontation and self-examination. The fragmentation and proliferation of identities that occurred around reunification is signaled by the newly specialized identities of their speakers. In the years 1990 and 1991, there appeared a collection of lesbian protocols, an anthology of theater women's voices, and a book of letters and dialogues by women writers, in addition to the three books of testimonials by what is still simply marked as "GDR women." The heterogenization of female identities indicates a sense of liberation from the leveling effects of egalitarianism even as they testify to the devastating effects the erosion of social equality had on women's biographies.[27] In the following section, I focus on two of those collections. Petra Lux and Erika Fischer's anthology *You Can't Make a State without Us* (1990) matches Wander's book in its range of ages, regions, and social strata and exceeds it because it includes many voices that had been suppressed.[28] Renate Ullrich's the book *I am My Own Capital* (1991) traces the impact of the historic changes on the lives and experiences of women in East Berlin theater.[29]

These "archeological texts" chronicle a system that has ceased to exist but continues to shape the lives of its former citizens.[30] They also track the

subjective effects of reunification on a population that was particularly hard
hit by processes of rationalization, both in the sense of dropping to the bot-
tom of the economic scale and in the sense of being cast as a stand-in for
socialism at large. The feminization of socialism and its depiction as a "fallen
woman," which became particularly pronounced in the 1990 controversy
around Christa Wolf, is one important aspect of a larger dynamic that could
be observed in inter-German relations in the years immediately following
reunification.[31] The existing Cold War rhetoric of totalitarianism facilitated
the interpretation of state socialism as the direct heir of the Third Reich.[32]
The ubiquitous talk-show trials on television, which echoed the
post–World War II tribunals, dramatized the shift from political debate and
controversy to moralizing admonitions, confessions, and absolutions. In
such a scenario, West German "hosts" played judge and jury while East
German "guests" were cast in the role of defendants who must prove their
innocence. That task became increasingly difficult since the interrogation
tended to repeat the self-righteous question "why did you stay?" and
implied that the only "good" GDR citizens were those who had abdicated
their citizenship or at the very least their party membership.

In the historical context of reunification, the term *protocol* took on the
ominous overtones of trial records. Especially in the later volume, Ullrich's
I Am My Own Capital, one can observe the consolidation of the scenario
described above and the gradual congealing of a monolithic GDR subject
marked "guilty." Insofar as interviewees identified with the role assigned to
them, the subjective documents presented in these anthologies merely
reflect the power dynamic between East and West that was perpetually
reenacted in the mass media. However, in the absence of public media that
conveyed the perspective of East Germans and enabled a dialogue among
them about their own history, the protocols contributed to the task of "col-
lecting diverse views of GDR history" (108). Together these anthologies
assemble a mosaic of observant, critical, sometimes dissident subjectivities
that eschewed the rhetorical ruts illustrated by a joke circulating in East
Berlin in 1990, that "at present, 15 million resistance fighters are persecut-
ing 15 million Stalinists" (50). The period from February 1990 to November 1991 covered by the two anthologies records the turning of relief and
self-confidence into guilt and shame—subjective responses to the larger
economic, ideological, and cultural developments that arose in the wake of
the GDR state.

Lux and Fischer's *You Can't Make a State* records the voices of GDR
women during February and March of 1990, a time when the oppositional

citizens' groups were operating in high gear, anticipating the elections that
would decide the GDR's future. It was also a time of vigorous feminist
organizing in the newly founded Unabhängiger Frauenverband (UFV,
Autonomous Women's Coalition), the umbrella organization for a growing
number of women's groups. The anthology, edited by two self-described
feminists from either side of the former Iron Curtain, acknowledges its allegiance to the GDR women's movement in its title (which quotes the UFV's
manifesto), in its concern with feminist issues (from the GDR's sociopolitical measures to underwear and sexual practices), and in its choice of interviewees, several of whom are long-time feminist activists. The collection
captures the brief moment of East-West feminist collaboration across ideological differences. Lux and Fischer's book endeavors to create a historical
retrospective of the GDR, and they deploy a feminist critique that is clearly
historicized as socialist in order to map a broad terrain of political subjectivities. Their joint venture also foreshadows the differences between eastern
and western feminism that led to the present strife and stall. "Whether a
woman likes or dislikes her breasts is no longer interesting to [western] feminists," East German journalist Petra Lux remarks wryly, and she begs to differ. Nanette Funk, a feminist scholar in the United States, points out that
terms like *women's equality* were "associated with contempt and disrespect
for women, rather than commitment to women's dignity and equal worth
as persons";[33] after the collapse of state socialism, many eastern feminists
wished to explore women's difference in the context of the newly created
women's culture. To West German feminists, that project seemed dated,
contributing to the prejudice that East German women were "behind" and
had to be taught about feminism. Lux's Austrian collaborator, Erica Fischer,
writes, "My superior technical equipment, my childlessness, my political
inactivity secured me advantages which my conscience did not always bear
easily." Other western feminists were less self-critical when they regarded
their eastern sisters as liabilities rather than partners in a shared learning
process.

The differences of both volumes from Wander's collection shed some
light on the (self-)censorship to which the earlier book had been subject but
also on the changes in GDR culture since the publication of *Good Morning,
Beautiful*. The women who speak to Lux, Fischer, and Ullrich neither share
a commitment to the defunct socialist state nor necessarily to socialist ideology. Some mourn the end of the SED regime while continuing to believe
in the Marxist critique, others question the survival of "the idea" without
people to realize it, and most express relief at the demise of the regime. In

contrast to Wander, the women in *You Can't Make a State* bracket neither politics nor sexuality in same-sex relationships. The collection provides a sense of the many ways in which women's feminist (and other critical) practices destabilized the socialist state and, conversely, were hampered by it in myriad ways in addition to enduring outright persecution. The collections reveal histories of political repression and dissidence. Avoiding the impression of an "army of resistance fighters," they nevertheless attempt to excavate those biographies that are at risk to be twice suppressed: once as the product of political undesirables under socialism, and again, after reunification, when West Germans granted dissident status to a select few while condemning the GDR population at large.

The focus of the collection is on the uncovering of feminist identities and organizations at odds with the hierarchical structures of the socialist ruling party as well as the male-dominated "revolutionary" citizens' groups. The feminist biographies in *You Can't Make a State* present a series of struggles with institutions as well as with internalized gender roles. The critique of patriarchal structures frequently moves across various sites of resistance. In the case of Petra L., this includes opposition to xenophobia. Her activism is contrasted with the government's lip service to "international solidarity," which did nothing to end the exclusion and discrimination of foreigners living in the GDR. The formation of critical identities, however, was continually checked by state control and intimidation. Salomea G., a German Jew who returned to the GDR after years of exile in Australia, testifies to the difficulties of organizing a women's consciousness-raising group in the late 1970s: after a few weeks and great fluctuation among the participants, "only four women were left, and two of them, perhaps even three, were sent by the secret police or at least reported back to them. Of course, that is not the right atmosphere for consciousness-raising" (137). Salomea's experience calls attention to the changing political topography of the GDR in the 1980s. The state and its security agencies created (or at least condoned) certain pockets of social space that were designated as "oppositional," "resistant," or "critical." Officially they were outside of its purview, but nevertheless they remained under its surveillance. The Church played an important role in this scenario, since much of the oppositional activity during the late 1970s and 1980s took place under its aegis, including feminist, pacifist, environmentalist, and homosexual organizations. At the same time, the state quelled the spontaneous, uncontrolled performance of dissident subjects and practices. Ursula Sillge, cofounder of the first non-church-affiliated gay and lesbian club in the GDR, reported the SED's attempts to sabotage that enterprise, preferring homosexuals to remain within the existing associations sponsored by the Church.[34] In this way, the state carefully engineered the invisibility of its dissenting citizens while allowing some measure of disagreement. Tracking the state's attempts at ideological containment, the protocols also note its failures.

Lux and Fischer's protocols map a complicated notion of sexual politics, no longer bound by the heterosexual mandate to which Wander had largely subscribed. Neither do they add up to a naive sexual glasnost in which a range of "liberated," open sexualities supplants the socialist state's instrumentalization of women's reproductive capacities and its tendency to restrict and taboo erotic expression. The women in *You Can't Make a State* describe the impoverishment and alienation of sexual relations subordinated to the state's agenda of population growth. The most illuminating testimonial in this respect is a text entitled "My life is Messed Up" by forty-five-year-old Silvia, an office worker in East Berlin. She points to the contradiction between the state's liberal sociopolitical measures and the lack of eroticism: "The joy of sex, sex as pleasure, was a taboo topic. It wasn't that the pill and officially sanctioned abortion rights created an openness for such an idea. . . . Day care and the kindergarten, all that worked out well so that these young mothers became something like breeding machines" (38). She concludes, "there was no eroticism, no humor, no drive. The uniformity of our lives has broken the men and made them indifferent" (40). She is excited by sex shops, lingerie, pornos, dildos, and vibrators, all of which for the first time became readily available to GDR citizens after the opening of the borders. Feeling cheated out of individualized options for erotic pleasure, Silvia constructs a narrative of sexual liberation that peaks in Beate Uhse's sex toy imperium, a chain that rapidly expanded eastward after reunification. Reacting to a lifetime of egalitarian gender ideology, which, to her mind, turned women into "worker bees," Silvia's longing for the celebration of difference culminates in the dream of complementary gender roles and codes of behavior, of gentlemen holding doors and ladies in makeup and fancy clothes.

Others, like the canteen manager Johanna B., are more critical of the "liberation" the West has to offer. At a West German train station, she was asked by three different men to turn a trick, which appalled her, because it illustrates that the benefits of "sexual freedom" for men do not necessarily extend to women. Her own experiences testify to a remarkable degree of sexual autonomy. Johanna reports that one day (before reunification) her husband bought an expensive pornographic magazine on the black market:

"He paid sixty Marks for it in a bar. I said, I'll cut your allowance for next week" (119). This remark highlights the contradiction between female self-confidence bought at the expense of a puritanical, sex-negative egalitarianism, on the one hand, and sexual liberation purchased at the price of gender inequality as well as class differences on the other. The situation of textile workers in a plant now manufacturing underwear for the prestigious West German Schiesser brand illustrates the same contradiction: their latest product, named Slipididu, is more attractively designed than the simple ribbed knickers of previous decades, which only came in two variations, pink and beige. Yet the women can no longer afford the sexy panties they sew, and it is questionable whether their sex lives will improve much considering their increased anxiety and exhaustion resulting from higher productivity demands. Silvia's interpretation of egalitarianism captures the social implications of instrumentalized sexuality: "If a girl doesn't take the pill and has a child at age sixteen, well, she has a child. There is no finger-pointing, not even if she's unmarried, not even if she has a black baby. That is indifference, no one cares" (38). In view of the resurgence of sexism, discrimination against single mothers, and racism since that time, her assertion points to the limits of sexual liberation under capitalism. The protocols in You Can't Make a State, by recording subjective damages resulting from a rationalistic ideology and instrumentalized social practice, and by refraining from giving or implying solutions (as Wander had done), called for sexual experimentation during a time of political change. Their open-endedness registers a brief period of much-needed reflection and the search for alternatives, which was short-circuited by the March 1990 elections in which the East German population voted overwhelmingly for the West German ruling party, the conservative Christian Democrats.

The groups whose histories are loosely sketched in Lux and Fischer's protocols developed a feminist critique of the socialist patriarchy and its contradictions that shaped the most intimate experiences of gender. The women who in 1989 organized the UFV participated in the project of the opposition movement, namely, to formulate an agenda for building democratic socialism. In addition, they recognized the importance of creating alternative forms of political organization, exemplified by the round table, minimal consensus, collective reflection, and gender quotas.[35] In the course of those months, however, feminist activists and programs were progressively marginalized "through the streamlining of politics toward professionalization and efficiency," resulting in a remasculinization of politics.[36]

In the liminal moment between socialism and capitalism, Lux and

Fischer assembled heterogeneous subjectivities and accounts of GDR history. In *You Can't Make a State,* the women take stock of a system that imposed difficulties and hardships on most of its citizens as well as dispensing privileges to some. Many voice resentment at having been cheated out of material comfort as well as professional or life-style choices. However, even in the deeply disorienting year of 1990, most women in *You Can't Make a State* pride themselves on having managed their personal and professional lives in a competent manner. In the face of looming unemployment, loss of financial security, and ideological reorientation, many refuse to be pressured into quick decisions but take the time to withdraw and recenter themselves. That step indicates a still-intact sense of security that is missing from *I Am My Own Capital,* assembled only a few months later. Despite the fear of an uncertain future that pervades most protocols, the optimistic title *You Can't Make a State Without Us* is programmatic, exuding a sense of self-assurance and confidence that is shared by some of the women Renate Ullrich began interviewing in October 1990. However, the sense of productive contradiction gradually fades from the later collection. The differentiated reckoning with forty years of GDR history is superseded by examinations of one's own complicity and guilt, which accompanied the daily, horrifying revelations of party mismanagement and abuse of power.

The contradictory evaluations and conclusions offered by the protocols in *You Can't Make a State* illuminate a politicized terrain of personal experience, engagement, and activism that defies the impression, conveyed by Western media, that the opposition movement in the GDR had suddenly sprung into existence in 1989. However, Lux and Fischer's attention to dissident biographies, a much-needed project, may lead one to romanticize the events of the fall of 1989 or to overestimate the practice of resistance garnered from *You Can't Make a State.* In 1991, GDR sociologist Hildegard Maria Nickel flatly stated that the women's movement in East Germany had done too little too late.[37] Whether that is correct or not, it appears useful and necessary to investigate those subjects who were predisposed to voicing criticism and who, in the fall of 1989, stood at the forefront of political change, and examine their relation to a feminist critique of the socialist state. *I Am My Own Capital,* published by the Center for Theater Documentation and Information, illustrates the East German notion of theater work as social work and, at best, as political activism. This also motivated the center's publication of the collected flyers, open letters, and pamphlets produced by theater artists during the fall of 1989 when artists were instrumental in creating public forums for discussions, both in the theater and in the street, turning the latter into a "tribunal of the people."[38] The protocols collected by Ullrich, a theater scholar from East Berlin, map the arrangement of critical, even oppositional, subjects within a paternalistic provider state, elucidating the paradox that, I believe, explains in part the opposition movement's failure to bring about the renewal of socialism as well as the swift implementation of capitalist principles and structures. My reading of Ullrich's protocols is guided by the assumption that, indeed, democratic socialism would not have been possible without a challenge to patriarchal structures, as the UFV (and Lux and Fischer) asserted. However, just as it is important to resist the tendency to heroicize the dissident speakers in *You Can't Make a State,* I would similarly refuse to dismiss Ullrich's partners as mere accomplices.

Assembled roughly a year after Ulrich's volume, *I Am My Own Capital* records not only the growing fears and existential uncertainty of its subjects but also a changed outlook on the past. The sense of an exploding multiplicity of voices and perspectives that characterizes *You Can't Make a State* is gradually replaced by the discovery of a shared identity as a GDR woman, a process that parallels the dismantling of the East German state, its institutions, and its social programs. Although both Ullrich and her interlocutors have lived in East Germany, the editor stages a series of East-West confrontations by phrasing her questions in the language of West German feminism. Since only one interviewee identifies herself as a feminist, feminism in this collection serves in some ways as a stand-in for the Western system with which theater artists have to contend, and the women's responses to Western feminist rhetoric frequently reflect the refusal to believe in any system of organized thought. "Another social utopia? Not for me," says the young actress Gabriele Streichhahn who tries to survive with a one-woman show (122). That disillusioned stance in part undergirded East German women's reluctance to mobilize against their disenfranchisement under West German law.

Ullrich's interviewees report the first tangible impact of capitalism on their lives, including unemployment and loss of child care. They record their first confrontations with homeless people and beggars in the streets and onstage, and they report their reactions to the resurgence of anti-Semitism and racism. The women describe their theaters' efforts to cope with the lack of funding, changed audiences, and a new role in a society that no longer privileged literature or theater and in which the stage suddenly was forced to compete with modern technology and mass-produced entertainment and information.

The production hierarchy of the theater provides an apt metaphor for social apparatuses in the GDR, foregrounding the subjective, individual reproduction of power relations while maintaining a focus on the material conditions framing them. The women in *I Am My Own Capital* address notions of collectivity, responsibility to an audience, and commitment to continued experimentation. They also discuss questions of privilege and complicity and of situating oneself within a bureaucracy that pursues a politics of inhibition, intimidation, and repression. These concerns are similar to those dominating the culture at large. Whereas the majority of women is critical of the institutionalized curtailment of the "creative, subversive" aspect of art (107), few are willing or able to articulate power differences in terms of patriarchal oppression. Ullrich, borrowing her vocabulary from West German theater women,[39] raises such issues as the gendered division between actor and director, women's performance of roles written by male playwrights, the relation between actresses as professional gender role models and spectators, and female-feminist perspectives on history. Only a small number of interviewees identifies the rivalry between actresses competing for a scarcity of roles and their dependence on male directors and administrators for patronage and support as instances of patriarchal injustice. Trained in applying materialist categories to social relations, several acknowledge covert financial disadvantages and deplore the shortage of "good" roles for women. In the course of the book, they also point to the effects of capitalism on women, while refusing to be driven into an adversarial position vis-à-vis men. Unfortunately, it would seem that these women's solidarity with their male comrades is unilateral, as the changing status particularly of women from the erstwhile GDR in the united Germany has shown.

The organization of the theater sheds light on two distinct modes in which power relations and socialist subjects were produced in the GDR. On one hand, the theater, like other bureaucratic apparatuses run by party functionaries, operated as a technology of repression, meting out privileges to those who demonstrated compliance and censoring the (political and dramatic) representation of dissident subjects. *I Am My Own Capital* provides numerous examples of biographies shaped by cultural-political repression and continual hindrances. Brigitte Soubeyran concludes that critical intelligence was usually punished and harangued, while mediocre opportunism was consistently rewarded.

On the other hand, the theater was defined as an institution that resisted state ideology, a position that was able to absorb the emotional and political energies of its participants and effectively solicit socialist identifications. Theater artists had worked under a stable system of censorship and oppositional readings, which produced stable, dissident subjects defined by their distance from official ideology. While relying on an adversarial relationship toward the state as the common, unspoken referent in the performers' interaction with the audience—a constellation that is now thrown into crisis—the theater institution is based on internal homogeneity, continuing to duplicate within its own walls the male-dominated hierarchy that characterizes the political culture at large. Bonding on the basis of their shared resistance to external pressures, its members resisted any critiques they perceived to be divisive. That structure prevented a feminist challenge to the male-dominated theater apparatus and neutralized critical impulses not directed against the enemy outside. In this way, these oppositional identities themselves served to stabilize a system built on unequal access to authority and power.

The designation of the theater as a critical, even dissident, space left other axes of power, such as gender, unquestioned, and it purchased stable, "oppositional" identities at the price of a feminist perspective or critique. Unlike the feminists introduced by Lux and Fischer, most of Ullrich's interlocutors agree with the official doctrine that in the GDR the secondary contradiction of gender inequality had been resolved. As artists, many of these women belonged to a somewhat privileged class, often enjoying the opportunity to travel even to Western countries and a measure of financial security unknown to most Western actors or directors. Like the sociopolitical measures that secured women's financial independence, these privileges were not negotiated or won but constituted rewards that were dispensed from above, assuring the acquiescence, even the gratitude, of those who benefited from the paternalistic "provider state."[40] That system facilitated these women's arrangement within extant power structures. The provider economy fostered an attitude that, according to GDR cultural critic Irene Dölling, was largely responsible for the lack of a sustained feminist critique or movement that could have halted the disappearance of the GDR's social net, which especially affected women.[41]

At the same time that Ullrich endeavors to record "diverse views of GDR history," her book charts the shrinking cultural-political ground for such a project. The signposts of politicized biographies, including party or dissident activism, which Lux and Fischer noted, tend to slip into justifications of party membership and a litany of dates of dissociation. Nevertheless, the protocol offers a feminist historiographical model not only in its concern with women's issues and organizations but in focusing on the margins of the dominant melodrama of Cold War heroes and villains and salvaging what has already fallen victim to the revision of postwar German history. Finally, these documents allow for a rigorous assessment of the question of whether we as materialist feminists should discard the notion of women's emancipation based on legal and economic equality. Feminist scholar Frigga Haug wonders: "In rejecting the former model of socialism, are we dismissing a model of women's emancipation whose fruits we have yet to harvest?"[42] The growth of feminist movements in Eastern European countries, shaped by decades of socialist rule as well as diverse indigenous traditions, has produced feminist strategies that differ drastically from those addressed to late capitalism. Since so many of the central assumptions held by materialist feminists in capitalist countries rest on notions that were part of hegemonic, and often oppressive, practices, women's experiences in socialist systems cannot help but inflect and inform the theorizing and politicking of Western feminists as well. I believe that the personal and critical documents charting socialist feminism, a frequently effaced discourse, offer a position of critical intervention in the current creation of a postcommunist world order in the arenas of national parliamentary politics, East-West leftist debates, and international dialogue among feminists.

NOTES

I wish to thank the Henschelverlag in the former East Berlin, especially Maria Tragelehn, for generously granting me access to its archive.

1. The Zentrum für Theaterdokumentation und -information, now renamed Haus Drama, in the former East Berlin, documented the revolutionary involvement of many theaters in the German Democratic Republic during the fall of 1989 as part of their publication *Theaterarbeit in der DDR. Wir treten aus unseren Rollen heraus: Dokumente des Aufbruchs Herbst '89.*

2. *Theaterarbeit,* 183. The editors list nine demonstrations initiated by theater professionals between November 4 and November 20, 1989.

3. See my article on two feminist plays on reunification written by a West German and an Austrian, respectively: "The Revolution Has Been Televised: Reconfiguring History and Identity in Post-Wall Germany," *Theatre Journal* 45, no. 1 (March 1993): 35–47. See also *DDR-Theater des Umbruchs,* an anthology of plays on reunification edited by Harald Müller (Frankfurt: Eichborn, 1991).

4. Erika Runge, a West German leftist and feminist, first used the term *protocol* in a collection of interviews that she conducted with workers in the industrial heartland of West Germany in 1968 (*Bottroper Protokolle* [Frankfurt: Suhrkamp, 1968]). The term usually refers to scientific transcripts and carries the authority of scientific, objective observation. Runge and later authors used the term in order to highlight the documentary

character of these subjective reports and thus validate the expression of communities whose lives and language are not commonly considered the subject of literature.

5. The family code of law, which was passed in 1965, had already signaled the reversal of earlier policies designed to integrate women into the labor force and socialize reproductive labor. In contrast, the family code of law reassigned primary responsibility for housework and child-rearing to women. See Susanne Stolt, "Leitbilder—Leidbilder: Zur Frauen- und Familienpolitik der SED," in *Irmtraud Morgner's Hexische Weltfahrt*, ed. Kristine von Soden, 92–100 (Berlin: Elefanten, 1991).

6. The official, party-affiliated women's organization was the Demokratischer Frauenbund Deutschlands (DFD, the Democratic Women's Union of Germany), founded in 1947.

7. The phrase "real existing socialism" is used to distinguish the socialist state from the idea(l) of socialism. It allowed critics of the GDR government to voice their doubts while still calling themselves socialists. This maneuver endeavored to preempt the accusation of counterrevolutionary thought or practice.

8. Ilse Nagelschmidt, "Sozialistische Frauenliteratur: Überlegungen zu einem Phänomen der DDR-Literatur in den siebziger und achtziger Jahren," *Weimarer Beiträge* 35, no. 3 (1989): 454.

9. Doris Paschiller, *Eine grosse Familie* (Berlin: Henschel, 1975), 68.

10. See Jutta Gysi, "Frauen in Partnerschaft und Familie: Sozialistisches Leitbild oder patriarchales Relikt?" In *Wir wollen mehr als ein "Vaterland": DDR-Frauen im Aufbruch*, ed. Gislinde Schwarz and Christine Zenner (Reinbek: Rowohlt, 1990), 106.

11. Irina Liebmann, another young author who began to write during the mid-1980s, resembles Maron in the use of those techniques. In her plays, too, surreal images function allegorically. See her *Quatschfresser: Theaterstücke* (Frankfurt: Frankfurter Verlagsanstalt, 1990).

12. Christa Wolf, the most prominent feminist writer in the GDR since the 1970s, addressed the self-destructive dynamic of "techno-scientific socialism" as a function of the patriarchy, not just a symptom of the "dialectic of enlightenment," as the scholars of the Frankfurt School had posited earlier. Her analysis informs much of her writing, most clearly, perhaps, in the novel *Störfall*, which concerns the Chernobyl nuclear catastrophe. See Lennox's remarks on Christa Wolf's critique of the Enlightenment in Sara Lennox, "'Nun ja! Das nächste Leben geht aber heute an': Prosa von Frauen und Frauenbefreiung in der DDR," in *Literatur in der DDR in den siebziger Jahren*, ed. P. U. Hohendahl and P. Herminghouse (Frankfurt: Suhrkamp, 1983), 231ff.

13. Paschiller, *Eine grosse Familie*, 40, my translation.

14. Lennox, "Nun ja!" 233, 234.

15. Monika Maron, *Ada und Evald: Ein Stück*, in *Das Mißverständnis: Vier Erzählungen und ein Stück* (Frankfurt: Fischer, 1981), 107, my translation.

16. Peter Reichel, "Anmerkungen zur DDR-Dramatik seit 1980. Teil 1," *Weimarer Beiträge* 29, no. 8 (1983). In my research at the archives of the drama publisher Henschelverlag I found only six plays by GDR women written between 1975 and 1985, four of which address gender issues. Maron's play was published in West Germany. It should be noted that these figures do not accurately represent women's dramatic production during this time span because other houses sometimes published plays. In addition, some theaters staged pieces that were not approved or published by Henschelverlag.

17. Maxie Wander, *Guten Morgen, Du Schöne: Frauen in der DDR. Protokolle. Mit einem Vorwort von Christa Wolf* (Darmstadt: Luchterhand, 1978). See also Sarah Kirsch, *Die Pantherfrau: Fünf unfrisierte Erzählungen aus dem Kassetten-Recorder* (Berlin and Weimar: Aufbau-Verlag, 1973); Gabriele Eckart, *So sehe ick die Sache: Protokolle aus der DDR* (Cologne: Kiepenheuer and Witsch, 1984); and Christine Müller, *James Dean lernt kochen: Männer in der DDR. Protokolle* (Berlin: Buchverlag Der Morgen, 1986).

18. Andreas Huyssen, "After the Wall: The Failure of German Intellectuals," *New German Critique* 52 (Winter 1991): 132.

19. Christa Wolf, "In Touch," in *German Feminism: Readings in Politics and Literature*, eds. Edith Hoshino Altbach et al. (Albany: State University of New York Press, 1984), 163. The essay was published as the foreword to Maxie Wander's collection of protocols.

20. Wander, *Guten Morgen*, 7. Further page references to this work are cited in the text.

21. See Sue-Ellen Case's chapter "Personal Theatre" in her *Feminism and Theatre* (London: Methuen, 1988).

22. For the protocols of women who wished to leave the GDR but were incarcerated after applying for an exit visa, see Ulrich Schacht, ed., *Hohenecker Protokolle: Aussagen zur Geschichte der politischen Verfolgung von Frauen in der DDR* (Zurich: Ammann Verlag, 1984). The title promises an examination of gender-specific persecution in the GDR, which the text does not deliver.

23. Ursula Sillge, *Un-Sichtbare Frauen: Lesben und ihre Emanzipation in der DDR* (Berlin: LinksDruck, 1991).

24. Wolf, "In Touch," 164.

25. Ilse Nagelschmidt, "Vom Wert des eigenen Erkennens," in *Wider das schlichte Vergessen: Der deutsch-deutsch Einigungsprozess: Frauen im Dialog*, eds. Christine Kulke, Meiai Kopp-Degethoff, Ulrike Ramming (Berlin: Orlanda, 1992), 171.

26. Recently some East European feminists proposed to recast the public-private split in terms of state and family as more appropriate to political culture in socialist societies. See Czechoslovakian feminist Hana Havelkova's discussion of civic consciousness in relation to the public and private spheres in Nanette Funk and Magda Mueller, eds., "A Few Prefeminist Thoughts," in *Gender Politics and Post-Communism* (New York: Routledge, 1993), 62–73.

27. Anna Mudry, ed., *Gute Nacht, Du Schöne: Autorinnen blicken zurück* (Frankfurt: Luchterhand, 1991); Kerstin Gutsche, *Ich ahnungsloser Engel: Lesbenprotokolle* (Berlin: Reiher, 1991); Helga Königsdorf, *Adieu, DDR: Protokolle eines Abschieds* (Reinbek: Rowohlt, 1990); Gabriele M. Grafenhorst, *Abbruch-Tabu: Lebensgeschichten nach Tonbandprotokollen* (Berlin: Neues Leben, 1990).

28. Erica Fischer and Petra Lux, *Ohne uns ist kein Staat zu machen: DDR-Frauen nach der Wende* (Cologne: Kiepenheuer und Witsch, 1990).

29. Renate Ullrich, *Mein Kapital bin ich selber: Gespräche mit Theaterfrauen in Berlin-O 1990/91* (Berlin: Zentrum für Theaterdokumentation und -information, 1991). Further page references to this work are indicated parenthetically in the text.

30. The term *archeological texts* is used by gay East German author Jürgen Lemke in Jeffrey M. Peck, "Being Gay in Germany: An Interview with Jürgen Lemke," *New German Critique* 52 (Winter 1991): 145.

31. See Huyssen, "After the Wall"; and Thomas Anz, ed., *"Es geht nicht um Christa Wolf"*: *der Literaturstreit im vereinten Deutschland* (Munich: Spangenberg, 1991). The controversy has recently been fueled by the disclosure of Wolf's collaboration with the GDR secret police from 1959 to 1962.

32. I have discussed the public staging of the East-West encounter in "The Revolution has been televised."

33. Funk and Mueller, 6.

34. Sillge, *Un-Sichtbare Frauen*, 102.

35. See also Tatiana Böhm, "The Women's Question as a Democratic Question: In Search of Civil Society," in *Gender Politics*, 151–59.

36. Sabine Wilke, "Wie die altdeutschen Herren ein Land neu verteilten: Die Geschichte der (Wieder?)-Vereinigung als Herrengeschichte," manuscript, 2.

37. Hildegard Maria Nickel, "Modernisierungsbrüche im Einigungsprozess—(k)ein einig Volk von Schwestern," in *Wider das schlichte Vergessen: Der deutsch-deutsch Einigungsprozess: Frauen im Dialog*, eds. Christine Kulke, Heidi Kopp-Degethoff, Ulrike Ramming, (Berlin: Orlanda, 1992), 41.

38. *Theaterarbeit*, 183.

39. Ullrich, like some of her interview partners, attended the symposium "Die Sprache des Theaters und die Frauen," organized by the West German association of theater women (Frauen im Theater, or FiT) in the summer of 1991, which brought together theater women from both Germanies for the first time. She acknowledges her debt to West German feminist discourse (Ullrich, *Mein Kapital*, 54).

40. Political scientist Christine Kulke coined the term *Versorgungsökonomie* (provider economy) in "Ferne Nähe: Zum Dialog unter Frauen im rationalisierten Einigungsprozeß," in *Wider das schlichte Vergessen*, 18.

41. Irene Dölling, "Frauenforschung mit Fragezeichen?: Perspektiven feministischer Wissenschaft," in *Wir wollen mehr als ein lVaterland«*, 43, 44.

42. Frigga Haug, *Beyond Female Masochism: Memory-Work and Politics* (London and New York: Verso, 1992), 259.

5.

Patricia R. Schroeder

Transforming Images of Blackness: Dramatic Representation, Women Playwrights, and the Harlem Renaissance

When Angelina Weld Grimké's play *Rachel* was first produced by the NAACP's Drama Committee in 1916, it became something of a cause célèbre in the African American theatrical community. According to the program notes, the play was "the first attempt to use the stage for race propaganda,"[1] suggesting that pressures from outside the African American community had prompted black artists to employ theater as a tool of protest. But not all African American theater artists agreed that resistance was the proper function of drama. In direct reaction to the production of *Rachel,* several prominent members of the NAACP Drama Committee left the group, provoking what one recent critic has called a "cultural war . . . [fought] over accurate depictions of the African American community."[2] As a result of this "war," a double tradition of African American drama emerged during the Harlem Renaissance (from about 1919 to about 1929) that has continued to influence African American playwrights throughout the twentieth century. Based on competing aesthetic theories, one that espoused realistic protest dramas and another promoting the celebration of black popular culture, this lingering double tradition is the product of three intertwining forces of the early twentieth century: the social pressures exerted upon African Americans by the dominant white culture; the controversies within the black artistic community over the appropriate aesthetic responses to those social pressures; and the awareness of African American

women playwrights of their unique place within these two arenas of struggle. As external pressures heated up the internal debates, the Harlem
Renaissance became a crucible of crisis for all African American playwrights
but especially for women.

The social tensions that affected African Americans during the first two
decades of the twentieth century were the direct result of the widespread
racism that lingered after Reconstruction in the South. The most brutal
manifestation of this racism was lynching: between 1885 and 1919, more
than three thousand African Americans were lynched in the United States,
enduring methods of torture that included shooting, drowning, hanging,
burning, and mutilation.[3] In part to avoid this apparently socially condoned
violence, and in part to seek improved economic opportunities, African
Americans from the southern states (where lynching was most prevalent)
increasingly migrated north. While violence may have been generally less
overt in the North, this large-scale population shift inevitably produced new
tensions and problems, as the established residents of the urban North perceived these newcomers as competitors for increasingly scarce jobs.[4] Violence seemed at times to be unavoidable, culminating in the last six months
of 1919 when the United States witnessed approximately fifty racially motivated riots.[5]

Specific national and international events also pressured African Americans in particular ways. The end of World War I brought new problems, as
African American war veterans' demands for equal treatment at home led to
renewed racism and the revival of the Ku Klux Klan.[6] The 1910s also saw
the height of the women's suffrage movement. Many African American
women fought for the vote, even though their work was often denigrated
by white female suffragists and by men of all races.[7] African American
women playwrights of the early twentieth century responded to all these
tensions in their work, writing plays—such as *Rachel*—that protested issues
like lynching, unfair economic limitations, and the trauma of black mothers
who are powerless to protect their children from psychological and physical
abuse.

Within the world of theater, African American artists struggled with
problems of representation and access—more subtle forms of racism, perhaps, but ones with insidious repercussions. During this era, Broadway
remained largely closed to African American dramatists. While Broadway
producers of the period began to be interested in depictions of African
American life, they continued to foster primarily white visions of that life.
While twenty plays "with Negro themes" reached Broadway during the

1920s,[8] only five of them were written by African American playwrights (all male), and among those five only Wallace Thurman's 1929 melodrama *Harlem,* written in collaboration with white author W. S. Rapp, achieved commercial success.[9] Compounding this problem of access was the problem of image: many African American characters in these white productions perpetuated the racist stereotypes of the minstrel tradition, which depicted blacks as "lazy, comic, pathetic, idiotic" and created "an image that was disastrous to the advancement of serious black theater."[10]

Not surprisingly, African American theater artists felt the need to counteract these demeaning stereotypes and construct alternative stage versions of the black experience. Writing in *The Crisis* in 1926, W. E. B. Du Bois outlined a program for African American theatrical practice that became something of a manifesto for the black theater companies of the period. He wrote:

> The plays of a Negro theatre must be: 1. About us. That is, they must have plots which reveal Negro life as it is. 2. By us. That is, they must be written by Negro authors who understand from birth and continued association just what it means to be a Negro today. 3. For us. That is, the theatre must cater primarily to Negro audiences and be supported and sustained by their entertainment and approval. 4. Near us. The theatre must be in a Negro neighborhood near the mass of ordinary Negro people.[11]

While not many plays fit this definition in 1926, the principles set forth in this statement—that black theater be centered in black consciousness, penned by black writers, and performed in black community spaces for black audiences—were widely supported by African American theater artists even before Du Bois codified them. Throughout the 1910s, 1920s, and 1930s, African Americans were founding their own theater companies in an attempt to redefine theater within an African American context.

There were, however, significant differences of opinion among these artists as to how that redefinition could best be accomplished in theatrical practice. While some groups, like Anita Bush's Lafayette Players, wanted to perform plays unrelated to black experience, others, notably Du Bois and his Krigwa Players, wanted to produce propaganda plays that would depict and so protest racial oppression. Others, like Alain Locke and his Howard Players, fought for artistic and imaginative depictions of black folk culture without a political agenda, while still others, like the Rose McClendon

Players, attempted to dramatize the similarities between blacks and whites when they are placed in similar conditions.[12]

As the specific controversy over the 1916 production of *Rachel* reveals, these strategic and aesthetic debates crystalized around two central figures of the Harlem Renaissance: Du Bois (who promoted the play) and Locke (who disparaged it). Their sometimes heated interchanges were published regularly in competing literary journals, *The Crisis* (Du Bois) and Opportunity (Locke), which also sponsored playwriting competitions for black artists and so offered publishing opportunities for aspiring dramatists. While both men agreed that black art should explore black life from a black perspective, disagreement arose when these principles began to be put into practice.

For Du Bois, all art was propaganda designed to incite social change. African American art, therefore, ought to depict such social problems faced by African Americans as racially motivated violence and limited economic opportunities in an appeal to white audiences with the power to redress injustice. In depicting worthy African American characters who are unfairly victimized by racism, theater would concomitantly offer positive representations of African Americans for black audiences, thereby supplying a corrective to minstrel stereotypes. As Rebecca Cureau explains it, Du Bois "took the middle-class position that characterization of black life should project a proper image of the Negro," a stance sometimes described as the "best-foot-forward" school or the "genteel tradition" of African American drama.[13] In retrospect, it is clear that much of the impetus of the "best-foot-forward" school came from class bias on the part of Du Bois and his followers, who criticized writers like Langston Hughes for their use of "low-life" characters that might reinforce degrading stereotypes.[14] Du Bois evidently wanted to record middle-class African Americans struggling to achieve conventional bourgeois success without judging the underlying assumptions and prejudices on which those middle-class norms are based.[15] Despite overlooking the tangled intersections of class and race, however, Du Bois did recognize the social function of art and fostered it in his support of "race" or "propaganda" plays designed to explore social problems and protest the racial violence of his era.

Because Alain Locke disagreed so vehemently about the function of drama, he defected from the NAACP Drama Committee after the 1916 production of *Rachel,* later joining Montgomery Gregory in founding the Howard Players. For Locke, individual expression—art for its own sake—was the only appropriate goal of creative endeavor. From our postmodern perspective, it may seem a naive maneuver on Locke's part to deny the ideological biases, the propaganda, inherent in all forms of creative expression. However, given the context of the Harlem Renaissance, Locke's aesthetic emphasis can be seen as providing an alternative to the African American artist's bind of facing a double audience: a white audience with stereotypical notions about blacks and a black audience eager to see its own experiences reflected onstage. As Locke wrote in a 1928 defense of his antipropaganda position:

> my chief objection to propaganda, apart from its besetting sin of monotony and disproportion, is that it perpetuates the position of group inferiority even in crying out against it. For it leaves and speaks under the shadow of a dominant majority who it harangues, cajoles, threatens or supplicates. It is too extroverted for balance or poise or inner dignity and self-respect.[16]

In fact, by pointing out that opposition to the status quo still signals dependence on it, Locke anticipates the position taken by many current materialist feminists.[17] And, together with Gregory, Locke developed an alternative to the propaganda play promoted by Du Bois: the folk play.

As delineated by Gregory and Locke, the folk play depicted authentic daily life without emphasizing racial oppression; it was to be a "drama of free expression and imaginative release . . . with no objective but to express beautifully and colorfully race folk life."[18] Focussing on the everyday experiences, customs, beliefs, traditions, and language of ordinary black people, the folk plays of the 1920s went a step beyond the humorous dialect plays of the 1910s (such as those of Paul Laurence Dunbar) because they treated the whole range of human experience, not just the comic.[19]

The dangers of Locke's approach to drama have been pointed out many times, both by Du Bois and his followers (who worried about perpetuating racist stereotypes of African American common people) and by critics today. Leslie Catherine Sanders, for instance, notes that the African American folk play was quickly appropriated by white writers in whose hands the characters became exotics; that many folk plays of rural life oversimplified the inherent problems (such as poverty) by imagining a false bucolic innocence; and that many of the characters did recapitulate traditional racist stereotypes.[20] Nonetheless, Locke and his associates made great strides in creating a black-centered stage reality, in assuming the presence of a black audience, in developing recognizably human black characters, and in fostering the work of many new African American voices in the theater.[21]

And how did women playwrights react to this debate over African American theater? That question is difficult to answer, since their chances for commercial success were even more limited than were those of their male counterparts, and as a result not all of their works have been preserved or recovered. Nellie McKay estimates that during the Harlem Renaissance eleven black women published twenty-one plays, but many more were evidently performed in community schools, auditoriums, and churches, and these were never published.[22] Gloria Hull's research suggests some reasons within the black artistic community for this failure to preserve women's plays. According to Hull, many New York–based patrons and mentors of Harlem writers were homosexual men who favored the work of male writers. Furthermore, much of Harlem's intellectual life took place in afterhours clubs, which respectable black women were not encouraged to frequent.[23] As a result, many women writers lacked access to literary and theatrical opportunities other than those offered by local church and community groups. Those female writers based in the Washington, D.C., area may also have faced gender restrictions. While Kathy Perkins credits Locke and Gregory with supporting a number of women playwrights in their Howard University playwriting classes, Hull suggests that Locke was something of a misogynist who actively favored male students and excluded women from his intellectual circle.[24]

In addition to this compounded problem of access, black women playwrights also faced extra complications in the area of representation, where they had to combat degrading sexual as well as racial stereotypes. In her work on African American women novelists, Barbara Christian has isolated four persistent stereotypes of black women: mammy, loose woman, tragic mulatta, and conjure woman.[25] These images have posed recurring problems for black women writers and performers. In a poignant 1925 essay on popular images of black women, Elise Johnson McDougald explained the psychological damage done to women who could not help but absorb the false but ubiquitous representations of them.

> [E]ven in New York, the general attitude of mind causes the Negro woman serious difficulty. She is conscious that what is left of chivalry is not directed at her. She realizes that the ideas of beauty, built up in the fine arts, have excluded her almost entirely. Instead, the grotesque Aunt Jemimas of the streetcar advertisements, proclaim only an ability to serve, without grace of loveliness. Nor does the drama catch her finest spirit. She is most often used to provoke the mirthless laugh of

ridicule; or to portray feminine viciousness or vulgarity not peculiar to Negroes. This is the shadow over her.[26]

Given this cultural climate, both on and off the stage, it is clear that replacing stereotypical images of African American women would be of paramount importance to these female playwrights.

While stereotypes of mammy and loose woman dominated representations of black women, the reality of African American women's lives before the twentieth century had been all but effaced from American history, their unique experiences and perspectives left unrecorded and unremarked. There are, of course, multiple reasons for such oversight, ranging from poor record keeping by slave owners to a widespread politics of silence—a "culture of dissemblance"[27]—among black women determined to protect their privacy and middle-class status. Given the secrecy and silence surrounding African American women's shared and individual histories, writing plays to reconstruct their lives was both challenging and important. For the black women playwrights of the Harlem Renaissance, therefore, a crucial first step in claiming the stage was to discover and depict the historical and cultural facts that black women had repressed or to which they had been denied access.

In responding to social pressures, counteracting stereotypes, and recovering lost history, African American women playwrights seemed less concerned about aesthetic form than about getting their messages across. Many of them, like Grimké, used realism and the genteel approach to protest social conditions. Others, like Georgia Douglas Johnson, May Miller, and Zora Neale Hurston, followed Locke's lead in writing folk plays to celebrate African American culture without specific reference to racial oppression. Still others, like Mary P. Burrill and Shirley Graham, combined elements of the two forms to protest existing conditions while simultaneously positing some intracultural solutions. A look at two plays from these different dramatic traditions—the infamous *Rachel* and Shirley Graham's *It's Morning*— will illustrate the ways African American women protested social inequity, re-created black female characters, recovered black women's history, and so developed a unique dramatic tradition out of the crises of the Harlem Renaissance.

Grimké's *Rachel* is an excellent example of the sort of "propaganda play" Du Bois espoused, illustrating the playwright's commitments to promoting African American equality, to replacing stereotypes (especially those of black women), and to showing how widespread social evils damage individuals. The story takes place behind the fourth wall of the Loving family parlor. A respectable, middle-class family consisting of a mother, her son Tom, and her daughter Rachel, the Lovings have come north after the lynching of the father and elder son, an incident that took place ten years prior to the action and of which Tom and Rachel know nothing at the beginning of the play. The title character is a vivacious teenager when we first meet her, devoted to her family and her education. Her dominant characteristics are a love for children (especially "the little black and brown babies") and a fervent desire someday to marry and raise a large family of her own.[28]

As she matures into a young woman in the second and third acts, however, her ideals become blighted. The changes in Rachel are prompted by a number of incidents, each revealing a different form of racial oppression common to the era. She discovers that her father and brother George were killed by a lynch mob; her brother Tom and his friend John Strong (with whom Rachel is in love) cannot find jobs equal to their college educations and must work as waiters to support their families; she meets a little black girl who has been so traumatized by the racism of her first-grade teacher and classmates that the child can no longer speak; and Rachel's young adopted son is physically bruised and spiritually wounded by a gang of white boys. Emotionally undone by the injuries inflicted upon the men in her life and upon the children around her, Rachel refuses Strong's marriage proposal, vowing never to marry and bring more black children into a world that will inevitably abuse them. The play thus illustrates the psychic repercussions of violence and bigotry and their potentially devastating effects on the African American family.

Augmenting the play's protest of racism in general is Grimké's attention to its particular impact on African American mothers. In commenting on her motives for writing the play, Grimké defines white women as her target audience and motherhood as the hook by which she would enlist their support in combating racial oppression.

> If anything can make all women sisters underneath their skins, it is motherhood. If then I could make the white women of this country see, feel, understand just what their prejudice and the prejudice of their fathers, brothers, husbands, sons were having on the souls of the colored mothers everywhere and upon the mothers that are to be, a great power to affect public opinion would be set free and the battle would be half won.[29]

In *Rachel,* then, motherhood itself becomes a crucible of crisis by which to enlist a white audience in promoting social reform. Grimké's attention to exploring the extraordinary tensions of motherhood for African American women has had lasting repercussions on African American drama, setting in place a tradition that persisted through Graham's 1940 *It's Morning* (as we shall see) and has continued, throughout the twentieth century, from Lorraine Hansberry's *A Raisin in the Sun* to Ntozake Shange's *For Colored Girls* to Adrienne Kennedy's *Ohio State Murders.*

Despite Grimké's avowed interest in engaging a white female audience, however, it is clear that she also subscribed to Du Bois's notion that a black audience "needed to see an image of its members . . . as they wished themselves to be."[30] In fact, Grimké created characters to represent (in her words) "the best type of colored people."[31] Her characters are middle-class paragons, conscientious about family, work, school, and upward mobility. Their apartment is decorated with prints by Raphael, Millet, and Burne-Jones. The characters value education, speak standard English, and Rachel takes pains to correct her adopted son's grammatical errors. In short, they are clear-cut examples of the "genteel" models advocated by Du Bois.

These genteel characters could be interpreted as just another form of stereotype—not a demeaning one, to be sure, but one guided by unchallenged bourgeois assumptions and middle-class aspirations. As James Hatch has remarked, "the author sees no conflict between middle class virtues and the beauties of being black."[32] But Grimké's challenge to the stereotypical images of black women takes on an added dimension in the character of Rachel, who reveals more complexity than a cardboard stereotype could bear. Rachel is, in Margaret Wilkerson's words, "the antithesis of the prevailing stereotypes," being "neither a superwoman nor of loose character; she is a tender, vulnerable person whom the evils of society overwhelm."[33] While some early critics of the play interpreted Rachel's refusal to marry as advocating race genocide,[34] Rachel's act is more one of autonomous self-definition. By rejecting Strong and refusing the marriage she has so long desired, Rachel transcends the prevailing stereotypes of black women as either mammies or wantons. Instead, Rachel's competing desires regarding Strong and her future children signify the internal conflicts faced by African American women in a violently racist society.

If the critical reception of *Rachel* was quite mixed at the time, it remains no less so today. While the play has begun to attract some recognition (especially from feminists), many reviewers of the past few decades have criticized the melodrama and sentimentality of the play or at best offer to forgive it these sins as endemic to its era.[35] A particular point of attack is Mrs. Loving's long narration describing the deaths of her husband and son. To some, this protracted monologue represents nothing more than clumsy exposition that impedes the action of the play.[36] Seen from within an African American cultural tradition that emphasizes the spoken word, however, Mrs. Loving's long tale *is* the action; that is, the scene offers a realistic enactment of the African American tradition of storytelling, of oral history in progress. Because their mother has never spoken of their father's death, Rachel and Tom believe she is concealing some disgraceful secret about him. When Mrs. Loving realizes that her children are ashamed, she shares the awful story, berating herself for maintaining a "culture of dissemblance" that was ultimately damaging. By means of this monologue, Mrs. Loving recovers lost family history, and Grimké documents the value of oral tradition for restoring racial pride.

The fact that Grimké's play has been so criticized for its long monologues probably has more to do with the realistic "propaganda" format she chose than with the monologues themselves; that is, long monologues seem intrusive when they disrupt a linear action designed to hammer home a particular point. While folk drama may have its own inherent problems (as we saw above), it better succeeds at embodying oral history and illustrating its power. Following the lead of Locke and Gregory, many playwrights of the Harlem Renaissance wrote folk plays, all of which presented common black people and their popular culture in a positive light. For example, Georgia Douglas Johnson explored the value of what white culture would call superstition in *Plumes* (1928). Eulalie Spence in *Fool's Errand* (1927) and Ruth Gaines-Shelton in *The Church Fight* (1927) showed the humorous side of African American church congregations, and May Miller satirized a rural black community's suspicion of education in *Riding the Goat* (1925). Most of these plays are short pieces, often humorous and sometimes poignant, in which the oral and performative aspects of black culture take center stage. To illustrate what folk elements can add even to a propaganda play, as well as to document the continuing influence of the 1920s folk play on twentieth-century African American drama, it is to Shirley Graham's 1940 play *It's Morning* that I now turn.

Graham's play, which takes place in a slave cabin on the last day of 1862, is an interesting amalgam of propaganda play and folk drama, illustrating the lasting impact of both forms and the creative ways in which they can be combined. Because she was married to W. E. B. Du Bois and was herself a classically trained musician, Graham had obvious links to the genteel tradition. She created admirable characters and a Christian framework for her story to put African Americans' "best foot forward" and to illustrate (as *Rachel* did) the effects of racism on the psyches of black mothers. However, in *It's Morning* she also used a number of folk elements that celebrate African American culture. During the course of the short play we hear both secular and religious songs, witness a variety of dances, and hear stories passed down orally through the generations. Because of this innovative embedding of African rhythms and oral culture within a traditional Aristotelian structure, Elizabeth Brown-Guillory has described *It's Morning* as "a major break-through in African-American drama."[37]

Most versions of the play begin with a party in the cabin of Cissie, slave mother of the light-hearted, fourteen-year-old Millie.[38] When the laughing dancers move offstage, we learn that Millie has been sold to a repulsive and lascivious creditor and that Cissie is hosting the party to give her innocent daughter one last day of joy. While Cissie is offstage, her distress at losing her daughter is explained by Grannie Lou, the oldest slave on the plantation, who offers two reminiscences to the assembled slave women. First she recalls Cissie's youth. To the astonishment of her current friends, the now-stolid Cissie was as cheerful and lively as her daughter until an overseer swore to "break huh will" (86) and evidently did so by raping her repeat-edly. Later, in Cissie's presence, Grannie Lou recounts the even older story of a queenly slave woman from Africa, noted for her strength in cutting down cane stalks, who lined up her three sons to watch the sunrise and beheaded them from behind—with one swoop of her cane knife—to pre-vent their being sold down the river. Cissie heeds Grannie Lou's repeated admonition that "She [Millie]—don'—hab—tuh—go!" (90), and, at dawn on the next day (New Year's Day), she kills Millie with a cane knife. The terrible story takes an ironic twist when the knock at the door that impelled Cissie's action turns out to be not the lustful creditor come to collect his prize but a young Union soldier who informs the slaves that they are free. The play ends with Cissie's proffering Millie's limp body to the horrified Yankee boy who would have released her from bondage, suggesting that the sunrise framing him in the doorway, symbol of a new day dawning for the freed slaves, will never obliterate the ghastly atrocities on which slavery was built.

As this brief summary suggests, *It's Morning* shares a variety of themes and strategies with *Rachel,* written more than twenty years before it. Most obviously, Graham's play includes a variety of admirable characters who do not conform to the demeaning stage stereotypes of African Americans. The neighbors are kind, helpful to each other, energetic, and deeply spiritual. Uncle Dave, the preacher who tries to talk Cissie out of murdering Millie, exemplifies traditional Christian values and religious faith in God's plan, sentiments echoed by the other characters. Above all, Cissie herself defies the traditional stereotypes of African American women. While Cissie's action is obviously a mercy killing designed to spare Millie the life of degradation that Cissie herself has suffered, murdering her own child as a safeguard against sexual abuse effectively undermines Cissie's status as either nurturing mammy or wanton whore.

Graham also followed Grimké's example of appealing to both black and white mothers to stop violence and racism. In a version of the play preserved only in manuscript, Cissie engages in a conversation with Mrs. Tilden, the wife of the absent plantation owner, in which they share the pains of motherhood for all women during a period of slavery and war.

> Cissie: Yo' heart am good—but yo' kain't know mah pain,
> Pain dat began when fus mah baby move, soft in mah bosom—pain dat growed big wid passen days.
> An' wen at las' Ah look into huh face, mah eyes run down in teahs an' covered huh, couse in mah arms Ah hold jus' one mo'—*slave.*
> Mrs. Tilden: Millie's your girl, and Charles was my boy.
> Do you forget how gayly he waved back, as he rode laughing off to war?
> Is my pain any less because he died a soldier?
> Cissie: But, he war free!
> Mrs. Tilden: Is that why men must die—
> That they be free? We women live—and so
> Our hearts are breaking.[39]

This conversation suggests that Graham, like Grimké, was aware of a double audience and attempted to override spectatorial racial differences by appealing to gender similarities, holding out the possibility of female solidarity, whether real or imagined, across race lines. Also like Grimké, Graham here appeals directly to black and white women—especially mothers—to stop the violence that jeopardizes both races. Graham's Civil War setting may provide the distance necessary to avoid *Rachel*'s didacticism, but it also offers a clear parallel to the savage racism of her own era.[40]

Given its affinity to the propagandistic *Rachel* and its inclusion of folk elements, *It's Morning* represents an amalgamation of African American drama's double tradition. Perhaps the most significant illustration of this combination of elements appears in the storytelling within the play, which functions both as a cultural practice and as a form of dramatic action. As we have seen, the storytelling monologues in *Rachel* are sometimes seen as disruptions of the action, which otherwise is realistically linear and causal. Because so many folk elements are already embedded in *It's Morning,* however, the interpolated tales seem a natural outgrowth of the action rather than impediments to it. Both Cissie's past and the legend of the noble African woman are communicated to the slave women and to the audience through Grannie Lou's unofficial history, a spoken tale related by one who claims she "ain't so ole dat Ah don' membah!" (90). Despite their lack of written documentation, Grannie's remembered truths are powerful: they explain Cissie's motives for killing Millie and provide a model (complete with choice of weapon) for the murder. To be sure, without Grannie Lou's oral history Cissie might never have taken her tragic action. However, in the context of the play, Grannie Lou's story emphasizes the heroism of the African mother and suggests the defiance and pride of black people who must use drastic measures to resist their enslavement.[41]

In *It's Morning,* then, Graham created a unique composite dramatic form that combined the two strands of a double tradition and solved some of the knotty problems inherent in each. By using a distant historical context as an analogy to her own, she was able to depict the physical and psychological effects of racism and violence without "perpetuat[ing] the position of group inferiority" (to borrow Locke's phrase) and without alienating white audiences who needed to hear the message. By incorporating Christian iconography into her imagery and traditional Christian values into her characters' motives, she was able to present African Americans in a positive light to middle-class audiences, both black and white. Finally, by including elements of folk drama, Graham was able to record some of the content of African American oral history, embody its interactive form, document its authority, and restore voice to long-silenced African American women.

In a 1992 essay on contemporary representations of African Americans, bell hooks writes, "Unless we transform images of blackness, of black people, our ways of looking and our ways of being seen, we cannot make radical interventions that will fundamentally alter our situation."[42] In this statement, hooks suggests that controlling how one is represented is an essential step in promoting social change; it can be a revolutionary act. Seen in this context, and against the backdrops of interracial violence, aesthetic controversy, and feminism, the theater artists discussed in this essay emerge as revolutionaries who fought to alter the ways African Americans were seen and saw themselves reflected. They were also progenitors of an important dramatic tradition that combines social protest and cultural celebration, a double tradition apparent today in the work of playwrights as diverse as Amiri Baraka and August Wilson, Alice Childress and Ntozake Shange. Through their attention to representations of blackness and to the various dramatic forms appropriate to that task, the theater artists of the Harlem Renaissance reconfigured the field of performance inherited by African American playwrights, forever transforming images of blackness.

NOTES

1. Quoted in Robert J. Fehrenbach, "An Early Twentieth-Century Problem Play of Life in Black America: Angelina Grimké's *Rachel,*" in *Wild Women in the Whirlwind: Afra-American Culture and the Contemporary Literary Renaissance,* ed. Joanne M. Braxton and Andrée Nicola McLaughlin (New Brunswick, N.J.: Rutgers University Press, 1990), 91.

2. Wahneema Lubiano, "But Compared to What? Reading Realism, Representation, and Essentialism in *School Daze, Do the Right Thing,* and the Spike Lee Discourse," *Black American Literature Forum* 25, no. 2 (1991): 263.

3. Arthur P. Davis and Michael W. Peplow, *The New Negro Renaissance* (New York: Holt, Rinehart and Winston, 1975), 21.

4. John Hope Franklin, *From Slavery to Freedom: A History of Negro Americans,* 4th ed. (New York: Knopf, 1980), 320–22.

5. Ibid., 357.

6. Ibid., 356.

7. Rosalyn Terborg-Penn, "Discrimination Against Afro-American Women in the Woman's Movement," in *The Afro-American Woman: Struggles and Images,* ed. Sharon Harley and Rosalyn Terborg-Penn (Port Washington, N.Y.: Kennikat, 1978), 17–27; Steven M. Buechler, *Women's Movements in the United States: Woman Suffrage, Equal Rights, and Beyond* (New Brunswick, N.J.: Rutgers University Press, 1990), 135–50.

8. James V. Hatch, ed., *Black Theater, U.S.A.: Forty-five Plays by Black Americans, 1847–1974* (New York: Macmillan, 1974), 209.

9. Freda L. Scott, "Black Drama and the Harlem Renaissance," *Theatre Journal* 37, no. 4 (1985): 438.

10. Nellie McKay, "Black Theater and Drama in the 1920s: Years of Growing Pains," *Massachusetts Review* 28, no. 4 (Winter 1987): 617.

11. W. E. B. Du Bois, "Krigwa Little Theatre Movement," *The Crisis* 32 (1926): 134.

12. McKay, "Black Theater," 617.

13. Rebecca T. Cureau, "Toward an Aesthetic of Black Folk Expression," in *Alain Locke: Reflections on a Modern Renaissance Man,* ed. Russell J. Linneman (Baton Rouge: Louisiana State University Press, 1982), 78.

14. Ibid., 85.

15. Writing in 1945 about African American depictions of the black middle class—and especially about the use of realism to portray it—Sterling Brown offered a useful summary of the conflicting demands that black artists face in balancing class aspirations and racial identity. His comment about realist fiction could easily illuminate the case against Du Bois's blindness to his own class assumptions: "There is certainly place in American fiction for treatment of the Negro middle-class. The precarious situation of this small group could well attract a realist of vision, not only to satirize its pretense, but also to record its dogged struggling. But to approve it in proportion to its resembling white middle-class life, is not the way of important realism" (quoted in Doris E. Abramson, *Negro Playwrights in the American Theatre, 1925–1959* [New York: Columbia University Press, 1969], 159).

16. Quoted in Nathan Irvin Huggins, *Voices from the Harlem Renaissance* (New York: Oxford University Press, 1976), 312–13.

17. See, for example, Sue-Ellen Case, ed., *Performing Feminisms: Feminist Critical Theory and Theatre* (Baltimore: Johns Hopkins University Press, 1990), 12.

18. Alain Locke, "The Negro in the American Theater," in *The Black Aesthetic*, ed. Addison Gayle Jr. (New York: Doubleday, 1971), 263–71.

19. Jeanne-Marie A. Miller, "Georgia Douglas Johnson and May Miller: Forgotten Playwrights of the New Negro Renaissance," *CLA Journal* 33, no. 4 (1990): 353.

20. Leslie Catherine Sanders, *The Development of Black Theater in America: From Shadows to Selves* (Baton Rouge: Louisiana State University Press, 1988), 9–10, 38.

21. In "Drama and the Dialogic Imagination: *The Heidi Chronicles* and *Fefu and Her Friends*," *Modern Drama* 34, no. 1 (1991): 88–106, Helene Keyssar examines folk drama (especially the Russian folk drama analyzed by Mikhail Bakhtin) as being somewhat more complex and dialogic than that described (at least overtly) by Locke and Gregory. While she does not specifically comment on the folk drama of the Harlem Renaissance, Keyssar makes the important point that much contemporary feminist and African American drama partakes of the very qualities Bakhtin applauded in folk drama. She says: "As Bakhtin implies about folk drama, the voices we hear in many black American dramas and feminist dramas are the voices of marginal folk, voices that are both in conflict with dominant ideological positions and resistant among themselves to the reductions of uniformity" (95). What this statement suggests to me is that perhaps Locke and Gregory were more "propagandistic" in their artistic endeavors than they acknowledged, using folk characters and situations as a site of resistance to dominant cultural images.

22. Nellie McKay, " 'What Were They Saying?': Black Women Playwrights of the Harlem Renaissance," in *The Harlem Renaissance Re-examined*, ed. Victor A. Kramer (New York: AMS, 1987), 129–48; Kathy A. Perkins, ed., *Black Female Playwrights: An Anthology of Plays Before 1950* (Bloomington: Indiana University Press, 1989), 281–85.

23. Gloria T. Hull, *Color, Sex, and Poetry: Three Women Writers of the Harlem Renaissance* (Bloomington: Indiana University Press, 1987), 8–15.

24. Perkins, *Black Female Playwrights*, 7; Hull, *Color, Sex, and Poetry*, 7–8.

25. Barbara Christian, *Black Women Novelists: The Development of a Tradition, 1892–1976* (Westport, Conn.: Greenwood, 1980), 10–19.

26. Elise Johnson McDougald, "The Task of Negro Womanhood," in *The New Negro: An Interpretation*, ed. Alain Locke (1925; rpt., New York: Arno, 1968), 370.

27. Darlene Clark Hine, "Rape and the Inner Lives of Black Women in the Middle West: Preliminary Thoughts on the Culture of Dissemblance," *Signs* 14, no. 4 (1989): 915.

28. Angelina Weld Grimké, "*Rachel*," in *Black Theater, U.S.A.: Forty-five Plays by Black Americans, 1847–1974*, ed. James V. Hatch (New York: Macmillan, 1974), 143. Subsequent page references to the play are cited in the text.

29. Angelina Weld Grimké, "*Rachel:* The Reason and Synopsis by the Author," *Competitor* 1, no. 1 (1920): 51–52.

30. Hatch, 137; see also Hull, 117–18.

31. Quoted in Jeanne-Marie A. Miller, "Angelina Weld Grimké: Playwright and Poet," *CLA Journal* 21, no. 4 (1978): 515.

32. Hatch, *Black Theater, U.S.A.*, 138.

33. Margaret B. Wilkerson, ed., *9 Plays by Black Women* (New York: Penguin, 1986), xvi.

34. Hull, *Color, Sex, and Poetry*, 121.

35. See, for example, Doris E. Abramson, "Angelina Weld Grimké, Mary T. Burrill, Georgia Douglas Johnson, and Marita O. Bonner: An Analysis of Their Plays," *Sage* 2, no. 1 (Spring 1985): 9; Fehrenbach, "Problem Play," 97–98; Hatch, *Black Theater, U.S.A.*, 138; and Miller, "Angelina Weld Grimké," 516.

36. Fehrenbach, "Problem Play," 101.

37. Elizabeth Brown-Guillory, ed., *Wines in the Wilderness: Plays by African American Women from the Harlem Renaissance to the Present* (New York: Greenwood, 1990), 82.

38. Many different versions of *It's Morning* exist in manuscript and in print. For three rather different published texts, see Perkins, *Black Female Playwrights;* Brown-Guillory, *Wines in the Wilderness;* and *Plays by American Women, 1930–1960*, ed. Judith Barlow (New York: Applause, 1994). In addition to these published versions, Judith Barlow has uncovered two others: a longer manuscript version with the subtitle "A Poetic Play" and a prompt book from the 1939 production at Yale. Complicating the matter further is the fact all these versions bear the title *It's Morning* except the Brown-Guillory version, which is called *It's Mornin'*. Unless otherwise noted, my citations refer to Shirley Graham, *It's Mornin'*, in Brown-Guillory, *Wines in the Wilderness*, 84–96, although I will use the standard title throughout my discussion. Page references are cited in the text.

39. Shirley Graham, *It's Morning: A Poetic Play*, manuscript, 9–10. This is the longest version of the play of which I am aware. I am grateful to Judith Barlow, who received the typescript from Graham's son, for sharing it with me.

40. Graham evidently wrote *It's Morning* in 1939, well after the period of violent lynching and race riots that Grimké lived through. Nonetheless, Graham's era suffered its own racially motivated hate crimes. Graham herself was particularly troubled by discrimination against black soldiers during World War II. Her civil rights activism eventually got her fired (in 1942) from her position as a YMCA-USO director—for "un-American" activities. See Brown-Guillory, *Wines in the Wilderness*, 80.

41. Ibid., 82.

42. bell hooks, *Black Looks: Race and Representation* (Boston: South End, 1992), 7.

6.

Loren Kruger

New African Drama and National Representation in South Africa: Notes from the 1930s to the Present Moment

Modern drama is not a mere emotional entertainment. It is a source of ideas, a cultural and educational factor, an agency for propaganda and, above all, it is literature. What part will the new African play in modern drama? On its physical side, he can contribute strong, fast rhythm, speedy action, expressive vigorous gesture and movement, powerful dramatic speech—no small contribution when modern plays drag so tediously. . . . We want African playwrights who will dramatize . . . African History. We want dramatic representations of African Serfdom, Oppression, Exploitation, and Metamorphosis. . . . The African dramatist . . . can expose evil and corruption and not suffer libel as newspapermen do; he can guide and preach to his people as preachers cannot do. To do this he must be an artist before a propagandist; a philosopher before a reformer, a psychologist before a patriot; be true to his African "self" and not be prey to exotic crudities.

This passage from Herbert Dhlomo's essay, "The Importance of African Drama" (1933), marks a crucial moment in the history of South African drama not only because it argues for plays that speak of and to the suffering and aspirations of Africans but also because it suggests the complex history of cultural developments now classified as "modern black drama in South Africa," illustrating the pitfalls as well as the potential of these developments for articulating an emergent national identity.[1] Dhlomo's dramatic work runs the gamut from an evangelical treatment of the Xhosa prophetess Nongqause in *The Girl Who Killed to Save* (1935), to the epic portrayal of historical African leaders such as *Moshoeshoe* or *Cetshwayo* (1936–37), to the indictments of contemporary race and class oppression in *The Workers* and *The Pass* (1941–43). In addition to this literary production, his activities as actor, director, journalist, and *animateur* make him a crucial point of reference for an investigation of the troubled relationship between theater and social change in South Africa.

As playwright, poet, and critic, as well as impresario for an Emancipation Centenary Celebration (commemorating in 1934 the centenary of the abolition of slavery in the British Empire), Dhlomo grappled with the oppositions between elite and popular, imported and indigenous, and literate and oral culture. Although dismissed by some present-day critics in search of authentic and univocal South African cultural expression, whether defined in terms of ethnic authenticity or in terms of a unified urban working class, as a writer of "sub-Wordsworthian" mission literature[2] or "sterile unimaginative plays bearing little relation to African theatrical expression,"[3] Dhlomo has been revived in South Africa as "the pioneer of modern black drama."[4] His revival as a source for a buried intercultural lineage that might have been more forceful now "had it been easier for him to publish or produce his work"[5] is not unproblematic, but it does bear witness to his role as interpreter of and participant in the formation of what he and his peers called the New African.

As a "detribalised, 'progressive,' adapted adaptor of the modern South Africa,"[6] in Tim Couzens's phrase, New Africans attempted to bring together European and African culture on equal terms at a time when the South African state's so-called European interests—selective modernization on the basis of racial discrimination—were becoming less rather than more accommodating to the advancement of the African majority. The New African thus represented the contradictions as well as the aspirations of men (and occasionally women) like Herbert Dhlomo. Trained in Anglo-American mission schools to admire the achievements of "European civilization" (such as parliamentary democracy and civil rights) and English culture (represented by Shakespeare and predominantly Romantic and Victorian literature), they were well aware of the discrepancy between the rhetoric of universal civilization and their actual exclusion from the neocolonial polity. Though their efforts to gain political and cultural legitimacy were thwarted by the systematization of racial discrimination over the first half of the twentieth century (by the end of the 1950s, organized cultural and social links between blacks and whites had been severed), New Africans recognized and celebrated the fundamentally international character of African national consciousness. As such, they represent not only an important attempt to bring a new South Africa into being but also a crucial reminder to race purists—now, as then—of the irreducibly complex character of South African identity.

In order to understand the contradictions in the New African formation and therefore in the political role proposed for theater, we should specify the character of the crisis in this period. The 1930s were years in which the South African state sharply curbed the economic, political, and cultural mobility of Africans. It was also a period of political and cultural fluidity in which different modes of resistance to and negotiation of this dispensation were played out. Beset by internal disputes and backed only unevenly by white liberals and an as yet only fitfully organized, partially proletarianized, black work force, African Nationalists struggled in vain against legislation such as the Urban Areas Act (1923) and the Slums Act (1934), which allowed for the clearance of urban slumyards while restricting African access to property or residence in urban areas, and the Native Representative Act (1935), which was to eliminate the last Africans from the Common Voters Roll. The conservative ascendancy in the African National Congress (ANC) at the time tended to see in the state's program of "separate development" an opportunity for what might be called "retraditionalization."[7] Retraditionalization in this context implies less a return to premodern rural life than a reappropriation of clan authority and custom as the means to a tangible if limited autonomy. This limited autonomy, always under the aegis of the neocolonial state, consolidated the power of the chiefs, which had been eroded by the emergence of the New Africans, on the one hand, and the mass migration of landless blacks to the cities, on the other.[8] It was thus not so much a rejection of modernity as an attempt to appropriate certain aspects of modernization, especially vernacular literacy and the technological reproduction or recording of traditional practices and artifacts, in order to reinvent habitual tribal affiliation as the natural respect for traditional authority.

New Africans, the small, urban, multilingual, intermediate class of clergymen, teachers, and other intellectuals that constituted an African elite of sorts (although under economic, social, and political constraints that prevented their full participation in the public sphere), began the decade still holding to the belief that the benefits of modernization would ultimately outweigh the disruption of communal life and tribal authority caused by colonization. Selope Thema, editor of the widely read *Bantu World,* defended African appropriation of the benefits of European civilization, such as literacy and individual rights, while acknowledging the value of traditional communal organization.[9] Reevaluating the authority of the chiefs, in particular the legendary power of Shaka over a now subdued Zulu nation, Herbert Dhlomo argued that those invoking Shaka defended the glories of a Zulu past rather than civil rights in the present and were advocating a "new kind of tribalism. . . [which] encourages non-progressive institutions among the people and made the government the supreme chief and dictator."[10] And, in *The Girl Who Killed to Save,* his only published play (1935), the exhortations of the Xhosa prophetess Nongqause, who urged the Xhosa to kill their cattle in anticipation of divine wrath on the colonizers, and the consequent starvation of the clan, are redeemed as the price paid for civilization.[11] Profoundly suspicious of European definitions of the authentic African promulgated by apologists for the "Native's own lines" of development, Thema, Dhlomo, and others urged their readers to bring together African and European traditions in institutions such as the Bantu Men's Social Centre (BMSC), the Gamma Sigma debating societies (founded in the 1920s), and the Eisteddfodau (founded 1932).

In this context, distinctions between indigenous and imported culture do not quite correspond to a clear-cut separation of the oppressed and dominant groups. On the one hand, appeals to African tradition were aggressively deployed by a government anxious to regulate (but not terminate) African migration to the cities. On the other, European culture, for Dhlomo and his contemporaries, represented access to drama, from Shakespeare to Shaw, as well as the opportunity to make informed comparisons between metropolitan and "tribal" dramatic forms. The hegemony of English high culture as disseminated by the mission schools was, however, continually challenged by American and African American popular cultural forms. These forms, including abolitionist melodrama and political rhetoric as well as the motley practices of jubilee singing, ragtime, jazz, and minstrelsy, reached a wide African audience that ranged from organizations such as the BMSC to the slumyards and dance halls frequented by city workers.[12]

These African American currents complicate any received dichotomy between imported art and indigenous practice or between modernity and its apparently premodern, "savage" other. The achievements of African Americans, or, in the Garveyite language borrowed by musician and critic Mark Radebe, "Africans in America," offered an array of references to urban, intercultural South Africans of a diversity of classes and social groups while testifying to "the enormous influence of Bantu rhythms on the world's music."[13] For New Africans, the metropolitan, modernizing impulse of the "New Negro" represented an alternative to a neocolonial retribalization and to the essentially antiurban Arnoldian version of English culture disseminated in mission schools and elite universities, on the one hand, and, on the other, to the allegedly degraded forms of jazz and minstrelry, which the African elite saw as corrupting the *abaphakathi* (the people in-between—neither assimilated to "European" modernity nor any longer at home with indigenous custom).[14] The distance traveled by African Americans from slavery to visible (if uneven) participation in American society also provided a crucial point of reference for criticizing the curtailment of civil rights for Africans in South Africa.

At a moment when political rights for even elite Africans were curtailed, culture, whether seen as arts or entertainment, became a crucial site for the contestation of the legitimacy of African participation in public. At its most instrumental, culture functioned as social control. For mining executives, controling the after-work activities of the "natives" meant a "good business investment" in the "moral and physical health of the workforce";[15] for missionaries, even liberal paternalists like Ray Phillips, author of the assimilationist *The Bantu Are Coming* (1930), activities from the elite BMSC to Chaplin evenings for mine workers might curb social and economic unrest and the "swaggering, sweeping claims of Communism" by "moralizing the leisure time of the natives."[16] More subtle, perhaps, were the aspirations of African retraditionalists such as John Dube, founder of Ohlange College (the South African Tuskegee), and Reuben Caluza, Dhlomo's cousin. A Columbia University graduate, and South Africa's premier composer of "African music," Caluza saw the state's interest in preserving "Native ways" as an occasion for reestablishing a coherent ethnic inheritance out of rural practices fractured by colonization. In the space between the instrumentalization of culture in the service of modernization and the evocation of culture as a retraditionalized refuge from the ravages of modernization lies the ambiguous notion of the disinterestedness of culture, disseminated by the mission schools, which offered an escape at once compelling and imaginary from daily humiliations.

This relative autonomy could and did give cultural production an affirmative cast, in Marcuse's sense of reinforcing the status quo by providing an imaginary refuge from it,[17] but it also constituted what could be called a "virtual public sphere." In this environment, which was increasingly hostile to African agency in a legitimate public sphere, theater offered a form of virtual publicity.[18] Operating in the subjunctive rather than indicative mood, theater offered not so much immediate political action as a testing ground for competing enactments of the nation, whether emphat-

ically, as in the protest drama that most contemporary metropolitan spectators take as South African theater per se, or more indirectly, as in the cultural work of the New Africans.

The variety of theater by and for Africans in 1930s Johannesburg highlights
the critical limits of familiar oppositions between elite and popular,
imported and indigenous, and literary and oral culture. *She Stoops to Conquer,* the Bantu Drama Society's inaugural production (1933), was perhaps
closest to the English genteel culture of the mission schools, but the "tribal
sketches" of the Lucky Stars and the All African Eisteddfodau, which combined European and African forms, were also indebted to missionary education. These sketches in turn inspired the commercially successful African
"revues" and pageants staged by the popular Darktown Strutters and its successor, De Pitch Black Follies, whose leader, Griffiths Motsieloa, also participated in the Eisteddfodau. On the other hand, the Bantu People's Players version of *The Hairy Ape* (1936)—which was to have been the Bantu
Drama Society's first production in 1933—combined the agitprop skills of
Belgian socialist Andre van Gyseghem, in South Africa as director of
pageants for the Empire Exhibition, with the local resonance of Fanagalo,
the pidgin used by miners and their bosses, to produce a more emphatic
representation of social and economic injustice. The Bantu Dramatic and
Operatic Society's production of *Moshoeshoe* (1939), Herbert Dhlomo's
dramatization of the charisma of the nineteenth-century Sotho leader,
attempted to bring together the "tribal sketch," the history play, and the
Eisteddfodau recital in a dramatic response to the ascendancy of segregationist ideology by the end of the decade.

   The hybrid character of these experiments resides not only in their use
of form but also in the tensions between form and occasion of performance,
especially in the representation of African tradition in the modern European
medium of naturalist drama. The reconstruction of a legitimate (rather than
verifiably "authentic") folk culture in this period relies heavily, as Veit Erlmann has demonstrated in his account of South African music, on the
invention of tradition and a "usable past" out of "the disparate remnants of
a shattered rural order."[19] In the creation of an African national theater, as
in that of an African music, finding a usable past was not so much an act of
pure discovery as a process of collection, recollection, and invention, of
grafting together African and European material in ways that would res-
onate with performers and audiences. The strict correspondence between
actor and embodied character, and the antirhetorical convention of individ-

ual interiority in a set designed to replicate an exterior or interior space characteristic of the early-twentieth-century metropolitan mainstream, had little in common with the more fluid and more overtly rhetorical relationship between performer, character, and location in the praise songs, folktales, and community dancing characteristic of Southern Bantu performance.[20]

The question of language, the hegemony of literary culture and genteel norms, and the weakness (relative to music) of an African American mediating term made the development of an African national theater more complicated than its musical counterpart. The central site for this "invention of tradition" was, paradoxically, also the crucible for "civilization": the mission schools, which encouraged performances of dramatic sketches, often as "reconstructions of tribal life."[21] These sketches provided the inspiration for the Lucky Stars, founded in 1929 by the Mthethwa brothers, who were educated, like Dhlomo, at Amanzimtoti College. Their sketches, presented in reconstructed Zulu costume and in the Zulu language, portrayed such subjects as *ukuqomisa* [courting] or *umthakathi* [the sorcerer]. Although formed in large part by an elite place and occasion (mission schools, the BMSC, and the like), the Lucky Stars were enthusiastically received by the *abaphakathi,* who found these "idealized images of a rural past" a welcome escape from their double alienation.[22]

But claims that the Lucky Stars were an early but unmistakable instance of critical black theater[23] or forerunners of the anti-apartheid protest theater of the 1970s[24] ought to be treated with caution. The origins of the sketches in the folkloric recuperation of the missions did not prevent them from being appropriated by a diverse popular audience, but their ethnic emphasis, even exclusiveness, was problematic, reflecting as much the Zulu pride of the performers, most of whom came from the Zulu-identified Amanzimtoti College, as a desire to challenge discrimination against all Africans.[25] Performed in the Zulu language and in historically reconstructed Zulu costume (rather than the range of traditional and modified attire worn in rural Zululand at the time), the exact satirical intent of the sketches would have been only partially accessible to speakers of other Bantu languages whose response may have been affected less by authentic detail than by the music (which was already a hybridization of urban and rural forms) and the tangible presence of African actors. The account of the Jewish South African impresario, Bertha Slosberg, who promoted the group from 1933 through its crowning appearance at the Empire Exhibition in 1936, emphasizes the spectacular as well as the folkloric dimension, the thrilling dancing as well as the need "to salvage from European influence, the remaining power, the native simplicity, the splendid savage grandeur of a dying pagan land."[26]

Whatever the influence of these sketches on "Johannesburg location productions," New African intellectuals such as Herbert Dhlomo and the poet and academic B. W. Vilakazi were skeptical of their value as the basis for an African national drama.[27] Dhlomo was particularly critical of the commodification of African tradition as "exotic crudities"[28] and its embalming in "static museum-like plays" ("Why Study Tribal Dramatic Forms?" *Literary Theory,* 39). Like Alain Locke, the self-declared New Negro who challenged white society's "sentimental interest" in black traditions and the "double standard" of the "philanthropic attitude" among white American liberals,[29] the New African was suspicious of those who expressed concern for "native" traditions while remaining either indifferent or hostile to black aspirations to transform society as a whole. African national theater should, as Dhlomo suggests in "The Importance of African Drama," the essay with which I began, neither capitulate to this reification nor abandon African concerns. It should instead explore the variety of forms from the European or American metropolis—from literary drama, to African American liturgy, to socialist agitprop—and appropriate those African (rather than strictly Zulu, Sotho, and so on) forms that lend themselves to a critical engagement between past and present. Appropriate subject matter should include the hopes and fears of contemporary Africans and the representation of African history, which had been repressed or distorted in the colonial record.

In numerous essays beginning with "The Importance of African Drama," Dhlomo defends the priority of literary drama while stressing the strong performative dimension of African oral traditions. He calls for the dramatic representation of social injustice but also argues that the modern African dramatist should be artist before propagandist. However indebted to British colonial education, this appeal to art before propaganda should not be read merely as a capitulation to imposed norms of gentility. Rather, it attempts to use the notion of artistic autonomy to negotiate cultural space for the contestation of oppression in an environment in which more direct action (from political mobilization to adversarial journalism) was increasingly curtailed. Framing the revitalization of indigenous tradition in the generalizing terms of African nationalism, Dhlomo challenges both white and black separatists when he argues, in "Why Study Tribal Dramatic Forms?" (1939), that this revitalization should transform not only African forms but also modern drama as a whole by "infus[ing] new blood into the weary limbs of the older dramatic forms of Europe" (*Literary Theory*, 35) to relieve the "tedium" of modern (by implication, English) plays. This disdain for the "acting plays" of the commercial theater (mostly touring companies from Britain) in favor of a "literary drama" (39) that might also be propaganda for social change echoes the aspirations of the advocates of the "new social drama" (Shaw, Galsworthy, and their contemporaries) in Britain, but, like them, it stops short of a radical abolition of aesthetics in the manner of Brecht's *Lehrstücke* or the proletarian agitprop of the United States and Britain during this period.[30]

The example of British social drama, with its attempt to be both literary and engaged, independent of the pressure to make a profit yet able to draw an audience, exercises a significant but not overwhelming influence on Dhlomo's reflections on drama and the African. Whereas Dhlomo's suggested themes may confirm the influence of Shaw or Galsworthy, his ideal institution of theater differs from that of the metropolitan "new drama," the producers of which relied on a modified version of the commercial theater. Dhlomo envisages performance legitimated as an occasion in the social life of a community. In "The Nature and Variety of Tribal Drama" (1939), he points to the close relationship between the occasion of performance and significant events, rites of passage, and seasonal festivals (*Literary Theory*, 28–35) and argues that traditional African drama shares with the classical Greek its integration into the social fabric (30). This evocation of a theater of ritual power does not entail a nostalgic revival of tribal community but rather the reverse. In "Why Study Tribal Dramatic Forms?" he warns, "The African artist cannot delve into the Past unless he has first grasped the Present. African art can grow and thrive not only by . . . excavating archaical art forms, but by grappling with present-day realities" (*Literary Theory*, 40).

Instead of "static museum-like drama based on primitive tradition and culture" (39), Dhlomo envisaged an African national theater that might appropriate those African performance forms that lend themselves to a critical engagement between past and present. While highlighting the public character of these forms, however, he insists that they be evaluated as "ends in themselves," in aesthetic as well as functional terms ("The Nature and Variety of Tribal Drama," *Literary Theory*, 27). He appropriates the courtly tradition of *izibongo* (praises—usually of the king or warrior) rather than the more demotic convention of *izinganekwane* (folktales), which suggests a desire to legitimate a tradition of high culture with a universal aesthetic status equivalent to that of Greek tragedy in the European pantheon. His appeal to tradition, however, rests on a distinctly modern invention of a term, *izibongelo,* to bolster his claim that the panegyric form contains within it the traces of dramatic structure and that its function, like that of drama, is to "tell the story of the nation" ("The Nature and Variety of Tribal Drama," *Literary Theory,* 23, 35).[31]

These essays record the impact of retraditionalist rhetoric in the appeal to a "sacred inheritance" ("Why Study Tribal Dramatic Forms?" *Literary Theory,* 37) and the "ground on which a great original African drama can be built" ("The Nature and Variety of Tribal Drama," *Literary Theory,* 35), even as they speak to New African suspicion of the construction of ethnicity as a museum exhibit. They also register the strain in New African faith in Europeanization, as the ineffectual response of most white liberals to the curtailment of African liberty and the spectacle of European savagery in Spain and Ethiopia progressively undermined the authority of "white civilization." Dhlomo's dramatic writing in this period responds more directly to the contradictory impulses of colonial modernity, between "European civilization" and the "white savage beneath,"[32] than does his evangelical *Girl Who Killed to Save.*

The play most often cited in this context is *Cetshwayo* (1936–37). Portraying the betrayal of the last autonomous Zulu king in the 1870s by Theophilus Shepstone, governor of Natal, and his ally, John Dunn, an "English adventurer" gone native, *Cetshwayo* is Dhlomo's most explicit indictment of segregation and disenfranchisement conducted in the name of civilization and Empire.[33] For all the argument for African forms and conventions, however, the dramaturgy of *Cetshwayo* is thoroughly Aristotelian, or, more precisely, Schillerian, in that it focuses on a national hero whose inability to see through the machinations of his enemies brings about his tragic defeat; African motifs, especially *izibongo* (praises) of the king, tend to be subordinated to the forward drive of the plot. Drawing on the Schillerian history play in its English derivation as well as the conventions of Victorian melodrama, especially in its treatment of the "white Zulu" Dunn, *Cetshwayo* makes for stirring reading today.[34] We can, however, only speculate on the contemporary effect of this play, since it was neither published nor performed.

Moshoeshoe, written in the same period, was performed by the Bantu Dramatic and Operatic Society at the BMSC in May 1939, in honor of Moshoeshoe Day, and it was the first indigenous drama combining the efforts of Zulu (Dhlomo and Caluza) and Sotho (choreographer A. P. Khutlang and songwriter Salome Masoleng).[35] Less adversarial than *Cetshwayo,*

Moshoeshoe portrayed the wisdom of the legendary Sotho statesman, revered not only for his ability to resolve conflicts between his subjects and refugees from the Difecane (the mass migration caused by Zulu expansionism under Shaka in the 1830s) but also as a model African leader whose perspicacity was sadly missed a century later. By placing at the center of his play a *pitso,* or people's assembly, Dhlomo called to mind the disputes of the African National Congress and its rival at the time, the All-African Convention (AAC). The play's emphasis on Moshoeshoe's criticism of ethnically divisive custom and the temptations of dictatorship highlighted the relative success with which the Basutoland Protectorate was managing to resist attempts at incorporation by the South African government.

The play was performed at the BMSC and not, for instance, in the mountain setting of Thaba Bosiu in Bastouland (now Lesotho) where Moshoeshoe held his *pitso,* or its namesake in Pimville, near Johannesburg, where political meetings were held.[36] Nonetheless, its loosely linked scenes—the *pitso* in the center, framed by suitors' quarrels and encounters between Sothos, a wandering bard, and refugees from the Difecane, and ending with a harvest festival—suggest a recurrent commemoration rather than a unique story. While we do not have access to the score for the performance, it is likely that it would have at least alluded to melodies already familiar to this audience from Caluza's extensive repertoire of national sorrow songs such as "iLand Act" and "Elamakosi" ("To the Chiefs"), which lament African dispossession and appeal to the chiefs for guidance. Dhlomo would have liked to legitimate his play by drawing on the immediate authority of the All-African Convention as well as the comparison with numerous Moshoeshoe Day rallies, but this legitimation was far from secure. While reviewers picked up the contemporary resonance of the *pitso,* and audiences would have made the connection between the *pitso* and the rallies, the harvest festival that concludes the play does not quite bring in the yield. The festival envelopes but cannot incorporate the British missionaries who praise Moshoeshoe's genius only to cast doubt on the enactment of his legacy: "Moshoeshoe . . . a man consumed by the smouldering and devastating fire of . . . great expectations unfulfilled, of plans and ambitions whose very attainment would give birth to plans and ambitions never to be attained" (260–61). This ambiguous praise strikes a cautionary note against the soaring *izibongo* at the end; the allusion to the citadel of Thaba Bosiu and to "Moshoeshoe the man-mountain, the mountain-mind" (265) carries traditional weight but not the force of historical inevitability.

In dramatizing the discrepancy between the celebration of the African exemplar and the implied deflection of his legacy without providing a resolution, *Moshoeshoe* represents the historical impasse faced by the New Africans. In 1934, an event like the Emancipation Centenary was still supported by New African faith in the liberating promise of European civilization. In 1939, however, this faith was fast evaporating in the white heat of European savagery at home and abroad. Dhlomo never quite concurred with those South Africans who understood these developments as a stage in the international class struggle or, in the words of one commentator in 1936, as "symptomatic of the world-wide travail of all repressed communities and dominated classes,"[37] but he was certainly influenced by the more militant African resistance to the South African state that was to emerge in the 1940s and 1950s under the conflicting guidance of the ANC Youth League and the Communist Party.[38] Dhlomo's redefinition of the New African to include not only "progressive intellectuals" but also "organized urban workers" registers this shift, as do two of his unperformed plays from the 1940s, *The Workers* (1941) and *The Pass* (1943).[39]

Although these plays register greater militancy among urban Africans, they can only with difficulty be seen as undisputed evidence of a political vanguard or emerging mass movement. *The Workers,* to be sure, "portrays working class conditions" after a fashion, but this abstract, often fragmented text does not really respond to the "need to develop proper unions as well as tactics for strike action."[40] Rather than either a naturalist or agitprop version of the play intended as a strike tool, *The Workers'* portrayal of the reification of factory workers more closely resembles the abstract, telegraphic style and dark, often elegiac treatment of the menace of a mechanized society and the alienation of labor characteristic in the expressionist tradition of drama such as Georg Kaiser's *Gas* trilogy. The opening of the play is significantly contradictory. The trade unionist, a chauffeur for the "Nigger-Exploitation Slave Crookpany," calls for union organization, but the impact of the massed workers is described in almost mystical terms, as Mpulo, the protagonist-worker, announces, "Don't speak of the close of day. It is here and now! Don't you see the workers? . . . Nothing will stop them."[41] The manager's defense of machines over men, "The machines must not stop . . . even if men die like flies. . . . Machines are rare and costly, men are cheap and common. . . . We no longer believe in the myth of the soul and the dignity of Man but we know that machines have a soul . . ." (216), likewise recalls the technological juggernaut of Karel Čapek's *RUR* (the play that introduced the word *robot*) rather than the workers' agitprop

of the European left of the 1920s and 1930s or its counterpart in South
Africa in the 1980s. Even though the manager's position is undermined by
stage directions that describe him as "almost hysterical" (216) and "childish"
(226) and by a concluding scene in which the workers physically overwhelm
management and the police only to die in large numbers in the final explo-
sion (227), the play suggests the expressionist apocalypse rather than the dis-
ciplined action of revolutionaries.

The Pass, on the other hand, offers more plausible evidence of "a writer
in touch with urban realities, capable of dialogue stripped of literary self-
consciousness and rooted in a more clearly defined political vision."[42]
Dhlomo's most documentary play, The Pass is also his most Aristotelian.
Compressed into less than twenty-four hours, the action of the play tracks
the impact of the pass laws and arbitrary police power on a group of Africans
arrested in a random sweep on one night in Durban. The strength of the
play lies not merely in its graphic portrayal of police brutality or in its expo-
sure of their venality but in the concrete representation of different cases,
including, among others, those of an elderly woman shamed by the arrest, a
burglar whose scorn for the police earns him a modicum of respect from
other men in the jail, and Edward Sithole, an educated professional who is
nonetheless not immune to arrest. Although Sithole is ultimately acquitted,
thanks to a soon-to-be-closed legal loophole that exempted educated
Africans from the obligation to carry passes, the play makes clear that the
institutionalized injustice of the pass laws will radicalize the otherwise qui-
escent population. As an unnamed woman detainee remarks, "The pain and
hate in our hearts will mould and be suckled by our children of the next
generation. When these children grow up, the white man will regret [it]"
("The Pass," Collected Works, 200). In this foreshadowing of the anger as
well as the suffering of blacks in South Africa, The Pass looks forward to the
Defiance Campaigns of the 1950s, in which Africans, especially African
women, burned their passes, and beyond to the culture of protest that has
characterized much South African drama since the early 1970s (before the
Soweto uprising brought the trend to the attention of metropolitan spectators).

Understood as harbingers of a revived black militancy, plays such as
Shanti by Mthuli Shezi (Peoples Educational Theatre, 1973), Egoli by Mat-
samela Manaka (1979), and Gangsters by Maishe Maponya (1984) can also be
seen as the symbolic progeny of The Pass, symbolic because Dhlomo's work
was not readily available until the publication of the Collected Works in 1985.
We should not, however, assume that the historical coincidence of a

renewed political and economic struggle in the 1970s, when black trade
unions and black political movements such as the Black Peoples Convention tested the limits of state tolerance for alternative public spheres, and a
revitalized political theater meant that this theater necessarily spoke to and
for the majority.[43] Indeed, as debates in South Africa since the "thaw" of
1990 have suggested, protest drama, including the work of Fugard and his
collaborators, has often been more effective in raising the consciousness of
white audiences than in mobilizing black audiences, who have historically
responded with more pleasure to melodrama and township musicals.[44] But
these debates have also foregrounded the complexity of cultural mediation
of political crisis by reminding audiences and producers alike that culture is
not simply and transparently politics and perhaps also that its political value
as virtual public sphere may depend on subjunctive rather than emphatically
indicative action.[45] Dhlomo's drama, with its juxtaposition of incompatible
elements, its lack of resolution—in short, its inauthenticity—is clearly no
cultural weapon, and it may seem anachronistic or irrelevant today.
Nonetheless, the very uneven and syncretic character of his work, read in
the interregnum of 1994, speaks more truly than any resounding fictional
triumph to the pressures and uncertainties of historical transformation in
South Africa.

NOTES

Unattributed articles are anonymous. The epigraph is from H. I. E. Dhlomo, "The
Importance of African Drama," *Bantu World*, October 21, 1933, 17.

1. In South Africa the term *African* commonly refers to Bantu-speaking people of
reputedly complete African ancestry, whether habitual speakers of English or of the ver-
naculars. The official government equivalent was *Native* until the 1950s when it was
replaced by *Bantu*. *Black*, in common usage since the 1970s as a term designating all those
disenfranchised by apartheid (as opposed to the official term, *nonwhite*), is thus a term of
political rather than racial or ethnic identification since it includes those of mixed (so-
called Coloured) and Asian descent, who do not habitually speak Bantu languages. Use
of the term *European*, until recently synonymous with *white*, is a sign not of origin but of
political and cultural hegemony and therefore implicitly intersects with "American" as
well as "English" culture.

2. Albert Gérard, *Four African Literatures* (Berkeley: University of California Press,
1971), 236.

3. David Coplan, *In Township Tonight!* (London: Longman, 1985), 125.

4. Nick Visser and Tim Couzens, "Introduction," in *Collected Works of H. I. E.
Dhlomo*, ed. Nick Visser and Tim Couzens (Johannesburg: Ravan, 1985), xv. See also

Ian Steadman, "Towards a Popular Theatre in South Africa," *Journal of Southern African Studies* 16, no. 2 (1990): 208–28; Bhekizizwe Peterson, "Apartheid and the Political Imagination," *Journal of Southern African Studies* 16, no. 2 (1990): 229–45; and Martin Orkin, *Drama and the South African State* (Manchester: Manchester University Press, 1991).

5. Orkin, *Drama and the South African State*, 49.

6. Tim Couzens, *The New African: A Study of the Life and Work of H. I. E. Dhlomo* (Johannesburg: Ravan, 1985), 36 (hereafter cited in the text as *The New African*).

7. Ali Mazrui and M. Tidy coined this term in *Nationalism and New States in Africa* (London: Heinemann, 1984), 282, to describe a tactical appeal to tradition made by leaders of new African states in the service of nationalist resistance to international models of modernization. V. I. Mudimbe redeploys the concept, in *The Invention of Africa* (Bloomington: Indiana University Press, 1988), 169, to reflect on the ambiguity of invoking tradition as a weapon in the service of modernization, albeit locally defined.

8. While the rhetoric of separate development appealed to chiefs keen to maintain their ebbing authority and also to those on the reserves understandably ambivalent about living conditions in the cities, despite extreme rural poverty brought about by the government's legalized land grab (Land Act of 1913), there can be no doubt that the government's interest in segregation, although rationalized by contradictory assertions about African self-determination and the vulnerability of the "child race," was firmly grounded in "European interests." See Saul Dubow, "Race, Civilization, and Culture: The Elaboration of Segregationist Discourse in the Inter-war Years," in *The Politics of Race, Class, and Nationalism in South Africa*, ed. Shula Marks and Stanley Trapido (London: Longman, 1989), 71–94. As Marks has shown, ethnic consciousness in South Africa "has been the product of intense ideological labour by the black intelligentsia and white ideologues" ("Patriotism, Patriarchy, and Purity: Natal and the Politics of Zulu Ethnic Consciousness," in *The Creation of Tribalism in Southern Africa*, ed. Leroy Vail [Berkeley: University of California Press, 1989], 217), as the close ties between the Natal ANC, the Zulu Cultural Society (founded in 1937), and the Department of Native Affairs confirms.

9. R. V. Selope Thema, "Before the Advent of the White Man, the Dead Ruled the Living with a Rod of Iron in Bantu Society," *Bantu World*, May 12, 1934, 8–9.

10. H. I. E. Dhlomo, "Tshaka—a Reevaluation," *Umteteli wa Bantu*, June 18, 1932, 4.

11. For a critical analysis of this play's negotiation of the tension between European civilization and the barbarity of colonization, see Orkin, *Drama and the South African State*, 32–36.

12. As historians of leisure in South African cities have indicated, class distinctions between elite and popular, or petit bourgeois and the working class, were solidifying in this period but by no means fixed. See Belinda Bozzoli's introduction to *Town and Countryside in the Transvaal: Capitalist Penetration and Popular Response* (Johannesburg: Ravan, 1983), 40. While those present at the Emancipation Celebration at the BMSC, for instance, were reluctant to associate themselves with the alleged immorality of jazz and *marabi* in the slumyards, but they might have gone to a Darktown Strutters show. Audiences at the show, on the other hand, may have been more likely to go to a *marabi* dance than to the Bantu Dramatic Society's production of *She Stoops to Conquer*.

13. [Mark Radebe,] "The All-African Music Festival," *Umteteli wa Bantu*, October 29, 1932, 2; "The Coming of Paul Robeson," *Umteteli wa Bantu,* June 1, 1933, 2.

14. Couzens's definition of the New African as "detribalised, 'progressive,' adapted adaptor of the modern South Africa" (*The New African,* 110) highlights the intermediary and therefore ambiguous class position of this formation. He points out that the New Africans' scorn for the *abaphakathi* was not without irony, since they, too, had come up through assimilation (36–37).

15. Eddie Koch, "'Without Visible Means of Subsistence': Slumyard Culture in Johannesburg, 1920–1940," in Bozzoli, *Town and Countryside in the Transvaal,* 167.

16. Ray Phillips, *The Bantu Are Coming* (New York: Richard Smith, 1930), 51, 58.

17. Herbert Marcuse, "On the Affirmative Character of Culture," in *Negations,* trans. Jeremy Shapiro (Boston: Beacon, 1968), 116.

18. As Negt and Kluge have argued in response to Habermas's classic conceptualization of bourgeois *Öffentlichkeit* ("public sphere" or "publicity"), publicity includes not only physical space for public activity (implied by the translation "public sphere") but also the civic and cultural mobilization necessary if the popular majority is to emerge as the public. It also acknowledges the experience of exclusion from public action that might precede such mobilization. See Jürgen Habermas, *Structural Transformation of the Public Sphere,* trans. Thomas Burger (Cambridge, Mass.: MIT Press, 1989); and Oskar Negt and Alexander Kluge, *Public Sphere and Experience,* trans. Peter Labanyi and Jamie Owen Daniel (Minneapolis: University of Minnesota Press, 1993). For a more thoroughgoing theory of theater as virtual public sphere, see Loren Kruger, *The National Stage: Theatre and Cultural Legitimation in England, France, and America* (Chicago: University of Chicago Press, 1992), 3–29.

19. Veit Erlmann, *African Stars* (Chicago: University of Chicago Press, 1991), 150. "Usable past" is the phrase employed by Eric Hobsbawm and Terence Ranger in the introduction to their edited volume *The Invention of Tradition* (Cambridge: Cambridge University Press, 1983), 3.

20. In her classic account, *Oral Literature in Africa* (Oxford and Nairobi: Oxford University Press, 1970), Ruth Finnegan points out that "while dramatic elements [such as impersonation, props, costumes, and the representation of interaction among characters] enter into several different categories of artistic activity in Africa . . . there are few or no forms which include all these elements" (501). South Bantu conventions, in particular, she argues, favor the sequential impersonations by the storyteller or praise poet rather than the dramatic imitation of several characters, each by a designated actor.

21. Erlmann, *African Stars,* 64. See also Peterson, "Apartheid and the Political Imagination in Black South African Theatre," 229–31.

22. Coplan, *In Township Tonight!* 127.

23. Gérard, *Four African Literatures,* 197.

24. Robert Kavanagh, *Theatre and Cultural Struggle in South Africa* (London: Zed, 1985), 45.

25. Erlmann's argument (*African Stars,* 76–78) that groups such as the Lucky Stars reflected an overall shift in educated African attitudes in favor of recovering ethnic traditions in response to the state's drive toward segregation accurately reflects the aspirations of the more ethnically militant Zulu intellectuals in Natal (see Marks, "Patriotism"), but it carries less weight in the much more ethnically diverse, urbanized, and class-conscious communities in the Transvaal, especially in the Johannesburg area.

26. Bertha Slosberg, *Pagan Tapestry* (London: Rich and Cravan, 1939), 192. Slosberg's plans for a triumphal London tour to follow this occasion were thwarted by the South African government's refusal to issue passports to the performers. The contradictions in Slosberg's enthusiasm for an authentic Zulu show and her willingness to challenge white South African taboos (from paying African performers a living wage to merely socializing with them) become unmistakable in her readiness, after the Lucky Stars dissolved in frustration in 1937, to devote the same enthusiasm to a series of dance numbers in a show at the Drury Lane called "The Sun Never Sets" [on the Empire?] performed mostly by Nigerians and British blacks trained by herself (*Pagan Tapestry*, 312–20). For the ambiguous position of the Lucky Stars between the primitivist nostalgia exemplified by Slosberg's "pagan tapestry" and the appropriation by other African showmen of what might be called national pageants, see Loren Kruger, "Placing 'New Africans' in the 'Old' South Africa: Drama, Modernity, and Racial Identities in Johannesburg, c. 1935," *Modernism/Modernity* 1, no. 2 (1994): 113–31.

27. B. W. Vilakazi, "Some Aspects of Zulu Literature," *African Studies* 1, no. 4 (1942): 270–74.

28. "Drama and the African" (written in 1936), in *Literary Theory and Criticism of H. I. E. Dhlomo*, ed. Nick Visser (special issue of *English in Africa* 4, no. 2 [1977]: 7). Quotations from this book are hereafter cited in the text as *Literary Theory*. Essay titles are included as needed.

29. Alain Locke, "Introduction," in *The New Negro* (written in 1925) (New York: Macmillan, 1992), 8–10. For the impact of New Negro formations on the New African, see Couzens, *The New African*, 110–12.

30. The connection between Dhlomo and the "new drama" is not accidental. Sybil Thorndyke, a major player at the Old Vic, a key venue for social drama in 1930s London, visited Johannesburg in 1935. In response to a performance for the Imperial Press Conference that included mineworkers performing *ingoma* (Zulu) dancing and singing hymns and *shebeen* songs, she urged white South Africans to learn from the "black races" ("There was Real Acting at Wemmer," *Bantu World*, March 2, 1935, 1). For further discussion of tensions between "new," or "social," drama and agitprop on metropolitan stages during this period, see Kruger, *The National Stage*, chaps. 3, 4.

31. *Izibongelo* appears to be derived from the verb *-bongela* (roughly "praise for or expressed directly to someone") and suggests a performance for a target audience. The target, in this context, appears to be not so much an individual object of praise as the nation as a whole (at once audience and subject of the representation).

32. The phrase "white savage" was attributed to D. D. T. Jabavu, president of the All African Convention, by M. L. Kabane in "The All African Convention," *South African Outlook* (August 1936): 187, in the wake of state indifference to the convention's call for repeal of the act of disenfranchisement. Other Africans, such as Selope Thema, were more cautious in their criticism but were more willing than ever to point out that tribalism was not a uniquely African problem, implying, however indirectly, that Europe, too, had emerged from savagery and might thence return (see editorial in *Bantu World*, January 18, 1936, 4).

33. For a detailed analysis of *Cetshwayo*, see Couzens, *The New African*, 125–42; and Orkin, *Drama and the South African State*, 39–43.

34. Although the direct impact of Schiller's drama on Dhlomo is difficult to prove, he was certainly more interested in history plays such as John Drinkwater's *Abraham Lin-*

coln, which may have influenced his view of Emancipation, than in the dramas of English manners of Harley Granville Barker, which may have been available to him (Steadman, "Towards a Popular Theatre," 214). His critical writing also reflects an interest in a theory of history that suggests, despite his understandable suspicion of German historians, at least the imprint of Hegelian notions: "Our ideas of Past, Present and Future do not rest on an unchangeable rock of finality, but on the plastic wax of time, conditions, progress. . . . Man's life is an unfolding, a revealing of new colours and designs. . . . It is this process of birth and revelation that writers should record" ("African Drama and Research," *Literary Theory,* 19–20).

35. Celebrated in the Basutoland Protectorate on March 12 in honor of the treaty in 1862, which made Moshoeshoe a subject of Queen Victoria, the date varied in South Africa, perhaps in response to debates about local sovereignty and the South African government's persistent but vain attempts to annex the protectorates. On the same day as the opening of *Moshoeshoe,* a celebration at Kroonstad praised the Basotho leader as an "embodiment of democracy" in an "undemocratic South Africa" ("Moshoeshoe Day: Celebrations in Kroonstad," *Umteteli wa Bantu,* May 6, 1939, 7). The reviews were mixed. *Bantu World* praised its evocation of Sotho custom and its entwinement of "legend and reality, action and philosophy" in the *pitso* (people's assembly) and surrounding action ("*Moshoeshoe:* Play Produced by Africans," *Bantu World,* May 6, 1939, 20). *Umteteli wa Bantu,* on the other hand, maintained that "there was too much of the refined" in the dialogue and accused the actors of not being "typically Masotho" ("Moshoeshoe," *Umteteli wa Bantu,* May 6, 1939, 4).

36. H. I. E. Dhlomo, "Moshoeshoe," *Collected Works,* 229–66. Subsequent page references are cited in the body of the text. Couzens (*The New African,* 161–62) notes the reference to Thaba Bosiu at the end of the play and speculates on the connection to its Pimville namesake. The publicity surrounding the Sotho chief Joel Molapo's speech at Western Native Township on Moshoeshoe Day (March 12, 1937) confirms the contemporary resonance of the occasion and, by implication, suggests at least a substitute place.

37. Kabane, "The All-African Convention," 188.

38. A full analysis of mass black rebellion in the 1940s and 1950s is impossible here but some points unfamiliar to non–South African readers are worth reiterating. The ANC Youth League, which included future leaders such as Nelson Mandela, demanded action on behalf of a much larger constituency than before. At the same time, increasing mass militancy was not only the work of this new elite but was also enabled by ever-greater numbers of industrial workers proletarianized by the war economy. The chilling effect of repression by the Nationalist government in the period leading up to the banning of the ANC and other organizations (1961–63) should not, however, be underestimated: mass black resistance went underground to reemerge only in the 1970s. Edward Roux's classic, if idiosyncratic, *Time Longer than Rope: The Black Man's Struggle for Freedom in South Africa,* 2d ed. (Madison: University of Wisconsin Press, 1964), offers a detailed account of the 1930s and 1940s; Tom Lodge's *Black Politics in South Africa since 1945* (London: Longman, 1985) provides a more systematic account up to the 1980s.

39. Dhlomo, "African Attitudes to Europeans," *The Democrat,* December 1, 1945, 21, 24.

40. Orkin, *Drama and the South African State,* 48.

41. Dhlomo, "The Workers," *Collected Works,* 211–27. Subsequent page references are cited in the body of the text.

42. Steadman, "Towards a Popular Theatre in South Africa," 216.

43. For an analysis of the discrepancies between the discourse of revolution in plays like *Shanti,* written by Black Consciousness students, and the relative indifference of working-class black audiences, whose tastes tended to favor township musicals and melodramas such as Gibson Kente's *Too Late!* and *How Long?,* see Kavanagh, *Theatre and Cultural Struggle,* 113–95.

44. For an analysis of the contradictions as well as the social-critical potential of township shows, see ibid. For a harsher criticism of the affirmative character of melodrama as a form of social control, see Andrew Horn, "Ideology and the Melodramatic Vision: Popular Theatre in Black South Africa and Nineteenth-Century America," *English in Africa* 12, no. 1 (1985): 1–10.

45. Documents in the debate on the protest paradigm, the erstwhile ANC slogan "Culture Is a Weapon," and the relevance of relevance are many and varied. See, especially, Njabulo Ndebele, "Redefining Relevance," *Pretexts* (University of Cape Town) 1, no. 1 (1989): 40–51; and the documents collected in Ingrid de Kok and Karen Press, eds., *Spring is Rebellious: Albie Sachs and the Debate about Cultural Freedom* (Cape Town: Buchu, 1990). For further commentary, see Loren Kruger, "'That Fluctuating Movement of National Consciousness': Nationalism, Publicity, and the Possibility of a Postcolonial Theater in South Africa," in *Imperialism and Theater,* ed. J. Ellen Gainor (London: Routledge, 1995).

7.

Anthony O'Brien

Staging Whiteness:
Beckett, Havel, Maponya

Radical black South African theater can be understood, in its relation to European (post)modernism, as a project of decolonizing the stage. Decolonizing the stage means not only a shift in historical and political consciousness away from a normative and oppressive whiteness but a strategic turn to the material cultural practices, the signifying systems, of a recovered indigenous theater that is also open to theatrical invention of every sort. To uncenter the whiteness of the white supremacist theater means, in the first instance, to *stage* that whiteness, to normalize it within a different set of rules. But that cannot be done without bringing in its wake an effect of retrospect on the white theater that has been decentered, the whiteness of its writing made newly legible. The *post* of *postcolonial* in this sense refers not only to the new products of a decolonizing culture but to a new periodization of the colonial or metropolitan text itself. And, if that text is also postmodern, the *post* of its postcoloniality is the same as the *post* of its postmodernity.[1] To see this is to make a postcolonial reading of the postmodern, a useful interpretive consequence of a decolonizing cultural project. This article explores at the same time an important political opportunity for a decolonizing theater, the possibility of displacing normative male heterosexist representation.[2]

A provocative instance of this general project is the intertextual chain that links three plays of the early 1980s: Samuel Beckett's *Catastrophe* (Paris, 1982), Václav Havel's *Mistake* (Prague, 1983), and Maishe Maponya's *Gangsters* (Johannesburg, 1984). *Gangsters,* Maponya's play about the death of Steve Biko in detention, brings into focus the question of how the postcolonial reads the postmodern because of its appropriation of the stage design and some passages from *Catastrophe*. Beckett's play, which was dedicated to Havel while he was in a Czech prison, shares with Maponya's the political aim of celebrating and vindicating a writer-activist in the hands of an enemy state. Havel's short play *Mistake*, a response to Beckett, was written after he was released from jail and performed in Stockholm on a double bill with *Catastrophe*. As both plays were published side by side in *Index on Censorship*—a journal much preoccupied in the early 1980s with censored South African writers—Maponya may have known the Havel play as well as he knew Beckett's.[3]

Looking at Maponya's appropriation of Beckett's Havel play in the context of Havel's response allows an exploration of the theatrical and political strategies the three playwrights have used to challenge the state with the power of the stage. Located as they are in three almost emblematically different cultural-political sites, the plays draw attention, first, to what the anthropologist Arjun Appadurai calls "heterogenization," or the way in which local cultures receive and adapt—resist by adapting, adapt by resisting—the ubiquitous products of the metropolitan centers in the "global cultural economy."[4] The roots of Maponya's Bahumutsi Drama Group in the Black Consciousness movement (of which Biko was a principal figure) highlight the heterogenizing impulse of his interest in an icon of Eurocentric postmodern theater such as Beckett. *Mistake*, too, is a revision by local knowledges of Beckett's ethnic and sexual politics.

It is equally important to trace the effects of Maponya's appropriation on the scene of Western reading. By analyzing the staging of race and gender as it circulates through first, second, and third World theaters, I mean to show that the decolonizing impulse can inform Western interpretation of Western texts and that postmodern theater—once we see it restaged by a South African theater of the dispossessed—is at the same time postcolonial.[5] What Maponya does, in effect, is not only appropriate postmodernism for a South African liberated theater but also in the same act reveal a new reading of the postmodern, just as Césaire, Lamming, and others compelled new readings of *The Tempest*.[6] My argument goes beyond the culturalist one that postmodernism gets acculturated heterogeneously. It is rather that Maponya's intervention makes visible a different reading of Beckett's and Havel's aesthetic transactions with race and with the European sex-gender system.

Race and gender function as mediations of power in *Catastrophe*, in which Beckett implies a confrontation between rival technologies of power and knowledge: the writer against the state, the theater against the prison.

The only direct reference to Havel is in the dedication,[7] and the plot is confined to the rehearsal of the ending ("catastrophe") of a play—the three characters being the Director (D), his Assistant (A), and a Protagonist (P). But it is clear that Beckett means the power relations between director and actor to figure the power struggle between the state and writers or political "actors" like Havel. In performance, the stage becomes a theatrical metaphor for the state. In such a scene gender and race mediate power, either the disciplinary "biopower" (in Foucault's terms)[8] of the state or the countervailing power of writing as political agency. But to ask how race and gender function in *Catastrophe* (as Maponya in South Africa must have asked) already begins to reposition Beckett "in other worlds." In the light of this postcolonial question it can be seen how *Catastrophe* must have drawn Maponya's attention.

In terms of gender, the accoutrements of male self-fashioning in the Director's furs, cigar, watch, and blustering speech contain a tacitly feminist critique, and D is set off against a different coding of the male (a different "stylization of the body") in the Protagonist—the male subject as vulnerable, stripped, feelingful.[9] P is abject under D's manipulation but recovers an aesthetic and epistemic energy in the spotlighting of his intense silent gaze out into the theater, displacing D's centrality as normative male figure as well as breaking the homosocial bonds of domination between them. We see a struggle between two versions of male gender performance deployed on the ground, matrix, or landscape of D's female Assistant, who remains as secondary to P at the end as she has been all along to D. A is an intermediary who executes D's orders yet sympathizes, not quite consciously, with P.

The resemblance of their triad to the nuclear family only makes more evident the fact that *Catastrophe* rehearses an Oedipal drama in the sense elaborated by Teresa de Lauretis in her theory of male narrative.[10] In the male narrative, women stand by to watch, assist, hinder, or function as origin or end of the male protagonist's quest to control the Lacanian symbolic order. In Beckett's play, with its self-conscious focus on theatrical signification, D and P battle for control of the symbolic order with a hyperreal clarity: control of closure, "catastrophe," and representation itself are the stakes of the game. P's unfilial stepping out of his role, the "anti-Oedipus" enacted by his raised head and the line of flight of his unveiled gaze, refuses the transfer of male privilege to good sons according to the established libidinal economy of the "law of the father." But, claiming that power anyway, P's antipatriarchy does not alter the structure of male desire that drives the stage action.

The male agon between D and P is fundamentally over the semiotic control of P's body; the political correlative is state control of civil society. To the extent that P's move for autonomy represents Havel's citizen resistance and responsibility, it is sobering to note that resistance and civic will are themselves thus silently encoded as male and politics marked as a male preserve. Acute in its grasp of the collusion between the powers of prison and theater, *Catastrophe* seems unaware that it underwrites a male monopoly of political power and the theatrical sign. It should be said that the same gap in consciousness is visible in Havel's political writings, so in this regard the political alliance between Havel and Beckett becomes a form of male bonding.[11] And to the degree that Beckett and Havel belong to the same European theatrical tradition, the fact that their thematics of power is mediated exclusively through the male gender position is a strong argument for revision of that whole tradition. One of the most arresting things about Maponya's *Gangsters,* to anticipate for a moment, is that we can observe him in the process of making such a revision of the male thematics of power.

Disturbing the gender iconography of *Catastrophe* by casting P as a woman, for example, would tilt the play alarmingly off its axis; the shock of a "female narrative," differently enigmatic, would complicate all the meanings of the play and put into strong relief its concept of power as uniquely male. It is interesting that, although Beckett's directions say that age and physique are unimportant in casting all three parts, he does specify the female gender of A: there is some measure taken here to question how gender interacts with power. The fact that A is a writer of sorts in the play, even if she mostly takes dictation in the notebook that is a sign of her ancillary status, also acknowledges "under erasure" that the female is excluded from the language of power and from power over language, an exclusion that founds the enunciating subject as male (as feminist thought at least since Cixous has claimed). A's presence as a woman in the margin of Beckett's theater of power is therefore not without emblematic force, jarring against its masculinist premises.

Questioning how *Catastrophe* constructs the racial subject reveals an effect, quite unlike the play's interest in gender hierarchies, of homogeneity, invisibility, and absence. Even in multiracial societies like that of France in 1982, where Le Pen's openly racist campaigns were beginning to make the politics of race, French nationality, and North African immigration as explosive as they remain today, all-white casts playing to mostly white audiences are often not perceived as "racial" at all. Where whiteness seems so much the norm as not even to be a race category, race seems a tendentious intrusion by the critic, even where the theater happens to be surrounded by the swirl of racial politics. But the fact that white audiences do not perceive the racial whiteness of the cast of *Catastrophe* itself signifies the Western ascription of race as an attribute to other people. Adrienne Rich, writing about race as a white feminist in "Disloyal to Civilization: Feminism, Racism, Gynephobia" (1978), analyzes this propensity as "white solipsism" or "snow-blindness" ("*Passive collusion:* Snow-blindness. White solipsism: To think, imagine and speak as if whiteness described the world").[12] bell hooks, in *Ain't I a Woman* (1981) and later writings, has deepened the analysis of this notion as central to white supremacy, including its contamination of feminist traditions,[13] and Marlon Riggs's video "Tongues Untied" (1991) extends the analysis to gay liberation theory.

In relation to Beckett's play, the point is that white solipsism fails even to describe or account for whiteness or rather describes it only from the point of view of its internal experience, radically decontextualized. Havel's and Maponya's reponses to the play's ethnopolitics raise this point in different ways. Maponya's, especially, suggests the need for interpretation to recontextualize and redescribe whiteness, to *stage* it, as a racial position rather than a racial norm (it being always a mark of privileged status to constitute the norm). Just as one uncovers gender politics by countercasting, one way of seeing what racially is "not there" in *Catastrophe*—and the consequences of its absence for Beckett's thinking about power—would be to imagine, at the 1982 Avignon theater festival, the Protagonist played by an Algerian or Senegalese or Martiniquan actor and to register the effect of that (including its reference to Havel's case) in the France of Le Pen. Unwriting the normativeness of whiteness and maleness in the play redescribes it, within obvious limits at least (the Mabou Mines female Lear showed that multiracial or cross-gender casting does not by itself work miracles of cultural criticism). Beckett's discussion of power without reference to race underwrites white solipsism in its silence about "other worlds" even though they are right outside the door of his theater in the form of French internal colonialism.

As an exchange between Western and Eastern European culture, *Catastrophe* constructs an alignment in which the East-West axis forms a bloc of white states and white cultures unconscious of their normative whiteness: a Eurocentric "civilization." It is equally apparent in Havel's political writings that for all his Heideggerian eco-political critique of modern postindustrial society or "technological civilization" he has not yet thought beyond a Eurocentric order as synonymous with civilization itself. Havel allows himself a terrifying innocence about racism and ethnocentrism, claiming at one point that Christianity has "that element of universality" that Indian religions lack and assuming throughout that what he calls "global civilization" is simply the internationalization of the Western technological model. One revealing passage concerns the use of a legal code by posttotalitarian states: "This could all be done, of course, without a legal code and its accessories, but only in some ephemeral dictatorship run by a Ugandan bandit, not in a system that embraces such a huge portion of civilized humankind and represents an integral, stable and respected part of the modern world."[14] Unfortunately, all the resonant terms of Havel's existentialist humanism—*life, truth, humanity, society, community, civilization, people, individual*—are here contaminated by a radical ethnocentric snow-blindness. Before each of these common nouns he does not seem to realize that he has silently placed a European proper name. *Catastrophe* may be less egregious, but in a postcolonial world the subtlety and profundity of its meditation on power are undercut by its normative unconcern with its own racial politics. The consequences of this "white" alliance between figures like Beckett and Havel are obviously far-reaching.

If we look more searchingly at *Catastrophe*, nevertheless, we notice at the center of the play, as so often in Beckett's work, a single obsessional image—P stands on his platform under the Director's appraising eye while the Assistant adjusts him—and we realize that at some level of deeply repressed memory this image derives from the life-world of racial slavery and colonialism: the auction block, the master's dining room, the colonial parade ground. (Claire Denis's film *Chocolat*, pairing the girl France and the servant Protée like Beckett's Assistant and Protagonist, is full of similar images from the French colonial context, and they are ubiquitous in British and North American culture.) Even without having P played by a black male or white or black female actor, the white male solipsism of *Catastrophe*'s iconography of domination is thus "shadowed," as Ralph Ellison and before him Herman Melville used the term, by gender and racial otherness, by the half-acknowledged presence of another history beyond the white quarrels between European socialism and capitalism or the European citizen and the state.

Given the political prehistory of this formalistic "plinth," the play's use of blackness and whiteness (again, like Melville's) looks different; no longer purely formal elements of minimalist theater idiom, the colors begin to make dialogical patterns, not so much of their traditional European symbolism (interestingly, black and white in *Catastrophe* both suggest the deathly, the moribund) as of their racial connotations: "To have him all black,"

"Whiten all flesh." The play turns so much on the thematics of the (male) body, and particularly the body surface, its colors of exposed and "whitened" skin against black or grey cloth, that a racial connotation, once glimpsed, comes to seem an inevitable, enigmatic component of the play's politics. It seems true, then, that just as the Assistant imports subversively into *Catastrophe* an emblematic female presence, so Beckett's shadow images of the auction block and racializing skin color insert a subtly unbalancing racial intertextuality into the play. Centrality, no matter how blithely assumed in the white writing of Beckett and Havel, always somehow evokes the half-seen and half-heard afterthought of the margin.

Though it may seem a slight sketch, Havel's *Mistake* is a considered response to *Catastrophe,* which he had read in a Polish translation Antoni Libera sent him just after his release from prison. (He had already written Beckett an appreciative letter for his act of solidarity at the Avignon festival.) It was Beckett and Ionesco who first inspired Havel to move from poetry to plays, and he said in a letter to his wife that "after Samuel Beckett, we live in a different world than we did before him."[15] Havel's affinity with Beckett, as the leading Eastern European exponent of Beckettian forms, ensured that *Mistake* was to him more than an occasional piece or a thank-you note. It reworks the terms of Beckett's comments on theater and prison, writer and state. The play begins with the newcomer, Xiboy, being confronted by three other prison inmates and a trusty (named King) because he has made the mistake of smoking before breakfast, unwittingly violating one of their cell rules. The whole fabric of prison life is laid bare in this event: its regimentation of individuated bodies through their willing submission to norms of time, space, functions, tasks, gestures, postures, pleasure, and work is a textbook illustration of Foucault's analysis of "carceral institutions," "docile bodies," and "the power of normalization" in *Discipline and Punish.* The veterans are bent on enforcing the norms and negotiating Xiboy's acculturation and submission. Xiboy responds with a puzzling silence, a second "mistake," which, even when it is interpreted as his not knowing their language, is about to be punished as the play ends with the four inmates closing in.

In *Mistake,* Havel's scene of the humiliated humiliating others is so obviously cast in gender and ethnic terms that one must speculate about how conscious a response *Mistake* is to those terms in Beckett's play. In the all-male prison milieu, an emasculated victim is preyed upon by exaggeratedly masculinist violence. Like torture that is accompanied by a relentless interrogation, this violence also hints at prison rape. Intertwined with this pattern, "foreign" silence is punished by nativist garrulity. Although Xiboy has the same shaven head and prison garb as the others (resembling Beckett's Protagonist in this, as in his muteness and impassivity), the blank language of his untattooed skin (like P's "whitened" skin) is a marker, in prison, of not taking part in a requisite male gender-game or a gendered display of toughness; there is presumably a narcissistic/homosocial sexual game involved as well, at least in the realm of the scopophilic (exhibitionism/ voyeurism), which the decorative play of tattooing enhances. Emasculation is also the burden of Xiboy's facial expressions, the "apprehension," "embarrassment," "puzzlement," and "apologetic smiles"—all features of feminized language styles—that lead the violently profane Second Prisoner to ask him, "What're you gawping at, you cunt?" And Xiboy's body language, his shrugs, slow movements, and refusal either to fight back or to enact the rituals of submission, mark off almost a gender difference from the dominant group.

But it is not quite a fiction of "feminization" that Xiboy deploys; rather, Xiboy is not properly "accountable" to his sex category, to use the terminology of the sociologists West and Zimmerman.[16] Lapses of gender accountability draw punishments to enforce gender solidarity and gender hierarchy, a process eminently theorizable in Foucauldian terms, in spite of Foucault's failure to include in his own work feminist theory of gender. In this case a gender code underlies the enforcement of a prison code, and a certain obligatory construction of masculinity (which itself would be quite difficult to describe, composed perhaps in equal parts of homophobia, a straight travesty of gay male sexuality, and genuine homoeroticism), a caricatural display of machismo, is seen to form part of the prison's discipline, its "anatomo-politics of the human body."[17] There are similar structures in *Catastrophe*, with its two contrasted styles of masculinity, one dominant over the other. What is different in *Mistake* is that there is no valorization of the less-macho style, as there is in P's "reversal"; the play closes grimly on a tableau of primitive enforcement. Again this can be read as a "mistake," Xiboy's gender category mistake, which points beyond itself to a more encompassing mistake, which is the tyranny of gender itself. The prison dynamic in which the humiliated humiliate is homologous with the gender dynamic in which the emasculated emasculate, to recover, as well as require, a fictional hypermasculinity.

Havel also revises Beckett's ethnopolitics. A border or barrier of ethnicity arises in the play as the "mistake" at its center. It does so through language alone, since there are no other signs of Xiboy's foreignness. The discovery of Xiboy's linguistic (and so ethnic or national) difference is not followed by understanding or empathy; the prisoners advance menacingly on him as though newly and more gravely incited to violence by this difference ("That's his funeral"). The play never positively confirms the Third Prisoner's guess that Xiboy must be foreign (he himself cannot testify), but the only other explanation, a less plausible one, would be that he is a deaf-mute. Perhaps that theoretical possibility only amplifies the point that difference is a barrier and an incitement to violence. Again, their mistaking his linguistic/ethnic identity turns out to be no mistake but (for them) an *explanation* of everything that is scandalous about Xiboy; torturers who cannot obtain a confession, they feel legitimately compelled to the last violence by the fact that the victim is unable to confess. In *Catastrophe* there is no ethnic implication in P's silence, which is explicable as the actor's participation in mime, and P's lack of voice is compensated by the power of his glance. Havel's conception of Xiboy seems to comment on P's silence by adducing a silence of another type, which expresses the powerlessness of ethnic marginality, doubly muted because Havel suppresses all countervailing body language. There is a dialogue of silences between Beckett and Havel: each silence is a differently chosen metaphor for the loss of power, in each case contrasted to an image of power as crude and "fallen" speech; in both plays, in different ways, the silence of the prison echoes in the theater, the place of speech, now self-violated by a usurping babble of power.

A silenced ethnicity as a political mistake: this motif is surely Havel's glance at the ethnic conflicts of Central Europe, not least in Czechoslovakia itself, and it is not impossible that it responds subliminally to what I have referred to as P's iconographical resemblance to the non-European slave or colonial servant. In the European context alone, ethnic difference and its political expression in nationalist bullying and recrimination are mostly a matter of land and language, not of "racial" markers. Yet, like *Catastrophe*, *Mistake* has selected a mark of dominated status, in this case language, which leaps outside of a purely European frame or rather reframes Europe in its history of linguistic imperialism. It is a clear implication of *Mistake* that, to survive, Xiboy would have had to unlearn his own language and learn the language of the "king," as many generations of colonized people have had to do. Not to speak the dominant language, in territorial or internal colonialism, is to be without social defenses, like Xiboy in his cell; failing to code switch when confronted by the arrogance of the linguistic norm is a "mistake" that, in the deep structure of Havel's play, always points further on, here to critique the world-historical mistake that is the colonialist dream of linguistic autarchy.

Havel's politicizing of linguistic competence in his Central and Eastern European context invokes the marginalized and colonial history of many peoples and nations in that region as well as the threat of micronationalist fragmentation there in the future (the future of 1983 has become the tragic present in the mid-1990s). But it also connects the play quite clearly, though how consciously one cannot say, to all the issues of decolonization of language in a global context, to the questions about Caliban's language and Ariel's song so eloquently rehearsed by Aimé Césaire, Rigoberta Menchú, Roberto Retamar, Ngugi wa Thiong'o, David Diop, and others. My argument here, as with Beckett's play, is not simply that a postcolonial interpretation "returned" to Europe must find these suggestive reterritorializings, these memories and afterimages, in European texts (though that is the case); the more essential claim is that such references are material, historical traces in the intertextuality of a European culture that has never been purely or only European, above all since the Portuguese voyagers set sail in the fifteenth century. The slave on the block or the colonized person without language are cultural residues of the European history of slavery and colonialism, which are activated somewhere in consciousness by Beckett's image or Havel's plot; interpellated by the postcolonial question, they rise up to give another account of themselves. The task of critics in the West who are persuaded by the problematic of the postcolonial is to ask the new question of this old history, to make conscious the operation of this European intertextuality, to admit that history is an object of critical reflection in every European text, and so move beyond solipsism and myths of centrality.

What has Maponya made of all these European transactions? *Gangsters* negotiates questions of power and representation differently because of its South African cultural location—not merely as a local or micropolitical difference but as a feature of the ways South Africa is integrated into the global cultural economy. (The global cultural boycott of South Africa at the time *Gangsters* and the two European plays were written is only one, paradoxical, feature of this integration.) In its inscription of race and gender, particularly, *Gangsters* is not merely local but global in its reference; the particular links and references the play has to *Catastrophe* and *Mistake* make this apparent, but there is a rule here not an exception. Dutch and British colonialisms have guaranteed historically that there is a cultural continuum, a single though differentiated history, between Europe and South Africa and between South Africa and other European settler colonies. The historic shift all but completed around 1960 from territorial colonialism to the current world system of transnational capital, with its attendant global mediatization of culture, has not erased the continuum laid down by colonialist history but simply built upon it. The meaning of a black South African play's treatment of race and gender therefore resonates through the postcolonial global cultural economy, particularly through the African diaspora and other multiracial societies. To see black South African theater in Los Angeles, London, Nairobi, Jerusalem, or Sydney is to see one's own race and gender system through that theater. The three plays examined here illustrate this general rule.

Gangsters, written in 1984 and performed in South African townships, Johannesburg, and theater festivals in London, Edinburgh, Dublin, and New York, is a play about the death of Steve Bantu Biko in prison seven years before. It works through a split temporality; interrogations of the Biko figure, Rasechaba, by the white and black security policemen, Whitebeard and Jonathan, are interspersed as flashbacks with the "rehearsal" scenes (later, in real time) in which Whitebeard and Jonathan try to touch up Rasechaba's body for the inquest. It is the idea of these rehearsal scenes that Maponya has taken from Beckett's *Catastrophe:* the triad of characters, the task of constructing a theatrical image from a passive stage body (in *Gangsters,* it is also a legal "image," a piece of false evidence), and a few of Beckett's incantatory lines such as "To have him all black."[18]

While the interrogation scenes (the bulk of the play) give powerful lines, political effectiveness, and moments of victory to Rasechaba, the use of Beckett's design to frame the play's opening and closing scenes is crucial to its elegiac tone and purpose. *Gangsters* breaks with the frame and mood of *Catastrophe* by setting elegy in a dialectic with heroic action, but Beckett is essential to the elegiac function of the play, its tribute to the fallen. *Gangsters* is thus, like all *imitatio,* a kind of tribute as well as an allusion to Beckett, just as Biko and Havel become political analogs through this associative link.

Of course, Maponya's play is centrally about black self-representation as the production of new, decolonized, theatrical images, and as such it comes up hard against the exclusions and absences, the hints and shadows, the colonialist residues and traces, in Beckett and Havel. But it is also a staging of racial whiteness, the decolonizing point of which criticism has to decode. bell hooks has written persuasively of this necessity, and South

African fiction by Coetzee, Brink, and Gordimer shows the decolonizing process at work in white consciousness.[19] "Whiteness" is a cultural code enmeshed in representation throughout the world system, and what someone like Maponya is saying about that code is not relevant only to white people in South Africa. Maponya's racial casting in *Gangsters* is especially interesting in a way that breaks with his own tradition and perhaps shows— as Njabulo Ndebele's cultural theory would predict[20]—how Black Consciousness, its project of autonomy carried out, has much to contribute to the other side of decolonization in South Africa, the difficult process of white repositioning in a nonracial "new nation"—if that is the outcome. Black theater before Maponya used black actors to play white roles, often with techniques of multiple characterization that are themselves full of meaning—such as the actor's slipping on of a pink clown nose, as in *Bopha!* and *Asinamali!*[21]—to denote his shift to a white role. Because of segregation in the theater, Maponya was the first black playwright in South Africa to direct white actors in white roles. An interesting sidelight on his venture is provided by Kavanagh's story of how Fugard, ten years before, reluctantly capitulated to the apartheid authorities' demand that he not play a white role in his collaborative play *No-Good Friday* when it was to be performed in black townships—and the disappointment of his collaborators Modisane and Nkosi at this self-censoring resegregation of their breakthrough "nonracial" theater.[22]

Read against *Catastrophe,* in which there is much business with skin and makeup, a thematics of the body surface, Maponya's casting decision to deploy white and black actors has important consequences. His white interrogator, Major Whitebeard, is not a cartoon like Beckett's Director but has dramatic force and menacing intelligence, particularly in contrast to the loss of force in Rasechaba, who is seen repeatedly as a dead figure hanging limply on a cross. The whiteness of the actor is thus not dismissively or derisively rendered. But in Maponya's design the dramatic force of his actor's whiteness is pointedly strategic: he has extended the thematic of the body surface from the target figure, Rasechaba (Beckett's P), to the power figure, Whitebeard, whose "raced" quality thus comes into focus. The act of exhibiting a white face, body, gestures, and language on the black stage, before an audience that in South Africa was mostly black, is in itself a claiming of power from the mystified domain of whiteness, white police, white prison, white nationalism, and white power for the new insurgent domain of blackness, black theater, black poetry, black political action, black nationalism, and black power.

The actor's whiteness, the magic of this supremacist fetish, is thus given room to have its full theatrical effect on Maponya's stage, while still being fully subordinated to a black artistic intentionality and Black Consciousness theatrical forms. This dynamic culminates in a struggle between Whitebeard and Rasechaba over the question of voice, of who speaks, who has the floor, who controls public discourse, and who determines the fate of black speech, black words, black texts. In their second encounter, Whitebeard forcibly (at gunpoint, inside the jail) removes one of Rasechaba's poems and insists, over the author's protests, on reading it himself. This emblematic act of power, expropriating a black text from its author and giving it an alienated voice, is then subjected to a double dramatic reversal. (Does Maponya here glance at his own "seizure" of Beckett's text?) First, Whitebeard's voice is, at the very moment he exhibits its power, molded to the black poetic text, Whitebeard becoming a vehicle for Rasechaba's words, which the audience is hearing for the first time. Then, as Rasechaba immediately reads another of his poems, Whitebeard's reading is overread, or erased, by Rasechaba's own voice. Fanon's psychology of decolonization gets a beautiful expression in this play of racial voices across and through each other's registers, as the fetishism of racial domination—and the psychology of torture/interrogation—is reexperienced by the black spectator in order to be demystified by the dramaturgy.

On the other hand, whiteness (blackness, too) is not an uncriticized, reified concept-metaphor in *Gangsters*. To begin with, "black" is primarily a political category, not a racial one, both in the anti-apartheid movement as a whole and (surprisingly, to a U.S. reader used to African American cultural nationalism, though not to a British reader familiar with *black* as a term of Afro-Asian unity in Britain) within the Black Consciousness Movement in particular.[23] That movement, as is clear in Biko's own writings and the studies by Robert Fatton and Anthony Marx, was not a politics of simple race consciousness or ethnic nationalism, ideologies fostered rather by the regime's tribalist policies, the "separate development" of autonomous "population groups," as the official discourse had it, and by the Zulu-separatist "cultural" organization Inkatha.[24] It was rather, in Fatton's words, "ideological resistance to white supremacy," something else altogether, logically entailing a deconstruction of the social construction "race." These are complex matters, and it will not do to obscure the important debates among traditional Pan-Africanism, which regarded the land as belonging uniquely to indigenous African people; a Black Consciousness that extended to all people of color who were targets of apartheid regardless of their ethnicity; the nonracial policies and vision of the ANC (which are far more radical, as in Ndebele's formulation, than their apparent resemblance to Western color-blind liberalism might lead one to believe); and leftist class-conscious analyses of "race."[25] It often seems that the major texts of South African writing shift constantly, even bewilderingly, back and forth between these various political subject-positions, whose interaction will undoubtedly determine the future of South Africa. It is a question of which decolonization, decolonization for whom, once apartheid and white supremacy are dismantled juridically.

Gangsters is, arguably, about the deconstruction of race as a category, from the vantage point of a Black Consciousness whose reflection deepened under the impact of radical nonracial struggle (e.g., by the United Democratic Front, the UDF) and massive trade union organization (in COSATU, the Congress of South African Trade Unions) in the South Africa of the mid-1980s.[26] One striking illustration of this is the way the play's representation of the black subject is, like Beckett's white Protagonist, "shadowed" or deconstructed by racial alterity, by its white shadow. Maponya's choice of the cross as an emblematic center, resiting Beckett's dais/auction block, introduces as Rasechaba/Biko's shadow the figure of Christ crucified. Within an ideal Christianity, of course, the figure of Christ is not white-identified. But the history of European Christian colonialism enforces precisely such a racial identification of Christ, nowhere more painfully than in South Africa, where until very recently white supremacy wore a theocratic mask and the Christian cult of the Afrikaner ascendancy could hardly be separated from its ideological cult of whiteness. The independent black churches in South Africa are devoted to a different figure of Christ. But what does this figure signify in a Black Consciousness play? If in Beckett the "shadow of the Negro" is an absent presence, Toni Morrison's "unspeakable things unspoken,"[27] or a kind of forgetting-to-remember/remembering-to-forget, in Maponya this white-coded Christological shadow of the tortured black artist is emphatically foregrounded, fully in focus, and deployed in the service of a critique of race.

There were close links among Biko himself (who never abandoned an occasional use of Christian frameworks), Black Consciousness, and the liberation theology of the University Christian Movement, which, along with the South African Student Organization (SASO), gave birth to Black Consciousness as an organized movement; Christian antiracists are a recognizable and important force in the anti-apartheid movement generally. Maponya's play may well not, unlike its predecessor, the first Black Consciousness play, *Shanti* (1973),[28] express a degree of Christian faith. But whether it does or not there is a complex intention to violate the cult of whiteness in Afrikaner nationalist religion by the very image of a black Christ, a revolutionary Christ, a "terrorist" Christ; such a Christ appears centrally in Mtwa and Ngema's *Woza Albert!* (1980) where he (as Morena, Lord) is confined to Robben Island as an "agitator." Putting Rasechaba/Biko on a cross decolonizes, if one may say so, the image of Christ, reterritorializing Christ as an insurgent in the theocratic white prison. It also inscribes Rasechaba/Biko in the homoerotic iconography of European paintings of the Deposition (e.g., Caravaggio's in the Vatican Pinacoteca, freely copied by Rubens, Fragonard, Géricault, and Cézanne)—acknowledging, perhaps, male homosocial leader-follower relations in the movement, like male actor-spectator relations in the theater.[29] (Jonathan can certainly be felt to respond in complex ways as the play returns him compulsively to Beckett's scene, studying the body of the hero he has killed.)

But it can also be said to confound or "cross" racial whiteness and blackness as supposedly distinct essences or categories. A policy of "confusing" race, or rather of recognizing its actual historical con-fusion, in a nation whose population is as racially mixed as in any other settler colony, is a powerful gesture against white supremacy and its fantasy of pure races. Beckett, and Havel with his thematic of power languages and muteness, may be said to do the same thing from their own vantage points, but with them it seems unconscious. Maponya's confounding of race is a conscious trope; it may be found as well in the blending/confounding of Whitebeard's voice with Rasechaba's words, in the State police uniform that clothes equally white officer and black subaltern, and, most hauntingly, in the psychic divisions within the black subaltern, Jonathan. What happens to the black policeman in the service of white supremacy? Percy Mtwa's play *Bopha!* (written the same year as *Gangsters*) explores this question at length, and shows a conversion and recuperation of the lost soul. Maponya is grimmer. A salvationist possibility for Jonathan is glimpsed, interestingly, in the church scene, but it is refused. Jonathan, racially black but politically "nonwhite" (to use the insult some Black Consciousness members directed at those who collaborated with white people), drowns in the confusion. Maponya is then very far from a glib nonracial stance (not that all nonracial stances are glib); race for him is perhaps a historical given, a contradiction that cannot be transcended but must be lived through. The project in this play would then be to achieve as much clarity as possible about the foundationlessness of race as a concept-metaphor, even while living through its painful historical reality.

The final words of Rasechaba's last poem in *Gangsters* carry further yet a deconstructive, anti-essentialist politics of race. The staging of these poetry readings, with Rasechaba alone on a blue-lit stage, is taken directly from one of the most powerful forms of conscientization that Black Conscious-ness developed in its community organizing work. The poetry reading, often to music, traced a line back to African orality and performance tradi-tions, while in its educated, urban tone it proposed a modern forward-look-ing black politics for its audience. (The same effect, in a very different set-ting, the industrial workplace and the union rally, is achieved by such oral worker-poets of COSATU as Hlatshwayo, Qabula, and Malange.)[30] Given this emphasis, then, and the sanction of the direct poetic voice, Rasechaba concludes:

> We loved this land
> And cared for all its people,
> White and black
> Free and unfree
>
> *(Woza Afrika!* 86)

In these lines the racial signifiers "white" and "black" float undetermined, like the related pair "free" and "unfree," in a swirl of motions and counter-motions. All objects of love and care, are they also, or which of them are also, the subject of the loving and caring that is Rasechaba's last definition of revolutionary action? The political and syntactic ground of the asser-tion—"we," "loved," "land," "people"—is fixed and firm, defining the collective revolutionary subject by its action, its object, its solidarity. Who may join? The modifiers of race, status, and class (we could take *free* and *unfree* as gender terms also) float in the semantic field of those who have yet to decide this for themselves. The lines echo and reinforce Maponya's design as a whole, rejecting any reified concept of race while figuring the revolutionary content of Black Consciousness as a dismantling of white supremacy.

From a slightly different angle, Maponya's staging of race throws another light on the European plays; it inserts race into their meditations on the relations between theater and the state. By quoting or importing *Cata-strophe's* central scene into *Gangsters,* with the two conspirators, Whitebeard and Jonathan, posing, costuming, and making up the body of Rasechaba in a cell, Maponya has critically disengaged the concept of (state) power from the concept of whiteness. And, equally, he has disengaged the concept of resistance from an essentialist identity with the concept of blackness. Race, achieving its own politics of deconstruction and tragic irony, is crucially distinguished from the politics of power in the nation-state (which entail class and gender issues alongside race, even under apartheid). In this way Maponya can engage in a spirited representation of the black voice, black unity, and black resistance and at the same time signal a politics of race beyond mere race, which maps out a further terrain of political struggle over power and representation.

Maponya has modified Beckett's metaphor of state-as-stage in another direction also. No less than the Director and his Assistant, Whitebeard and Jonathan are engaged in a true rehearsal, cooking the evidence for the coroner's court, that theater of falsification. *Gangsters,* like Brecht (the title is also Brechtian), exposes state processes as themselves theatrical, as "social dramas" in the anthropologist Victor Turner's phrase. The social drama of the state in its juridical forms is here shown caught in the supposed antinomy of law and violence, the rituals of law undone, and rendered more nakedly theatrical, by the prevailing operation of state terror. Again, Maponya is closer to Havel on the surface of the plays, which agree that the prison itself is an adequate scene of power for their purposes. But in a strange way Maponya's adaptation of Beckett, even though it refuses his metaphor, comes back to it in reverse by means of this stress not on the power relations of the theater that were the vehicle of Beckett's metaphor but on the theatrical structure of the text of state power.

The inscription of gender in *Gangsters* shows the influence of feminist consciousness in the anti-apartheid movement. As first written and performed, the play was all-male, and I have discussed it on that basis. But a feminist critique of some of the same gender effects as were noticed in Beckett and Havel is forestalled by Maponya's autocritique. In the 1986 New York production, staged as part of a festival of black South African plays, *Gangsters* was cast with the actress Nomathemba Nomvume Mdini in the role of Rasechaba, now named Masechaba, "mother [not father] of the nation." (There is a poem, "Masechaba," by the Black Consciousness poet Ilva Mackay, in an issue of *Staffrider* devoted to commemorating Women's Day, the great protest rally of women in Pretoria on August 9, 1956: its theme is Africa as political mother of political children.)[31] Maponya said of this casting change that "Women have long symbolized the strength of our movement, refusing to break under the yoke of oppression and sacrificing their very lives for the liberation. I thought a woman was more appropriate for the role for the overall sensitivity she would bring to the part."[32] These formulations are problematic with their typecasting of women as selfless servants of the cause and their apparent belief in gender traits such as sensitivity.[33] They still leave many questions about the staging of gender in the play, the construction of a female political subject, and the substitutability of a woman in a male role otherwise unchanged.

But the main point is that something in South African cultural politics in the mid-1980s, the rise in the influence of a women's movement within the anti-apartheid movement, has impelled Maponya to tackle these questions of gender politics head-on, his public self-correction underscoring the solidarity between women and men of the movement, the high stakes involved, and the strength of the liberating impulse at work. Does his rewriting of the gender code of power, putting the female subject as poet and revolutionary in the place of the male, giving her the site of enunciation, and making her the subject in the deep structure of the play's narrative, take the play out of the mode of male narrative in which *Catastrophe* and *Mistake* are written? It is too simple to believe that that could occur, as if by magic, without a fundamental reconceiving of the play. The poems, for example, are Maponya's own and distinctly in a male voice: voicing that poetry as a woman's with a woman delivering the lines onstage would seem to deny gender difference in a kind of speaking-for, a ventriloquism. Wouldn't the casting change require a woman's poems? And yet these questions are being asked not only by Western feminism as questions of interpretation but by South African feminists as questions of cultural production. A special issue of the Durban journal *Current Writing* devoted to feminisms in South Africa contains a representative selection of these new voices, and the necessary complications of cross-race feminisms are being fought through in conferences where sharp criticism of white essentialist feminism is being made.[34] Such questions are essential, on both ends of the process, for negotiating an exchange between third world writing and first world reading and for a revolution in gender relations inside third world revolutions; both kinds of questioning coexist in tension with each other.

To show Masechaba, the black female subject of the interrogation scenes, vanquishing Whitebeard with an art of words is a significant reordering of gender and enunciative space in the play consistent with its interventionist, power-seizing dramaturgy. It literalizes the metaphor of the Other's shadow, left offstage in *Mistake* and confined to a subaltern role in *Catastrophe:* here the shadow, Masechaba, has suddenly taken over the space where the white or black male "body" was. Her physical struggles with the police and the spectacle of her abject body (another "crossing" trope, as she occupies the space of a now female African Christ) also reposition the female protagonist in the political sphere. There is a gathering of energies about the new possibilities of Maponya's Masechaba that defers some of the questions that undoubtedly remain about his tactic of substitution. Clearly the effect is to seek a way to break out of the solipsism of heterosexist male theater. Rewriting his own patriarchal script, Maponya has made his widest swerve away from Beckett and Havel and hinted at gender liberation as the secret heart of an aesthetic of the dispossessed.

NOTES

1. See Kwame Anthony Appiah's discussion of "The Postcolonial and the Postmodern" in his *In My Father's House: Africa in the Philosophy of Culture* (New York: Oxford University Press, 1992), 137–57. On the word *post,* see also Geoffrey Bennington, "Postal Politics and the Institution of the Nation," in *Nation and Narration,* ed. Homi K. Bhabha (London and New York: Routledge, 1990), 121–37.

2. Maponya's *Gangsters*—as revised for the New York production—is an instance of male repositioning in response to feminism within a decolonizing cultural politics, but this is more the exception than the rule. The fiction of Achmat Dangor and Mongane Serote are, arguably, other South African examples, and Martin Orkin points to the significance of Mbongeni Ngema's *Sarafina!,* which focuses on women protagonists (teacher and student) in its account of the 1976 uprisings (*Drama and the South African State* [Johannesburg: Witwatersrand University Press; Manchester and New York: Manchester University Press, 1991], 232–33). The struggles of feminism against the patriarchy of liberation movements are analyzed in Marie Aimée Helie-Lucas, "Women, Nationalism, and Religion in the Algerian Liberation Struggle," in *Opening the Gates: A Century of Arab Feminist Writing,* ed. Margot Badran and Miriam Cooke (Bloomington: Indiana University Press, 1990), 104–14; Margaret Randall, *Gathering Rage: The Failure of 20th Century Revolutions to Develop a Feminist Agenda* (New York: Monthly Review, 1992); and Anne McClintock, " 'No Longer in a Future Heaven': Women and Nationalism in South Africa," *Transition* 51 (1991): 104–23. In South Africa today, feminism is putting the politics of the nation (the "new nation") under intense scrutiny.

3. Samuel Beckett, "Catastrophe (for Václav Havel)," *Index on Censorship* 1, no. 84 (1984): 11–12; Samuel Beckett, *Ohio Impromptu, Catastrophe, and What Where* (New York: Grove, 1984); Václav Havel, *"Mistake,"* *Index on Censorship* 1, no. 84 (1984): 13–14; Maishe Maponya, *"Gangsters,"* in *Woza Afrika! An Anthology of South African Plays,* ed. Duma Ndlovu (New York: Braziller, 1986), 55–87.

4. Arjun Appadurai, "Disjuncture and Difference in the Global Cultural Economy," *Public Culture* 2, no. 2 (1990): 5ff.

5. This is an extension of Fredric Jameson's argument that the modernist text is colonial ("Modernism and Imperialism," in *Nationalism, Colonialism, and Literature* [Min-

neapolis: University of Minnesota Press, 1990], 43–66). Ella Shohat has criticized the depoliticizing use of *postcolonial* in "Notes on the 'Postcolonial' " (*Social Text* 31, no. 32 [Spring 1992]: 99–113), but I mean here to keep the term's political valence as a contestatory term, implying not merely *after* but *above and beyond* (neo)colonialism. See also Bennington, "Postal Politics," 122.

6. See Barbara Bowen, "Writing Caliban: Anti-Colonial Appropriations of *The Tempest*," forthcoming in *Current Writing* (Durban, South Africa); and Rob Nixon, "Caribbean and African Appropriations of *The Tempest*," *Cultural Inquiry* 13 (Spring 1987): 557–78.

7. In the premiere at the 1982 Avignon festival, the Havel connection to Beckett's Protagonist (P) was made clearer by other tributes to Havel printed in the program, by Arthur Miller, Harold Pinter, and Tom Stoppard. P's dress also suggests the image of a prison inmate, and the unplayed play the ending of which is being rehearsed in *Catastrophe* may well be "about" P as a victim of imprisonment, interrogation, or torture. But whereas in Beckett all this is contained by the structuring metaphor of state-as-stage, the set in Havel's and Maponya's plays is a metonymic prison cell, the state-as-prison.

8. See Michel Foucault, *The History of Sexuality*, Vol. 1, trans. Robert Hurley (New York: Vintage, 1980), 140.

9. According to Judith Butler, "Gender is the repeated stylization of the body" (*Gender Trouble: Feminism and the Subversion of Identity* [New York and London: Routledge, 1990], 33).

10. Teresa de Lauretis, "Desire in Narrative," in *Alice Doesn't: Feminism, Semiotics, Cinema* (Bloomington: Indiana University Press, 1984), 103–15.

11. Margaret Randall argues that the new social movements in Eastern Europe, to recover from the failure of socialism —which she ascribes to the failure of its feminist imagination—need to break through precisely on this point (Margaret Randall, *Gathering Rage*, 37, 101–9, 114–18.)

12. Adrienne Rich, *On Lies, Secrets, and Silence: Selected Prose, 1966–1978* (New York: Norton, 1979), 299.

13. bell hooks, *Ain't I a Woman? Black Women and Feminism* (Boston: South End, 1981), 125–48.

14. Václav Havel, "The Power of the Powerless," in *Living in Truth*, ed. Jan Vladislav (London: Faber and Faber, 1987), 97 (see also 104, 114–17).

15. Václav Havel, *Letters to Olga*, trans. Paul Wilson (New York: Henry Holt, 1989), 276.

16. Candace West and Don H. Zimmerman, "Doing Gender," *Gender and Society* 1, no. 2 (June 1987): 125–51.

17. Michel Foucault, *History of Sexuality*, 1:139.

18. The issue of plagiarism prompts two reflections here. First, it is a case of allusion and appropriation rather than plagiarism *stricto sensu*, since Beckett's play had just been performed and published in several Western countries (including Britain and the United States, where *Gangsters* played), and the borrowings could hardly escape the attention of anyone who had seen or read *Catastrophe*. There is clearly no attempt to conceal indebtedness, though the clumsiness of a bald acknowledgment is avoided. Second, the thoughtful dissection of the power/knowledge relationships between texts and authors in Marilyn Randall's "Appropriate(d) Discourse: Plagiarism and Decolonization" (*New*

Literary History 22, no. 3 [Summer 1991]: 525–41) suggests that a literalist and heavy-handed wielding of plagiarism claims as a repressive weapon against decolonizing texts is simply "a strategy of institutional self-validation" (525). The relationship between *Gangsters* and *Catastrophe* is an absorbing case of the issues Randall discusses.

19. bell hooks, *Yearning: Race, Gender, and Cultural Politics* (Boston: South End, 1990); Andre Brink, *A Dry White Season* (London: W. H. Allen, 1979); J. M. Coetzee, *Waiting for the Barbarians* (London: Secker and Warburg, 1980); Nadine Gordimer, *Burger's Daughter* (London: Jonathan Cape, 1979).

20. Anthony O'Brien, "Literature in Another South Africa: Njabulo Ndebele's Theory of Emergent Culture," *diacritics* 22, no. 1 (Spring 1992): 72ff. See especially Njabulo Ndebele, "Artistic and Political Mirage: Mtshali's *Sounds of a Cowhide Drum*," in *Soweto Poetry*, ed. Michael Chapman (Johannesburg: McGraw-Hill, 1982), 190–93; and "The English Language and Social Change in South Africa," in *From South Africa: New Writing, Photographs and Art*, ed. David Bunn and Jane Taylor (Evanston: Northwestern University Press, 1987), 217–35.

21. Percy Mtwa, *Bopha!* and Mbongeni Ngema, *Asinamali!* Both plays are in *Ndlovu, Woza Afrika!*.

22. Robert Kavanagh, *Theatre and Cultural Struggle in South Africa* (London: Zed, 1985), 62.

23. Paul Gilroy, *"There Ain't No Black in the Union Jack": The Cultural Politics of Race and Nation* (Chicago: University of Chicago Press, 1991), 39. Gilroy suggests that this inclusive political identification of "black" in Britain is being lost, but in South Africa it has continued into the era of the United Democratic Front and beyond.

24. Steve Biko, *Black Consciousness in South Africa*, ed. Millard Arnold (New York: Random House, 1978); Robert Fatton Jr., *Black Consciousness in South Africa: The Dialectics of Ideological Resistance to White Supremacy* (Albany: State University of New York Press, 1986); Anthony Marx, *Lessons of Struggle: South African Internal Opposition, 1960–1990* (New York: Oxford University Press, 1992).

25. Paul Gilroy's careful distinction between older, reductive forms of class analysis of race and the necessary new analysis of the "formation" of both class and race as historically open categories I take as exemplary of this last position (*"There Ain't No Black in the Union Jack,"* 20–40).

26. Mongane Serote, writing in 1989 as a former Black Consciousness member who (like Ndebele) became a cultural spokesperson for the nonracial ANC, suggests that this deepening of Black Consciousness also derived from increasing knowledge of the *history* of resistance struggles, a history of which the young adherents of Black Consciousness were deprived during the repressive 1960s. See "Culture, Literature and Liberation," in Serote's *On the Horizon* (Fordsburg: Congress of South African Writers, 1990), 22–26.

27. Toni Morrison, "Unspeakable Things Unspoken: The Afro-American Presence in American Literature," *Michigan Quarterly Review* 28, no. 1 (Winter 1989): 1–34.

28. Mthuli Shezi, *Shanti*, in *South African People's Plays*, ed. Robert Mshengu Kavanagh (London: Heinemann, 1981), 63–84.

29. Martin Orkin points out the influence of black theology on the theater of Ngema and Mtwa (*Drama and the South African State*, 221–26). For Caravaggio's *Deposition*, see Giorgio Bonsanti, *Caravaggio* (Florence: Scala, 1984), 46–50.

30. See selections from *Black Mamba Rising: South African Worker Poets in Struggle* (edited by Ari Sitas), in Bunn and Taylor, *From South Africa: New Writing, Photographs and Art*, 273–304; and Alfred Temba Qabula, *Cruel Beyond Belief: A Working Life* (Durban: National Union of Metalworkers of South Africa, 1989).

31. *Staffrider* 6, no. 4 (1983): 23.

32. *Gangsters,* program notes by Duma Ndlovu for the *Woza Afrika!* festival production, Lincoln Center, New York, 1986.

33. Cf. Ketu H. Katrak's critique of Ghandi's use of the woman as sacrificial figure in the Satyagraha movement, with its mixed results for Indian feminism, in "Indian Nationalism, Ghandian 'Satyagraha,' and Representations of Female Sexuality," in *Nationalisms and Sexualities*, ed. Andrew Parker et al. (New York and London: Routledge, 1992), 395–406.

34. *Current Writing* 2 (1990). See also Desiree Lewis, "The Politics of Feminism in South Africa" (*Staffrider* 10, no. 3 [1992]: 15–21), a critical review of the first conference on women and gender in southern Africa, held at the University of Natal in 1991.

8.

W. B. Worthen

Convicted Reading: *The Island,*
Hybridity, Performance

Scene from a play: *Two sacks onstage. Goad enters from right, and prods sack on
right. A man gets out of the sack and prays. He dresses slowly, picks up both sacks and
moves them to center stage. He places his empty sack to the left of the other sack,
undresses, leaves his clothes in a heap, and enters the sack. Goad enters from right, and
prods sack on right. A man gets out of the sack, exercises vigorously, dresses quickly,
picks up both sacks and moves them to the left side of the stage. He places his empty
sack to the left of the other sack, undresses, leaves his clothes neatly folded, and enters
the sack. Goad enters from right, and prods sack on right. The first man gets out of the
sack and prays.*

Scene from a play: *Two men asleep onstage, both wearing identical, nondescript costumes—khaki shirt, short pants. Their heads are shaven. They rise. Mime: each
mimes digging, filling a wheelbarrow, pushing it to where the other man is digging.
This routine continues for some time. Whistle. The men stop digging and stand side
by side. Whistle. They begin running in strict, but mirrored unison, as though each
were linked to the other by the wrist and ankle.*

I have tried to describe the opening action of two plays, more or less from
the point of view of an audience: the first is Samuel Beckett's *Act Without
Words II;* the second is the opening mime of Athol Fugard, John Kani, and
Winston Ntshona's *The Island.* The resemblance between the two plays is
hardly accidental. Fugard had directed Kani and Ntshona in the Serpent
Players' production of Genet's *Death Watch* in 1968, and Fugard's own
involvement with the theater of the absurd extends at least from his all-black
production of *Waiting for Godot* in 1962 through the Beckettian resonance of
Boesman and Lena, first staged in 1969. Indeed, Fugard's initial notes for *The
Island* draw the themes of the play into a neat constellation with the absurd
and glance at one of Fugard's favorite writers, Albert Camus: "*Meaningless
Absurd Labour:* Punishment. Sisyphus."[1] "Tied" like Pozzo and Lucky, John

and Winston evoke the familiar pseudocouple of Beckett and his silent film progenitors: "[T]he classic double act: They evoke Laurel and Hardy or Didi and Gogo; John is the comic and Winston the straight man."[2] This absurdist texture is visible in the theater as well as on the page. Reviewing the 1974 New York production, Clive Barnes found the opening mime "hopelessly prolonged, until slowly one realizes one is being given a touch of tedium, a small, painless hint of the boredom that is the prisoner's most constant companion."[3] The Island uses the conventions of absurdist theater both to represent and—in a highly mediated, theatrical simulacrum—to reproduce the dehumanizing experience of prison life, the absurd feel of its appalling, arbitrary routine.[4]

The Island represents the carceral body, the body subject to the racialized power/knowledge of apartheid, through one of the dominant modes of modern Western theatrical representation, the technology of the absurd. Indeed, The Island is a palimpsest of forms and provides a particularly forceful instance of the ideological and interpretive challenges posed by the formal hybridity of resistant theatrical production. The Island shapes its critique of state authority through a variety of means, some drawn from the dominant modes of Western theater (theater of the absurd, the avant-garde aesthetics of Jerzy Grotowski's "poor theater," the classical model of Sophocles' Antigone) while others (storytelling and oral performance traditions, conventions of direct address and individual performance) are drawn from popular and indigenous performance genres. This formal hybridity is characteristic of South African theater, a theater in which various boundaries between indigenous and imported, traditional and contemporary, communal and elite are typically in play. Yet Temple Hauptfleisch's recent outline of the "interrelated polysystem of performance" in South Africa in the 1970s and 1980s suggests the difficulty of generalizing about the ideological work of hybrid forms.[5] In one respect, for instance, The Island's formal hybridity seems consistent with the "central and dominant form within the South African theatre system" (75), plays that use "local content" and "Western theatrical forms to produce plays intended for presentation to elite bourgeois audiences schooled in Western concepts of theatre and theatrical convention" (74). At the same time, it also illustrates the impact of "alternative" theater, using "techniques developed elsewhere, in order to confront the realities of South African society" (76), especially "experimental, non-mainstream improvisational performances based on Brechtian and Grotowskian models" (67). Hauptfleisch rightly argues that "it is at times difficult to separate out the provenance of the individual techniques used, as the new hybrid work truly constitutes a gestalt of its own" (77).

This sense of hybridity—of a syncretic art reflecting "concern with social change and with the relations between indigenous and foreign"— points, however, not to a bland blending of depoliticized forms but to an arena in which cultural hegemony is contested through the contestation of its instruments, the forms through which dominant culture represents and extends its authority.[6] In this sense, the role attributed to "dominant" or "hegemonic" forms in constituting the "meaning" of the hybrid whole is particularly problematic. For to derive the meaning of a hybrid work from privileged (Western) forms of signification—the absurd, poor theater, *Antigone*—is precisely to repress the agency of local speech and to "reincorporate postcolonial culture to a new internationalist and universalist paradigm" that maintains the relative privilege of Western cultural forms.[7] At the same time, to ignore the history of such forms, the ways they have conventionally been seen to signify, and so to privilege, certain modes of interpretation, is to enact a willing blindness to the working of hegemony, which typically naturalizes the instruments of its enforced consensus. Of course, the work of form is historically bound. To think of "realistic" theater in Norway in the 1880s, in New York in the 1930s, or in Buenos Aires in the 1970s is to recognize the dialectical relationship between the temporality of form and the immediacy of performance. The politics of theater is irreducibly local, arising from a specific event taking place here, tonight, with these performers and this audience. Yet the immediacy of theatrical performance is dialectically related to the history of forms, both literary or dramatic forms and the formal conventions of performance history. Performance enunciates an interpretive dissonance between the historical and the immediate, between the formal ideology of genre and the differential politics of its concrete implementation. To speak of absurdist drama or poor theater is to summon modes of representation cunningly inscribed with their own critical history, a sense of the kinds of uses and meanings these forms legitimately produce. Although this history need not determine the meaning of any performance, a performance is often traced by the ways such forms are thought to construct meaning by both performers and audiences. Indeed, "forms," like "canons," are the effect of interpretation, the application of interpretive practices that identify "similarities" between various works and privilege those features as the determining signs of form or genre. The ideological work of form lies less in the essential or innate nature of form itself than in the ways that notions of form are used to legitimate certain kinds of interpretation and repress others.

These questions are raised with particular urgency by plays like *The Island*, in which the apparently "resistant" invocation of hegemonic forms asks us to consider how—or whether—forms can be redirected, made to perform different kinds of work. As Ian Steadman suggests, in South African theater "cultural expression arising out of the dominant traditions does not necessarily simply exhibit the elitist concerns of a marginalised minority."[8] Hybrid works like *The Island* invite an interrogation of the work of form in history. Here, then, I want to reconsider the signification of Western performance forms—poor theater and especially theater of the absurd—rather than assume their significance to ask how the relations of authority typical of poor theater are represented in Fugard, Kani, and Ntshona's collaboration and how "absurd" representation and the kinds of interpretation it has historically privileged may be subjected to critique by being repositioned within (not above) the hybridized, politicized arena of the play's performance.

Fugard's invocation of Jerzy Grotowski's "poor theater" is well known in this regard and can be used to sketch some of the challenges posed by hybridized invocation of the forms of dominant culture. Loren Kruger has aptly characterized the use of poor theater techniques—"few actors with a minimum of props performing in a variety of multipurpose spaces"—as "not so much the attributes of artistic experimentation in the European avant-garde tradition of Grotowski or Brecht as the means of an 'intermediate technology' for the dissemination of information and the symbolic enactment of particular local issues."[9] This account points to the ease with which performance forms—poor theater, Brechtian alienation—can be dissolved from their original aesthetic and political affiliations and adapted to different purposes. In this sense, plays like *The Island* and Percy Mtwa, Mbongeni Ngema, and Barney Simon's *Woza Albert!* transform Grotowski's purely aesthetic "acceptance of poverty in theatre"[10] by marking poverty not as the sign of a chosen aesthetic discipline but as the enforced discipline of political oppression. When access to "rich theater" is publicly denied or forbidden (as of 1992 there were still no actual theater buildings in the townships of South Africa),[11] the exigencies of poor theater become functionally subversive. "*The actor is a man who works in public with his body, offering it publicly.*"[12] The apartheid state overdetermines the racialized public body, assigning racial identity as a means of controling the social agency of its subjects. In this context, the subversiveness of poor theater stems in part from its urgent display of the *black* body's exuberant, transformative power.[13]

As Stephen Gray suggests, "the influence of Grotowski alone does not explain Fugard's changing attitudes to the possibilities of theatre in South Africa" in the 1970s, and a full account of the working of poor theater would engage its reciprocal likeness to various indigenous forms of performance.[14] Yet Fugard singles out Grotowski as "in every sense the *agent provocateur* at that moment in my career," and the deployment of poor theater in *The Island* also illustrates the difficulty of assuming that modes of hegemonic cultural production can be easily or fully refunctioned.[15] Fugard makes it clear that he responded strongly to Grotowski's central emphasis on an actor-centered theater, one in which the actor's extreme self-confrontation lays the groundwork for a fully vulnerable act of self-disclosure, the "total gift of himself" to the audience (*Towards a Poor Theatre*, 16). Yet, despite Fugard's allusion to "the holy actor as opposed to the courtesan actor—truth versus pretence—the 'poor' theatre as opposed to the 'rich' theatre, etc.," the deepest relationship between Fugard's work and Grotowski's lies in the relations of authority—between author/director, performers, and text—governing the production of poor theater.[16] The politics of poor theater are marked by its essential confrontation between the actor and the spectator, a suspension of the construction of "self" and "other" that might align poor theater with a Derridean critique of the metaphysics of presence and open a more searching deconstruction of the naturalized hierarchies of identity structuring Western ideology. In practice, though, poor theater is also traced by a fidelity to authority—the authority of a recoverable self, the authorized functions and relations of theatrical production, the cultural authority of canonized texts, the author—in ways that blunt its claims to such a foundational critique.

Poor theater is insistently a director's theater. Grotowski describes a complex channel of guidance and response between director ("producer" in this translation) and performer: "The producer, while guiding and inspiring the actor, must at the same time allow himself to be guided and inspired by him. It is a question of freedom, partnership, and this does not imply a lack of discipline but a respect for the autonomy of others" (258). Although Grotowski clearly avoids the classic model of the director-dictator (epitomized by Stanislavski and Reinhardt), responsibility for the shape of the production is lodged firmly in the production's auteur. The auteur of poor theater trains the actors, produces the textual collage that structures the performance—in Grotowski's work, a collage layered on narratives drawn from the canon of

European drama such as Calderón's *The Constant Prince,* Marlowe's *Doctor Faustus,* Wyspianski's *Akropolis,* and the mélange of texts in *Apocalypsis cum figuris*—and designs the environmental mise en scène that positions the audience within the performance space.

While Fugard politicizes its aesthetics, his sense of poor theater is haunted by the principles of authority animating Grotowski's work. Fugard's account of his first experiment in poor theater is revealing. He took "an idea involving an incident in our recent South African history . . . a young man took a bomb into the Johannesburg station concourse as an act of protest."

> It killed an old woman. He was eventually caught and hanged. I super-
> imposed, almost in the sense of a palimpsest, this image on that of
> Clytemnestra and her two children, Orestes and Electra. There was no
> text. No single piece of paper passed between myself and the actors.
> Three of them. Anyway, after about twelve weeks of totally private
> rehearsals we got around to what we called our first "exposure." This
> was an experience that lasted for sixty minutes, had about 300 words, a
> lot of action—strange, almost somnambulistic action—and silence. It
> was called *Orestes.*[17]

As he would in his later work on *The Island,* Fugard follows Grotowski in positioning himself as the performers' guide, using classical narratives as the formative images to structure the actors' work. Without providing a written text, Fugard nonetheless composes the performance: "What was so marvellous in working on this project, along lines suggested by Grotowski and my own experience, was just how pristine, what weight you gave to a line, a word, a gesture, if you set it in silence."

In practice, poor theater (Fugard's as well as Grotowski's) emerges as a logocentric, theological theater surprisingly at odds with Artaud's theater of cruelty; poor theater is traced by the logos, the palpable authority of an absent text, a text that allusively gathers the immediate performance into the web of classical textuality. Despite its appropriation by the theatrical avant-garde of the 1960s and 1970s, poor theater is fundamentally modernist in its conception of performance. Its environmental, participatory aesthetic implies a critique of representation by blurring the line between performer and spectator, by infecting the space of representation with the audience's presence. Yet this critique is lodged within a final commitment to the performers' self-presence and a cognate sense of the elusive wholeness of Western literary and cultural tradition, a tradition that can still be evoked (in whatever ruptured and refracted form) for its explanatory power, fragments shored against the ruin. This modernist dissociation between the aesthetic and the political is entwined with *The Island*'s complex involvement with poor theater. For, while *The Island* is an example of poor theater, it also stages poor theater in John and Winston's production of *Antigone,* and these two registers of poor theater operate differently in the hybrid context of the play. The characters' dramatized *Antigone* represents poor theater's complicity in the modernist trajectory I have outlined: their "poor" performance is a resistant gesture but is fully contained by the apparatus of apartheid culture. Although Winston's performance as Antigone stages a moral opposition to state domination, it also implies that to speak the voice of dominant culture is to be threatened with a comic and feminizing mimicry; beyond that, the play concludes with a final absurdist vignette of pointless and exhausting abjection.[18] As Loren Kruger has shrewdly remarked of the Serpent Players' 1965 performance of *Antigone,* the "poor" production of *Antigone* in *The Island* represents "an extension of access, rather than a *popular appropriation* of hegemonic forms." But *The Island* itself is also a version of poor theater, a performance the politics of which originally emerged less from the invocation of *Antigone* than from the "*actors'* collective defiance in performing banned information about the Island" rather than on "the isolated *character's* position as victim."[19]

These two hybridizations of poor theater are not completely independent, though, for the work of cultural authorization and containment implied in John and Winston's production of *Antigone* is in some ways duplicated by the crisis of authority surrounding the production of *The Island* itself.[20] The instability of the characters' use of *Antigone* as a strategy of resistance enacts an instability in the play's status as property, for, despite the appearance of the names Athol Fugard, John Kani, and Winston Ntshona on the title page of the play, collaborative authorship is at once asserted and withheld: *The Island* is "devised by" Fugard, Kani, and Ntshona rather than being "written by"—or merely "by"—them. The narrative of *The Island*'s devising is beset by questions of authority. As Peter Rosenwald reports in his 1974 interview with Kani and Ntshona,

> To create the metaphor of this "sacred ground," Fugard took a large blanket and spread it outside his house on the grass. He asked Winston and John to explore its space, to stand in the centre, to walk around its

edge. Time and again Fugard would halve the space of the blanket until at last there was just room for the two actors to stand. Then he asked them: "What do you think it means?" Their answer was that it was a cell, that he had shrunk their liberty to move. They knew instantly where this was leading and they decided to follow: "To take the island and to say something about it. We joined our hands, closed the garage door and after two weeks, fourteen days, we were on stage in Cape Town," Kani says.[21]

As in the *Orestes* project, the "poor" improvisation is guided by Fugard's absent text—Rosenwald suggests that "the idea of 'The Island' was lurking in Athol Fugard's thoughts" after the success of *Sizwe Bansi is Dead*—which Kani and Ntshona are urged to "discover." Kani remarks that "Athol came up with the idea that there is a place we never talk about, no one can write about, the press cannot talk about, not even white South Africans, free as they are can talk about. It is the nightmare of every member of Parliament. What will happen to it in the end? That is, Robben Island" (the island prison, which could not be mentioned by name in the press, or in other public media like the theater).[22] Yet Kani also suggests that the period of writing and exploration was often tense, with Fugard asking questions that implied to Kani and Ntshona that "maybe he doesn't understand us as we thought he did. [. . .] Athol is a white man in South Africa. John and Winston are black men in South Africa. Sometimes it is difficult or even impossible for us to understand what operates in those little white boxes. And we fought, and we got very mad and yelled and cried."[23] And in a 1976 interview Kani responded to the question "You are more responsible for the play?" with a clear "Yes! We selected an issue as artists and used ourselves to deal with certain issues that affect our lives in a special context, our country."[24] For his part, Fugard regards the play as fully collaborative and typically describes the collaboration as one requiring him to suspend an "authorial" will to power over the text in order to assimilate the performative contribution of Kani and Ntshona. When asked whether he would have written *Sizwe Bansi* or *The Island* differently had he not collaborated, Fugard remarked, "On the credit side, I think they might have had a more economical structure. On the debit side, having written them and having presented them to actors, such as John and Winston, the very special energy that they use in performance might have been inhibited." While he appreciates the contribution of his collaborators, Fugard seems wistful for the closure of an authorized text. While Kani and Ntshona's work enhances the success of the performance, their involvement tends to violate the formal integrity of the literary product, the formal work: a "looseness and skimpy structural organization informs both those plays. Because you rely on the actor so much, there's a danger also of losing that marvelous ambiguity of metaphor."[25]

Much as the politics of *The Island* may originally have derived from the circumstances of its performance—rather than the events of the drama—so the politics of its use of poor theater may also arise in part from the working relations, and the proprietary relations, it created. John and Winston's production of *Antigone* in the play engages them in a ventriloquized conversation with cultural authority; the "devising" of *The Island* seems to have involved Fugard, Kani, and Ntshona in the strikingly asymmetrical dialogue of authority between actors and auteur characteristic of poor theater and finally unresolved by the play's subsequent history. The controversial matter of authorship is engaged in different ways by Fugard, Kani, and Ntshona, and the play's critics, and it points to a continuing desire to locate an author, "that principle of closure, of semiotic inhibition, employed in the conflict of interpretations to privilege certain readings and control 'unruly meanings.'"[26] Hybridizing poor theater in several ways, *The Island* involves this mode of dominant cultural reproduction as an arena of cultural contestation; poor theater emerges as a means of political theater at those moments— authorship, performance—in which its form is implemented locally: in working relations, property relations, and the political engagements of mutual theatrical production.

But poor theater might also seem a special case, an "experimental" genre already marginal to dominant culture and so perhaps more readily adaptable to resistant theater. *The Island*'s relationship to the theater of the absurd is more complex in this regard; not only is absurd theater a more widely recognized and disseminated dramatic and performance genre, but it has a more articulate and consistent critical history as well. Yet the hybridization of the absurd in *The Island* enacts the dialectic of form and performance in ways analogous to the play's unstable and contradictory relation to poor theater. Let me return, then, to my synopsis of the initial mime of *The Island*. In part, perhaps, because it is mimed, the opening vignette seems to supply the materials of absurdist signification: an existential plateau, generalized characters who assume the status of allegorical everymen, and repetitive action as the sign of the pointless and arbitrary routines of human life. To read the khaki costumes, for example, in the register of the absurd is to read them under the sign of this allegorizing, universalizing discourse. Like the indistinguishable long gray or black garments worn by characters in Beckett's later plays—*Ohio Impromptu, What Where,* and *Catastrophe* come to mind—the characters' shaved heads and identical clothing claim the individual body for the dominant thematic and symbolic concerns of the text, producing a symbolic image onstage. "I produce an object," Beckett once remarked, "What people make of it is not my concern."[27] At the same time, this identification of the absurd involves a complex erasure of the historical and cultural particularity of the stage image, an erasure perhaps more easily imagined in New York or London than in Cape Town and Johannesburg. Absurd interpretation, in this sense, may work to express the existential despair of prison life, but it does so precisely by erasing the material specificity of the scene: by rendering the *"prison uniform"* as a costume,[28] by assimilating the guard's whistle to the apparatus of the property closet (on a shelf alongside the mysterious whistle of *Act Without Words I* and the jarring bell of *Happy Days*) rather than the equipment locker of the prison, and by overlooking the race of the characters as interpretively significant—"whitening" them, to recall Beckett's Director, by identifying them with the universals of the absurd rather than with the specificity of Robben Island.[29]

To see the play's affiliation with the absurd, then, as Anglo-American criticism has often done, is to assert the possibility of a particular kind of hybrid reading, the effort to hold both the local (Robben Island) and the "universal" (the arbitrariness of the absurd) in hand at once, to see the absurdist texture qualifying, enlarging, and explaining the local, historical scene of South African apartheid. Albert Wertheim, for example, implies as much when he enlarges the absurd scene to the nation itself: "The Island is not merely Robben Island but South Africa itself, an absurd prison with absurd rules enforced by absurd officials."[30] Yet, for an audience inclined to read the signifiers of the stage more locally (as, perhaps, the play's Johannesburg and Cape Town audiences were inclined to do), this absurd register is positioned differently relative to the play's meaning. Readers of the play, of course, are alerted to its location immediately—"*Centre stage: a raised area representing a cell on Robben Island*" (47)—but this signifier is not directly available to theater audiences. Indeed, in 1973 it was illegal to discuss Robben Island openly. As John Kani remarks, the setting of *The Island* was literally ob-scene, a site "we never talk about, no one can write about, the press cannot talk about, not even white South Africans, free as they are can talk about."[31] In this sense, absurdist abstraction functioned less to universalize or allegorize the subjects of representation than to make a local reading possible: "The work was devised to survive certain regulations and conditions and the work was devised to live in that situation."[32]

(A) Absurdist everymen. (B) Prisoners of the politics of race. (C) All of the above. It's inviting to pursue the third alternative, the both/and interpretation favored by most Fugard critics and implied in Fugard's notes on the play. This vision of the play may be almost inevitable when it is produced in Europe, the United States, or other venues where the legacy of absurdist theater is familiar. But this reading carefully avoids the problematic Brechtian question, the question also posed by John and Winston's production of *Antigone*—"which is the pretext for what?"[33] From its inception—at least from Martin Esslin's *The Theatre of the Absurd,* published in 1961—interpretation of absurd theater has authorized the local as the sign of the universal, the abstract, and the arbitrary. More recently, this gesture has been used to represent the "arbitrary" working of totalitarian state oppression, as though the techniques that represent the allegorized everyman's confrontation with the arbitrariness of existence are akin to the instruments of a very particular state of being, the state of state control, whether in San Quentin, Robben Island, Mrozek's Poland, Stoppard and Havel's pre–Velvet Revolution Czechoslovakia, or the unnamed states of Pinter's *One for the Road* and *Mountain Language,* or even Beckett's *Catastrophe.* But this likeness raises a troubling possibility: perhaps the theater of the absurd is not merely a way to stage authoritarian oppression but an extension of it, a literal and a figurative ideological state apparatus. In this view, the ideology of the absurd, with its universalizing tendency, represses local, political, resistant signification and implies a much more contestatory relationship between the performance modes hybridized in *The Island.* Anthony O'Brien, for example, observes that the central image of *Catastrophe*—the Protagonist standing on his block "under the Director's appraising eye while the Assistant adjusts him"—derives "from the life-world of racial slavery and colonialism: the auction-block, the master's dining-room, the colonial parade ground."[34] More to the point, to see the absurdist texture of *The Island* as a decoy, a means of enabling the subversive reading of the obscene, is to suggest not so much that prison is an instance of the metaphysics of the absurd nor that the politics of apartheid are absurd. It is to suggest instead that the ideology of the absurd is invisible to the apparatus of the apartheid state. As Lukács remarks, "The only ideology which men will not feel to be an ideology is one

which prevails absolutely and tolerates no opposition or doubt; only such a one ceases to be abstract and intellectual and is entirely transformed into feeling."[35] In *The Island,* the metaphysic of the absurd is the ideology of the state.

This interpretive tension dates to the critical origins of the theater of the absurd. Indeed, the particular formulation of the local and immediate as the sign of "metaphysical anguish" owes itself less to Beckett's *Waiting for Godot* than to Martin Esslin's landmark study. Robben Island is, of course, not the first prison in which Didi and Gogo have appeared.

> On 19 November 1957, a group of worried actors were preparing to face their audience. The actors were members of the company of the San Francisco Actors' Workshop. The audience consisted of fourteen hundred convicts at the San Quentin penitentiary. No live play had been performed at San Quentin since Sarah Bernhardt appeared there in 1913. Now, forty-four years later, the play that had been chosen, largely because no woman appeared in it, was Samuel Beckett's *Waiting for Godot.*[36]

Esslin uses this remarkable production to outline the signal immediacy of the play, how "what had bewildered the sophisticated audiences of Paris, London, and New York was immediately grasped by an audience of convicts." To illustrate, he cites several of the convicts' responses to a *San Francisco Chronicle* reporter: "One prisoner told him, 'Godot is society.' Said another: 'He's the outside.' A teacher at the prison was quoted as saying, 'They know what is meant by waiting.'" Esslin concludes this fascinating account by citing an article from the prison newspaper as exemplary of "how clearly the writer had understood the meaning of the play."

> It was an expression, symbolic in order to avoid all personal error, by an author who expected each member of his audience to draw his own conclusions, make his own errors. It asked nothing in point, it forced no dramatized moral on the viewer, it held out no specific hope. . . . We're still waiting for Godot, and shall continue to wait. When the scenery gets too drab and the action too slow, we'll call each other names and swear to part forever—but then, there's no place to go!
> (2–3)

In fact, "turns of phrase and characters from the play, have since become a permanent part of the private language, the institutional mythology of San Quentin" (3), an eerie anticipation of the later course of absurdist theater itself.

Esslin implies that the first audience to grasp the play did so precisely by reading the play in light of its own immediate, local, and material situation. Chosen precisely in order to avoid inflaming the audience of a men's penitentiary—"largely because no woman appeared in it"—*Godot* confronted the inmates "with a situation in some ways analogous to their own" (3).[37] Yet, despite his scorn for those sophisticated metropolitan audiences, Esslin is reluctant to grant special interpretive authority to the prisoners of San Quentin, whose ability to read the themes, gestures, language, and atmosphere of arbitrary constraint clearly arises from their circumstances. For, in the words of "'Godot' Gets Around," one of Esslin's sources,

> A favorite character with the audience was Lucky, the slave. Said one member, "I just don't know . . . but I'd go back to see it tomorrow night. Anyway, maybe they'll bring something else over here. Maybe next month, or next year—or whenever. Like the man said, 'Nothing happens.'"
>
> Michael Harris of the San Francisco *Chronicle,* one of the reporters permitted to watch the performance, noted that the identification of Godot himself seemed somewhat easier for the San Quentin audience than for the average group. One prisoner told him, "Godot is society." Said another: "He's the Outside."[38]

A day, a month, a year: at the moment that *Godot* signifies the local, the prisoners' sympathy with Lucky's servitude and their understanding of the social context of their seemingly endless waiting, Esslin argues that legitimate interpretation should read through the densely immediate texture of this performance to find that *Godot,* like the plays of Adamov, Ionesco, Genet, and others, concerns the "sense of metaphysical anguish at the absurdity of the human condition" (5).

Granted, the theater of the absurd is less apparently invested in intellectual abstraction than the theater of Camus or Sartre, who articulate an existentialist thematics through the formal, literary complexity of plot and character. Instead, the theater of the absurd "strives to express its sense of the senselessness of the human condition and the inadequacy of the rational approach by the open abandonment of rational devices and discursive thought" (6), largely by presenting its themes "in being—that is, in terms of concrete stage images" that cast the spectator in a position of interpretive aporia akin to that felt by the characters. The thematics of the absurd arise less from the interpretation of the drama than from the experience of the theater itself. But, while we might expect this account of how absurd theater signifies to valorize the material specificity of theatrical performance—in San Quentin or elsewhere—Esslin locates its meaning in dramatic conventions shaped by the aesthetics of international modernism and "broadly based on ancient strands of the Western tradition" (8). Indeed, Esslin argues that the only way to understand a "completely new and revolutionary convention" (10) is to place it "within its historical context"; an "examination of the works themselves" reveals absurd theater to be "part of an old tradition that may at times have been submerged but that can be traced back to antiquity" (9). Despite the fact that the San Quentin convicts seemed to find plenty of immediate relevance in the play, Esslin argues that only a universalizing interpretive paradigm—recourse either to the thematics of "metaphysical anguish" or to an equally universalizing understanding of literary history—can enable the "relevance and force" of the theater of the absurd to "emerge as clearly to the reader as *Waiting for Godot* did to the convicts of San Quentin" (10).

Yet the convicts' interpretation of *Godot* is "relevant" in another sense, implying its own critique of the metaphysics of the absurd. For the inmates' impression that Godot is "society" or the "Outside" points to a deeply political reading of the play, one perhaps enabled by their own captivity. Much as the absent Godot is the principle that organizes the lives of Didi and Gogo, at once determining their experience and evacuating it of meaning, so "society" at once determines and evacuates the lives of its inmates (those in San Quentin as well as those "Outside"), operating through a similarly oppressive strategy—mystifying its arbitrary authority by claiming it as inevitable, natural, existential, and metaphysical. In this sense, *The Island*'s contradictory invocation of the politics of the absurd is traced in the origin of the "theater of the absurd" itself. Esslin invites us to read through the local, material events and bodies onstage, to see them as the sign, the image of a metaphysical and abstract meaning. The convicts see the experience of the bodies onstage as more directly relevant to their immediate, local, social condition, and the gesture to the "metaphysical" itself enacts the structure of power that deprives the local—the staged bodies, their bodies—of meaning and value.

To construct stage action as absurd is to read through the local to the

metaphysical or universal. In *The Island,* however, this universalizing interpretive practice—in addition to the arbitrary thematics of the absurd—is
itself closely aligned with the rhetoric of apartheid. How, then, are we to
read the opening and closing vignettes of *The Island* when the absurd is at
once partly a vehicle of political critique and—as the diversion that enables
the critique to take place—complicit in the reproduction of the state it
seems to criticize? I say "we" advisedly here, not meaning to homogenize
the very different situation of the play's various audiences, nor to claim a
factitious identification between Anglo-American criticism and the interpretation of any South African audience, nor merely to note my own social
and cultural positioning (white, male, privileged, American) relative to the
play's original production or its subject matter. Part of *The Island*'s purchase
as a critique of apartheid appears to involve a critical invocation of familiar
forms of hegemonic stage and literary representation, forms of cultural
reproduction that are part of the history of modernity, a history of which I
am a part, and of which in all probability you—*hypocrite lecteur*—are a part as
well, whatever our different configurations in relation to that history may
be.[39] How are "we" to understand the various potentialities of hybrid forms
like *The Island,* two of which I have tried to outline here? Although these
concerns were certainly inflected differently in 1973 in Cape Town and are
inflected differently by various ways of performing the text—onstage, in
reading, in cultural critique—the play's complex theorization of the politics
of hybrid production cannot be assigned in any pure or final way to a single
moment or site of production. In theory, as well as in performance, *The
Island* continues to enact the problematic relation of the modes of cultural
production it puts into play. In place of a bland hybridity, the performative
discourses in *The Island* seem internally confrontational, suggestive of a
larger paradigm of the third world's relation to modernity itself. As Homi K.
Bhabha argues, postcolonial perspectives "intervene in those ideological discourses of modernity that attempt to give a hegemonic 'normality' to the
uneven development and the differential, often disadvantaged, histories of
nations, races, communities, peoples."[40] Hybridity in this sense enables not
only an interrogation of the changing use of form, but a critical intervention
in the ongoing performance of the forms of modern culture.

NOTES

1. Athol Fugard, *Notebooks, 1960–1977* (Johannesburg: AD. Donker, 1983), 212.
Subsequent page references to Fugard's *Notebooks* are to this edition and appear in the
text.

2. Russell Vandenbroucke, *Truths the Hand Can Touch: The Theatre of Athol Fugard* (New York: Theatre Communications Group, 1985), 129.

3. Clive Barnes, "'*The Island*,' A Powerful Tale of Prison Life," *New York Times*, November 25, 1974.

4. Criticism of *The Island* has repeatedly drawn the play's absurdist opening texture into a realistic account of prison life. Erroll Durbach, in "Sophocles in South Africa: Athol Fugard's *The Island*" (*Comparative Drama* 18 [1984]: 256), compares the opening mime to Beckett's *Play* and more specifically to "the absurdity of meaningless repetition" in *Endgame*. In a similar vein, Albert Wertheim remarks that "The Island is not merely Robben Island but South Africa itself, an absurd prison with absurd rules enforced by absurd officials" ("Political Acting and Political Action: Athol Fugard's *The Island*," *World Literature Written in English* 26 [1982]: 251). For a convenient chronology of Fugard's plays in production, see Stephen Gray, *Athol Fugard* (Johannesburg: McGraw-Hill, 1982), 3–14.

5. Temple Hauptfleisch, "Post-Colonial Criticism, Performance Theory, and the Evolving Forms of South African Theatre," *South African Theatre Journal* 6, no. 2 (September 1992): 66. Subsequent page references to this article appear in the text.

6. As Karin Barber remarks, "All art produced in present-day Africa is to some degree syncretic. All of it reflects some concern with social change and with the relations between the indigenous and the foreign. All performance art is concerned with establishing intimate responsive contact with the audience. And all art whatsoever is communicated through shared conventions which are to a greater or lesser degree elusive, changing and difficult to establish. . . . Modern popular arts are essentially syncretic; the conventions shared by their creators and audiences, because always emergent and undefined by any official canon of criticism, are exceptionally difficult to establish; their performance style, because it is designed to overcome the anonymity of the new urban crowd, is intensely concerned with the dissolution of distance, the creation or recreation of a rapport which traditional performers could take for granted. This gives modern urban popular forms from widely separated geographical areas with quite different traditional cultures a common style: a similarity of form, theme and presentation which makes them more like each other than they are like the 'traditional' or 'elite' arts of their own culture." Barber is quoted by Ian Steadman, in "The Uses of Theatre," *South African Theatre Journal* 6, no. 1 (May 1992): 35.

7. Bill Ashcroft, Gareth Griffiths, and Helen Tiffin, *The Empire Writes Back: Theory and Practice in Post-colonial Literatures* (London: Routledge, 1989), 155–56.

8. Steadman, "The Uses of Theatre," 38. As Steadman remarks, developing Raymond Williams's discussion of emergent, dominant, and residual elements of culture, "no area of culture is independent, no element of culture is spontaneously generated: there are continually changing relationships with other elements" (34). Yet, despite an incisive sense of the hybridity of South African performance, Steadman tends to see forms as "products" and popular cultural performance modes as processual and informal. This seems to misrepresent the way that dramatic forms operate in the theater, in which they are always processual, always being put into play, and also to sort oddly with the sense of the hybrid relations between performance forms that sustains this fine essay. For a careful discrimination between modes of "dominant" and "hegemonic" culture, see

Abdul R. JanMohamed, "The Economy of Manichean Allegory: The Function of Racial Difference in Colonialist Literature," in *"Race," Writing, and Difference,* ed. Henry Louis Gates, Jr. (Chicago: University of Chicago Press, 1986), 80–81.

9. Loren Kruger, "Apartheid on Display: South Africa Performs for New York," *Diaspora* 1, no. 2 (Fall 1991): 196.

10. Jerzy Grotowski, *Towards a Poor Theatre* (New York: Simon and Schuster, 1968), 21. Subsequent page references appear in the text and are to this edition.

11. Martin Orkin, "Whose Popular Theatre and Performance?" *South African Theatre Journal* 6, no. 2 (September 1992): 34.

12. Grotowski, *Towards a Poor Theatre,* 33, my emphasis.

13. Indeed, as Biodun Jeyifo argues, Fugard's thematization of poor theater is one of the ways his collaborative plays challenge "the inhuman claustrophobic space" typical of earlier plays; "the artificial, fragmented totalisation of experience which the walls erected by apartheid social-fascism create are negated," and replaced by a more fluid and flexible form that is "one of his most important contributions to contemporary drama. It would seem that Fugard has by this principle dialectically converted an initial disadvantage, and initial restrictive structure, into a dramaturgic technique of lasting value" (Biodun Jeyifo, *The Truthful Lie: Essays in a Sociology of African Drama* [London: Port of Spain, 1985], 102–3).

14. Gray continues, "Euro- and albicentric critics, one should add, who attribute all useful theatrical invention to the West, fail here to notice that Fugard might also have learned techniques of story-telling and methods of communally evolving dramatic ritual with its own unique structures from his African acquaintances as well. With the Serpent Players in New Brighton, Port Elizabeth, starting as early as 1963, 'poor theatre' without the elaborate machinery of modern playhouses was the norm, and the elevation of the actor from mere interpreter into co-creator had always been an element in Fugard's productions, even of the chamber plays. What distinguishes this new period, then, is the admission of the raw material of the lives of others into the very creative process; the 'writer' is demoted into a 'scribe' or go-between, a catalyst and a recording organiser" (Gray, *Athol Fugard,* 20).

15. Athol Fugard, "Introduction," in *Statements: Two Workshop Productions Devised by Athol Fugard, John Kani, and Winston Ntshona,* Sizwe Bansi Is Dead *and* The Island, *and a New Play,* Statements After an Arrest Under the Immorality Act (Oxford: Oxford University Press, 1974). The main lines of Grotowski's theatrical experimentation have— since the early 1970s, the period of their widest dissemination—faded somewhat, and may be worth recalling here. Grotowski's work with the Laboratory Theater responded to a sense of cultural crisis, a kind of alienation: "The rhythm of life in modern civilisation is characterised by pace, tension, a feeling of doom, the wish to hide our personal motives and the assumption of a variety of roles and masks in life" (*Towards a Poor Theatre,* 255). The theater's "therapeutic function" (256) emerges when the actor is able to become fully exposed to himself and to the spectator, through what Grotowski calls the *via negativa,* removing culturally imposed barriers to complete self-recognition, to make a "total gift of himself" (16). That is, while Grotowski's training—both the physical and the psychological—is directed toward removing the actor's desire to "act"—that is, conceal, mask, falsify himself—this theater is fundamentally collaborative.

It is true that the actor accomplishes this act, but he can only do so through an encounter with the spectator—intimately, visibly, not hiding behind a cameraman, wardrobe mistress, stage designer or make-up girl—in direct confrontation with him, and somehow "instead of" him. The actor's act—discarding half measures, revealing, opening up, emerging from himself as opposed to closing up—is an invitation to the spectator. This act could be compared to an act of the most deeply rooted, genuine love between two human beings—this is just a comparison since we can only refer to this "emergence from oneself" through analogy. This act, paradoxical and borderline, we call a total act. In our opinion it epitomizes the actor's deepest calling. (256)

It might be noted that reviews of Fugard, Kani, and Ntshona's collaborations suggest the success of Fugard's assimilation of Grotowski. Elsa Joubert, for example, reviewing *Statements after an Arrest under the Immorality Act*, suggests that "In your intense involvement you forget that this is play acting—rather, something is occurring before you." Describing the 1975 London production of *Sizwe Bansi is Dead*, Alastair Niven describes the audience being "made to suffer just for a moment the kind of humiliation which is permanent for the passbook-bearing African." Both reviews are quoted in Gray, *Athol Fugard*, 86, 89, respectively.

16. Fugard, *Notebooks*, 201. Fugard remarks in his introduction to *Statements* that he had not seen Grotowski's company perform but had been inspired by his reading of *Towards a Poor Theatre*. Vandenbroucke also reports that Fugard, who was without a passport during the period of Grotowski's theater work, received copies of *Towards a Poor Theatre*, notes on Grotowski's New York lectures, and Jean-Claude van Itallie's *The Serpent* from Barney Simon (*Truths*, 108). Fugard, too, has linked the two notions of "poor theater": "My aesthetic probably comes out of having a theatre in South Africa with nothing, but even if I had resources, my inclination may be not to use them" (quoted in Vandenbroucke, *Truths*, 109).

17. Fugard, "Introduction," n.p.

18. I am thinking, of course, of Homi K. Bhabha's argument in "Of Mimicry and Man: The Ambivalence of Colonial Discourse," in *The Location of Culture* (London: Routledge, 1994), 85–92.

19. Loren Kruger, "Placing the Occasion: Raymond Williams and Performing Culture," in *Views Beyond the Border Country: Raymond Williams and Cultural Politics*, ed. Dennis L. Dworkin and Leslie G. Rowan (London: Routledge, 1993), 63–64.

20. I am not echoing Robert Mshengu Kavanagh's critique of Fugard's participation in dominant elites and their strategies of representation here; I am arguing instead that producers and audiences who are familiar with Grotowski's poor theater will have to confront the metaphysics and ideology it exemplifies in contemporary performance. Kavanagh comments on Fugard in *Theatre and Cultural Struggle in South Africa* (London: Zed, 1985), 101–4, 202.

21. Peter Rosenwald, "Separate Fables," *Guardian*, January 8, 1974, 10.

22. Most critics have followed this lead in attributing the play mainly to Fugard. Erroll Durbach remarks, "His *Notebooks* make it clear that the ideas, dramatic structure, and the basic source material for *The Island* are Fugard's own" ("Sophocles in South

Africa," 263 n.1). Russell Vandenbroucke characterizes Fugard as a "'scribe' for the collaborative works" (*Truths*, 110) and reports Kani claiming that they "worked very directly with [Fugard] in the creation of the play" (126 n.19).

23. Rosenwald, "Separate Fables," 10.

24. John Kani and Winston Ntshona, "Art Is Life, Life Is Art: An Interview with John Kani and Winston Ntshona of The Serpent Players from South Africa," *UFAHAMU* 6, no. 2 (1976): 7.

25. Fugard is quoted in Vandenbroucke, *Truths*, 131, 132 n.22. Fugard's sensitivity here may have a pragmatic rationale as well. Writing about the Market Theatre (founded in 1976), David Graver and Loren Kruger note that, while even theaters like the Market, which "clearly oppose the policy established with the South African National Theatre Organization (1947–63), as perpetuated by the present provincial arts boards, whereby the government subsidizes only theatre by whites based on European models, they are nonetheless caught up in the structures of cultural hegemony in South Africa, which continue to designate as legitimate theatre those dramatic texts that can be validated as literary works. This legitimation tends to render illegitimate those theatre events whose value emerges from their actual significance as counter-hegemonic occasions for community self-representation by celebration or protest" (David Graver and Loren Kruger, "South Africa's National Theatre: The Market or the Street?" *New Theatre Quarterly* 5 [August 1989]: 274).

26. Harry Berger Jr., "Bodies and Texts," *Representations* 17 (Winter 1987): 153.

27. Beckett is quoted in Dougald McMillan and Martha Fehsenfeld, eds., *Beckett in the Theatre, vol. 1: From* Waiting for Godot *to* Krapp's Last Tape (London: John Calder; New York: Riverrun, 1988), 15.

28. Athol Fugard, John Kani, and Winston Ntshona, *The Island*, in Fugard, Kani, and Ntshona, *Statements*, 47. Subsequent page references to *The Island* appear in the text, and are to this edition.

29. See Samuel Beckett, *Catastrophe*, in *Collected Shorter Plays* (New York: Grove Weidenfeld, 1984), 299.

30. Wertheim, "Political Acting and Political Action," 251.

31. Rosenwald, "Separate Fables," 10.

32. Kani and Ntshona, "Art Is Life, Life Is Art," 7.

33. Bertolt Brecht, *Brecht on Theatre: The Development of an Aesthetic*, ed. and trans. John Willett (New York: Hill and Wang, 1964; London: Methuen, 1978), 37.

34. Anthony O'Brien, "Staging Whiteness: Beckett, Havel, Maponya," *Theatre Journal* 46 (1994): 50. See also this volume, pp. 148.

35. George Lukács, "The Sociology of Modern Drama," trans. Lee Baxandall, in *The Theory of the Modern Stage: An Introduction to Modern Theatre and Drama*, ed. Eric Bentley (Harmondsworth: Penguin, 1976), 443.

36. Martin Esslin, *The Theatre of the Absurd*, rev. ed. (New York: Anchor, 1969), 1. Subsequent page references appear in the text and are to this edition.

37. In Esslin's source—"'Godot' Gets Around," *Theatre Arts* 42, no. 7 (July 1958): 73–74—the unidentified writer remarks on the necessity of producing an all-male play: "Obviously the rules and regulations have changed since Bernhardt's day, for women are now not permitted within the prison walls" (73).

38. "'Godot' Gets Around," 74. Esslin's account adds much detail from the San Quentin *News* about the audience's composition but does not include these remarks about the prisoners' identification with Lucky.

39. It should be clear here that I am attempting to characterize the relationship between formal features of *The Island* and the interpretive conventions that produce those forms. I am trying to avoid what Elin Diamond has called "the unrigorous 'we' of the traditional critic who projects her/his subjective impressions and analyses on all members of the theater audience—as in 'we feel [Hamlet's] remorse' or 'we understand [Hedda's] frustration.' One of the effects of such rhetoric (in which the emotions and thoughts of others are assumed to follow our model) is a factitious but powerful sense of community which buttresses but also conceals the narcissistic claims of the critic" ("The Violence of 'We': Politicizing Identification," in *Critical Theory and Performance,* ed. Janelle G. Reinelt and Joseph R. Roach [Ann Arbor: University of Michigan Press, 1992], 390). David Coplan is also to the point here: "While I concur in the implicit rejection of class-based, socially emasculated Western formalist drama criticism, my experience compels me to maintain that a consciously formulated performance aesthetic is as important as social realism and ideological context in heightening the political and cultural consciousness of black audiences" (*In Township Tonight! South Africa's Black City Music and Theatre* [Johannesburg: Ravan, 1985], 228).

40. Homi K. Bhabha, "The Postcolonial and the Postmodern: The Question of Agency," in Bhabha, *The Location of Culture,* 171.

9.

Gregg Dion

From No Man's Land to No Man's Theater: The Theatre of the 8th Day Returns to Capitalist Poland

It's hard to tell which is worse: political terror or the terror of the market.
—Tadeusz Kantor

In the summer of 1989, the Polish theater collective known as the Theatre of the 8th Day (Teatr Ósmego Dnia) surreptitiously ended four years of exile by performing in a tent in a Warsaw park as part of Mir Caravane, an international theater circus trekking from Moscow to France via Warsaw and Berlin. Although it was an unofficial homecoming, political change was in the air, and the 8th Day performers relished thoughts of returning to their roots, their families, and, as actor Adam Borowski recalled, "the forests where we once walked with friends."[1] Indeed, soon the first Solidarity government was formed and the Theatre of the 8th Day was invited back to Poznán, thanks to the combined influence of Prime Minister Tadeusz Mazowiecki, the Cultural Ministry, and Pope John Paul II (Karol Wojtyla).[2]

But of the three, only the Pope remains in his position today. In the tumultuous political and social milieu of postcommunist Eastern Europe, where one crisis inevitably begets another, the Theatre of the 8th Day finds itself in a bizarre dilemma: now that it has become a fully established cultural institution, it may be closer than ever to collapse. With Poland's plunge into the murky waters of late capitalism, all cultural institutions have felt new challenges to staying afloat despite declining governmental and popular support. But the avant-garde, once symbolic, if not instrumental, in the political revolution, has been further stripped of its social function and identity. For the 8th Day company, founded on Grotowski's principles of the "holy" performance and preoccupied with a search for authenticity, finding a new voice with which to address postmodern existence is especially daunting. Moreover, their experience raises broader questions about how the avant-garde—so characteristically eloquent in states of conflict—functions in a state of crisis, about how oppositional artists may be consumed by a (micro)hegemony of revolutionary politics, and about artistic integrity and collaboration under the divisive influences of capitalism.

Among as many as two hundred student and alternative theater groups that formed in the wake of the nationwide student rebellion of March 1968, none rivaled the moral and artistic authority of the Theatre of the 8th Day.[3] Originally organized in 1964 as a student theater of poetry in collaboration with Stanislaw Barańczak, the 8th Day's reputation as a major Polish alternative theater ensemble (with requisite manifestos and ties to Grotowski's Laboratory) may be attributed to the leadership of Lech Raczak, who functioned as the group's artistic director through most of its history. Raczak was one of the 8th Day's actors (performing roles such as Coulmier in *Marat/Sade*) before taking on the responsibility of stage directing in 1968. The events of that year were pivotal for the Theatre of the 8th Day, as Raczak recalled.

> As in the West, there were student protests here and a strong opposition was formed to the present "reality." We felt it was indispensible to continue the work inspired by Grotowski on the Self, but a new desire was born—a kind of duty—to cut ourselves free from those mythical concerns and move towards our contemporary problems.[4]

The Theatre of the 8th Day helped initiate the trend of politically subversive student theater in Poland as early as 1970 with the production of *An Introduction To . . . (Wprowadzenie do)*, an ironic protest against conformity in the form of a grotesque parody of the public celebrations of Lenin's birthday.[5] The following year they introduced *In One Breath (Jednym tchem)*, a collective expression of protest against the "spiritual violence" of "official lies" by the communist regime in response to the December 1970 revolt in Gdánsk.[6] Successive creations like *We Have to Confine Ourselves to What Has Been Called 'Paradise on Earth' . . . ?* (1975), *Discounts for Everyone* (1977), and *Oh, How Nobly We Lived* (1979) confirmed the ensemble's stature as "a moral guide for that generation," while prompting increased harassment by the authorities.[7] Political tensions rose dramatically in Poland in the summer of 1976 after widespread workers strikes and a major riot in Radom. The 8th Day troupe was openly sympathetic with the KOR—the Committee for the Defense of the Workers' Rights—a small but significant pressure group of leading Polish intellectuals, including Barańczak.[8] The authorities took notice, and as a consequence from 1976 to 1979 the 8th Day group was denied mention in the Polish press and other publicity and company members were often subjected to short-term detention without charges.

Current company members Ewa Wójciak, Marcin Kęszycki, Adam Borowski, and Tadeusz Janiszewski all made their acting debuts in the early 1970s and have made their performing careers exclusively with the Theatre of the 8th Day. Asked about their backgrounds, they characteristically take some pride in the fact that not one is an institutionally trained actor—an expression of contempt for the complacent Polish repertory system in general.[9] Although the student theater movement in Poland occasionally included students from the dramatic academies—Teatr STU in Kraków is the most notable example, a group formed by theater students in rebellion against the rigid training methods and repertoire of the conservatory—most commonly the participants were theatrical amateurs from a variety of university disciplines. Like many of the student theaters formed in Poland in the 1970s, the performers in Theatre of the 8th Day shared a sense of social obligation, a familiarity with the work of Jerzy Grotowski, and, in the aftermath of the 1968 revolt against the government's closing of the National Theatre of Warsaw's production of Adam Mickiewicz's classic *Forefathers' Eve (Dziady),* a perception of theater as a site of political contestation.[10] But the 8th Day was exceptional—exceptionally talented amateurs, working intensely under the exceptional guidance of Raczak and sharing a commitment to their work and an ability to work together that would last two decades. As Raczak once explained,

> The company is based on personal ties. From the outside we seem an anomaly because it is rare that a group based primarily on friendship continues for so many years and plans to keep existing in the future . . . . There have been a few changes in our group, but not many, nothing significant. For us the chance to speak through the theatre is a fundamental value, even a necessity. We have all arranged our private lives in such a way that the theatre is at the center.[11]

In 1979, the Theatre of the 8th Day turned professional with financial backing from the Poznan Stage Performers Association. This was managed despite the fact that the 8th Day members were then on trial for "economic fraud" among other dubious charges. Ironically, it was a project of the Cultural Ministry, which simultaneously "promoted" five of the major student theater groups in Poland, including Teatr STU, Teatr 77 in Lódź, Kalambur ("Pun") in Wroclaw, and Academia Ruchu ("Movement Academy") in Warsaw.[12] As Taduesz Janiszewski recalled, this was a thinly disguised political maneuver.

> Our influence on student groups was always rather strong, so the authorities thought it might be an advantage to create a distance between us and the students by making us professional—by buying us. We became part of an establishment, Estrada, whose main business was circus and striptease. They thought we would like more and more money and would agree to more and more control in exchange.[13]

The tactic was relatively successful in neutralizing the other groups (especially Teatr STU and Kalambur), but it failed to placate the Theatre of the 8th Day. Critic Elżbieta Morawiec observed in 1980 that the new productions of the other groups in 1979 already seemed to be responding to "pressure to find a place in the country's cultural life" and exhibiting a turn toward naturalistic acting or laboratory "research." The 8th Day alone had remained the "theatre of action."[14] As a professional company it still remained homeless, renting performance facilities as needed, but was allowed to perform in festivals in Scandinavia, Europe, and Mexico.

After the declaration of Martial Law by General Wojciech Jaruzelski in December 1981 (which remained in effect until July 1983), however, alternative theater was characterized as a threat to "public order" by the ruling militia and tolerated accordingly. The independent student union NZS, which had supported most of the student theater groups in Poland in conjunction with Solidarity, was banned, leaving student theater not only officially "illegitimate" but without a material foundation.[15] Several 8th Day works were banned, actors were jailed, and Communist Party officials routinely persuaded managers of theaters to deny them performance space or even to cancel scheduled presentations.[16] Invitations to perform in festivals abroad often disappeared in the mail, and acceptance was usually rendered impossible by the Polish authorities' refusal to grant passports.

Theatre of the 8th Day nevertheless developed two new works in 1982—*Ascension*, about the life and death (in a Soviet prison camp) of the poet Osip Mandelstam, and *A Fable*, based on William Faulkner's morality tale—and in 1983 premiered a day-long project, *Report from a City under Siege,* in Jelenia Gora for the International Festival of Street Theatres. Martial Law had a discouraging effect, however, as for the first time since the 1960s the company resorted to literary source material:

> because we couldn't find our own language faced with such a situation. We didn't have enough courage. We weren't sure if there was any justification for the theatre's existence. That's why we looked for a literary example that could be similar to the terrible Polish situation of camps, prisons, and internments.[17]

Report from a City under Siege was based on poetry by Barańczak and Zbigniew Herbert. Since the most significant poems had come from uncensored underground *samizdat* publications, further outsmarting of the local theatrical censor was required. If not directly addressing the political situation in Poland at that time, these three works each stressed the importance of individual conscience in the face of authoritarianism, a theme that in the context of the Martial Law could be provocative. Regarding *Siege,* for example, Halina Filipowicz observed that the performance "never allowed spectators to relax from their unease at watching a transformation of their life under martial law into art,"[18] while another critic (anonymously) noted that in the final scene of the mythical city's destruction the audience could not help but associate the Four Horsemen of the Apocalypse with the familiar riot police (Zomo-boys) and feel a personal "moral imperative to struggle for what is right."[19]

Theatre of the 8th Day was eventually granted its own premises in May of 1984, only to have the offer rescinded two months later along with a revocation of its financial support and actors' stipends. Reportedly, the company's appeals to the Cultural Ministry were denied with the admonition that it had maintained too close a relationship with the dissident writer Adam Michnik.[20] The group was ultimately forced underground, performing for invited audiences in Catholic churches. The church performances were often problematic, at times challenging the ensemble to play before as many as two thousand spectators and implying that it had aligned itself with another (more metaphysical) authority. However, the association with the Church afforded the Theatre of the 8th Day not only performance venues free of police interference but an opportunity to perform for audiences uninhibited by conditioned theater behavior. Early in 1986, the actor Marcin Kęszycki observed:

We play for absolutely new people. Before we were functioning in student circles—so our audiences were recruited from [among the] students, intellectuals, and intelligentsia. During Solidarity we played in
factories—in Gdansk we played in the shipyards. Now we play for
people who come to the theatre for the first time. In my opinion these
people are the most interesting. They are like Kaspar Hauser: they see
what they see. They laugh if something is funny, they cry when they
are sad.[21]

In 1985, six members of Theatre of the 8th Day were granted passports
to perform in Western Europe while four were refused. The company temporarily split to enable the tour to proceed. The company won the Fringe
First Award at the Edinburgh Fringe Festival that year (protested by Polish
cultural representatives, who claimed that the group did not officially exist)
among other accolades garnered in this first tour outside Poland since 1981.
Making a joint decision to defy the restrictions on their passports, the core
members reunited as exiles a year later in Italy where until the decline of the
Polish communist regime they lived and worked, performing and conducting workshops, often in conjunction with the Teatro Nucleo of Ferrara.[22]
They were also joined by an Italian performer and journalist, Daria Anfelli.
The years in Italy afforded them opportunities to experiment and work with
other theatrical companies without the political distractions of the Polish
scene and at the same time to advance their artistic reputation by touring
throughout Western Europe. But the life—often on the road—was
demanding, and exile was rarely glamorous. Always looking forward to an
eventual return to Poland, the 8th Day actors never even inquired about
asylum. Said Borowski, "We were more like tourists who wished to stay
and work awhile."

Their personal experiences and feelings about the years in exile became
the basis of their first new work after the fall of the Communists, *No Man's
Land* (*Ziemia niczyja*), which premiered in January of 1991. The title refers
to the vacant strip of land inside the Berlin Wall, which serves as a metaphor
for the experience of exile in a cultural no-man's-land between Western and
Eastern European mentalities. Raczak has described this as:

a place between Poland and the West, until recently obstructed by
wires. . . . At the same time it is a spiritual abyss splitting Europe into
two parts, which remain so. Spiritually we belong to pre-war of even
nineteenth century Europe. That Europe doesn't exist anymore, so we

have become anachronistic. For 40 years our minds have been transformed to such a degree that we are not able to understand the alterations which happened in the West in this time.[23]

In performance *No Man's Land* takes the form of a fluid series of vignettes and images augmented by a parade of stage props. At first, terrorized Eastern European figures dance stiffly and self-consciously, stand writhing in windows, and are denounced for seeking passports. A comic sequence follows, composed of escape attempts resembling those of the East Germans—hiding in a car, tunneling, walking a tightrope, and fashioning homemade airplanes and submarines. As refugees, they are dazzled by the splendor of the West but correspondingly inhibited, intimidated, and prostituted. Finally, haunted by the ghostly torments of Van Gogh, Nietzsche, Artaud, and other oversensitive Europeans, they withdraw from the "New Europe" in a literal shower of dirt.

With the decline of Polish Communism and the rise of the Solidarity government, virtually every well-known adversary of the former regime was lionized and customarily rewarded with the spoils, such as they were, of position, sanction, or financial support. Most notoriously, the debt to the Catholic clergy was repaid in part with broad access to the Wałesa administration and representatives in the Sejm, leading not only to new abortion restrictions but to widespread fears of an emerging theocracy. The Theatre of the 8th Day was welcomed home to Poznan in 1990 and provided with a spacious floor in a centrally located building, money for renovations and equipment, and base salaries for its members, including one office administrator and a theater technician. Although it had resisted the label "Solidarity's theater" for many years, the company was understandably receptive to the new government's financial support in its hope of establishing a theatrical home.

When I first visited with members of the Theatre of the 8th Day in 1992, they were still settling into these facilities and admitted that they hadn't found much use yet for their new computer and fax machine. They were performing regularly in Poland and Western Europe and otherwise seemed preoccupied with remodeling several rooms in their facility. The performance hall was set up for rehearsals of *No Man's Land*.

But it had been eighteen months since *No Man's Land* had premiered, and still no new works were in progress. At that time the Theatre of the 8th Day could take comfort in having a functional base of operations and an

FIG. I. *No Man's Land* was a play of displacement, depicting a cultural void, part autobiographical, as felt by exiles. (Photo by Andrzej Szozda.)

intact company; most other Polish alternative theater groups had lost founding members, disbanded, or become pale imitations of themselves.[24] But
individual members of the group confided that many serious anxieties had
come with the company's new status as an "institutional" theater. Some
expressed fears for the company's integrity in the face of impending competition for audiences, a lack of inspiration for new improvisationally developed works, suspicions that an administrative hierarchy might emerge, and
even the possibility that members would leave for more rewarding pursuits.
Although the Theatre of the 8th Day had survived twenty years of attack by
devoting itself to a common purpose, in the new capitalist society a single
purpose might not sustain it.[25] The company had found itself in yet another
"no man's land."

Much has been said about the Polish theater's covenant with audiences
in opposition to the communist regime; less attention has been paid outside
of the Polish press to the drastic decline in theater attendance (despite relatively stable ticket prices) since the fall of communism. To some extent this

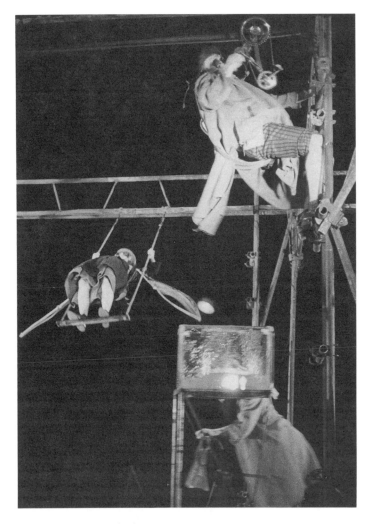

FIG. 2. *No Man's Land* culminates in an ironic spectacle of desperate attempts actually used by East Germans to escape to the West, from hang gliders to high-wire crossings to homemade submarines. (Photo by Weodzimierz Kwiecinski.)

drop can be explained as the result of a natural and temporary shakedown period, as Poles come to grips with the anxieties of rampant capitalism, particularly those of declining real income among public employees and epidemic unemployment.[26] But a greater anxiety for theater managers and artists arises from fears of an unprecedented post-modern shift away from live theater as a form of representation.[27] What is obvious, in the words of Halina Filipowicz, is that "the theatre which participated and intervened in the social and political reality—the theatre which served as a group therapy, an ethical guide, and a forum for national debate—has been abandoned by its audiences."[28] To the extent that they once fulfilled such a social function, members of the Theatre of the 8th Day have become acutely aware of their superfluousness in the new order. In a 1993 interview, Marcin Kęszycki described this Polish "postmodern condition" in stark contrast to his earlier description of the actor-audience relationship in church performances.

> Most important to us is the change in the way people are thinking, working, and living. The next performance we do will be in the street because people don't want to come to the theater. Before, the theater was full of people because it was a place of freedom where an actor spoke in the name of the people and identification was very easy. But now people are only looking for ways to make money. They live very separately—they sit in the same churches but they are separate. So for performers there is also a separation from their audience—they are less involved, more distanced. The theater is not so necessary as before.[29]

Kęszycki's language reveals a continued concern with authenticity, calling to mind Peter Bürger's theories on the relationship of avant-garde art to "life-praxis." But, whereas Kęszcyki laments the passing of the theater as a site of authentic interaction, his description of the contemporary inability of Polish spectators to participate in the performance event, if not in social life generally, would seem to prevent or substantially inhibit the kind of audience reception he desires in any venue. Under such circumstances, how can theater on the street be any more "necessary"?

In the West, of course, we are more accustomed to distanced spectators and the notion that in our society, as Peter Brook put it, "the role of art is nebulous."[30] So we tend to idealize the theater, perpetuating a belief in the power (if largely negative in our current discourse) of theatrical representation and its potential for community impact. I mean to suggest that what might seem a naive and vain striving for authenticity—in performance, reception, and life—to the Western poststructuralist may have been in the not-so-distant past a kind of reality for many East European artists. Avant-garde movements are notoriously unaware of their own historicity, so we might expect the artist for whom an expression of the truth was once regarded as a political act to now question the political impotence of truth telling rather than the ideological role of truth teller. Having once experienced an audience rapport and cause célèbre status unrivaled (if not unimaginable) in the West, the 8th Day performers now are confronting the construction of their former identity in a seemingly desperate attempt to free themselves from the contemporary limitations of that passé role. Ironically, the 8th Day company now has what Lech Raczak described in 1985 as a typically Western "identity problem."

> In Poland we are in an enviable position. In our oppressive political situation we do not have any trouble choosing our values. In the West the situation is more complicated and many theatres are hopelessly muddled—Western alternative theatres have identity problems. I know what I'm doing, while many theatre workers in the West are frantically looking for something to do.[31]

Raczak's comparison serves to point out a useful distinction between conflict and crisis. Whereas a protracted conflict along clear ideological lines might leave an oppositional theater group dead or alive, its identity and purpose nourish its activities. Muddled and unstable ideologies, however, make for muddled alternatives and a crisis of uncertainty.

Unlike theater groups in the West, the Theatre of the 8th Day's current problem is not simply that of forging an identity and purpose; it also feels compelled to shed an obsolete one. Piotr Gruszczyński, for example, has recently written that "The alternative theatres' raison d'etre was political involvement, their opposition to the regime."[32] This simplistic notion is dominant in Poland as well as in the West, and it is indicative of the way journalists and scholars alike have priviledged the politics of the avant-garde. But to the 8th Day performers such statements are an insult to their artistic commitment and their participation in a broader social movement. Gruszczyński further exhorted them to "reclaim the spirit of revolt" and "reclaim the canon," expressing an ignorance of their working methods and theatrical principles as well as their history.[33] While the ensemble satisfied a revolutionary social demand and is undeniably complicit in the construction of this received view, its members insist that they have always seen their true, or ideal, function as one that transcends a black-and-white political situation. As Raczak once said, "If we are political it is in this sense: we want to make a dent in the monopoly of thought imposed by the system."[34] A 1982 manifesto published by the 8th Day company declared that:

The imperative urge to participate actively in the making of reality
cannot lead the theater astray toward a facile political propaganda. Art
should not—according to us—limit itself to experience and the comment of a hic et nunc.[35]

But that same pamphlet (which included a prefatory passage from Simone
Weil) also asserted:

If practical experiences of human social activity testify to many com-
promises, limitations, and surrenders, art—again, according to us—
should never be allowed to surrender utopia, dreaming, and a violent
revolt against daily treasons, even if social reality and our daily experiences rapaciously strangle us, calling for a total surrender of all "other
realities."

Whatever they meant by "other realities," or, for that matter, whatever the
manifesto meant by the "duty of an active participation in the shaping of the
world," the 8th Day ensemble invariably represented itself as an idealistic,
radical alternative in the form of theater.

But this belief in "theater as an independent force, as a value," could
never be distinguished from its realpolitik social function. What the company attempted to present in a theatrical "universal language" was inevitably
heard as specifically Polish.[36] In my interviews (1992, 1993) with members
of the 8th Day, I was never told a single anecdote of their revolutionary
activities, nor did anyone wish to romanticize their experience in that
regard. Ewa Wójciak admitted,

It was not our aim to be heroes, nor was it some kind of love-in as
some people think. We were not so sure about what we were doing
. . . . We were absolutely accepted by our audiences, and at times our
performances in the churches were very interesting, very touching and
beautiful. But we were perceived rather more like heroes of anticom-
munism in that context than as artists. Sometimes I have some bitter-
ness when I see people who don't understand that [politics] was not
our raison d'etre. . . . They don't understand us, but that is our history.[37]

Others in the company concurred, insisting that they had always sought to
dramatize universal themes. According to Borowski,

Prior to 1990, if anyone attempted to tell or show something like a truth about what was going on, it was instantly political because the state was a complete liar—always double, always false. Any person who started to tell truths was first considered "oppositional," and then "dangerous," and so on. . . . Even in our most political performances, we were always thinking of metaphysical questions—looking for some universals.[38]

Recent revivals of *Ascension* and *Wormwood* (1985), two works that were attacked by censors in the early 1980s, were received on another level by many 1990s spectators, according to Kęszycki.

Originally we felt these works were very much consumed by the concrete political situation. But when we experimented by performing them in a new situation, completely out of that historical context, they still worked. To us it means these performances were more universal than we could have known during the communist period. So in such ways we are better off now.[39]

Kęszycki acknowledged, however, that their repertoire may be doomed to become "classics" now; the task ahead is to prevent the 8th Day from succumbing to its own reputation.

The question of change—how much and in what ways?—has imposed itself on the Theatre of the 8th Day no less than it has on Poland as a nation, further prompting the group's ongoing concern with authenticity. In 1992, Lech Raczak observed that the ensemble, like Poland generally, was suddenly confronted with a multiplying array of choices and competing truths: "In this situation we must do what we did 10 and 20 years ago—we have to find our own truth, within the group."[40] Within the year, however, Raczak left the Theatre of the 8th Day, along with Daria Anfelli, due to unresolvable conflicts within the company over its artistic mission in the new Polish society. Tensions first surfaced during the work on *No Man's Land,* based initially on disagreements over how favorably Western Europe should be depicted in light of the members' collective experiences there. In one significant scene, Janiszewski plays a transvestite who describes Western Europe in terms of social exclusion and alienation. Raczak and Anfelli reportedly felt that a more balanced point of view was warranted, while the others stressed the importance of presenting a specifically Eastern European perspective on the so-called New Europe.[41] But they soon found them-

FIG. 3. *Wormwood* had 13 illegal performances in Polish churches in 1985. It toured Europe in 1988. Still, in 1989, a series of performances could only be held in Jesuit venues in Poznan. It was not performed in a Polish theater until 1991. (Photo by Leszek Sczaniecki.)

selves further divided over the imperative question of how and whether the Theatre of the 8th Day should change, a crisis and an impasse not unlike those that prompted the undoing of a succession of Polish governments. Most members of the company felt a responsibility to continue some "participation in social reality," taking new performances to the streets.[42] Raczak and Anfelli insisted that the situation had completely changed, calling for a reexamination of their working methods and direction. "They wanted to continue," as Raczak saw it, "the same motifs of conflict, repeating our old thoughts, gestures, and means of expression."[43] The rift, after two decades of collaboration, can be read as a remarkable indicator of the severity of Poland's cultural crisis or as the inevitable parting of the ways of artists once they are freed of political responsibility. For those involved, it could only be immediately viewed as personal, although Raczak admitted that "the disappearance of outside pressures and dangers (such as police and censors) made our former relationships relaxed and stimulated interpersonal

FIG. 4. A street performance prepared with the thought of a tour in the Soviet Union and East Europe, *Meat* addressed the myth of revolution symbolized by the crew of the battleship Potemkin. (Photo by Andrzej Szozda.)

processes."[44] It also may remind us that the rhetoric of "authenticity" involves both the characteristic and the spontaneous aspects of the subject.

In July of 1994, the Theatre of the 8th Day premiered a new open-air performance, *Sabbath*, before four thousand people in the center of Poznan; Raczak and Anfelli, meanwhile, were working in Poland with a small new international ensemble named "Sekta" (which included four other former associates of 8th Day) on a more cosmic piece called *Orbis Tertius*.

Other major problems facing the Theatre of the 8th Day at the present time seem to revolve around the core question of whether the group has the ability to change without seriously compromising itself, no small task in the whirligig of instantaneous capitalism.

During the communist years, when we began working on a performance the last thing we thought about was finding money to finance

it, usually because it was clear there was none. But now—it's a paradox—when we start to think about a new performance the very first
questions are about where we'll get the money.[45]

On the surface, the Theatre of the 8th Day seems relatively unfazed by
financial problems, having learned long ago to make do with less. It believes
its modest needs provide an advantage in its competition for support with
the mainstream theater. Poznan's Teatr Polski (Theater of Poland), for
example, maintains fifty resident actors and a support staff of double that
number. But financial support from the government has not been sufficient
to fund larger production budgets for the 8th Day Theatre, or to pay the
technical staff and extra performers that the *Sabbath* project required. The
company worries over someday losing its newly won facility and is well
aware of the immediate pressures that have led companies like the Teatr
Polski to offer a commercial repertoire of farces and musicals. The Theatre
of the 8th Day is not experienced in fund-raising, and Poland's nouveau
riche are not inclined toward patronage. As Kęszycki explained,

> We don't really know how to look for funding, how to find private
> sponsors or how to speak with them. We have to learn how to create
> tax deductions and other legalities. But the private sector has money
> *because* they don't give it away—they're still investing in their own
> growth and can't give until they're fat.[46]

Funding for a special project can be sought by way of a local authority with
political connections, but the 8th Day has already found that "if the proposed project is not in line with their politics, they are not very enthusiastic."[47]

If somewhat disdainful of its reputation for mere agitprop, the troupe
shows few signs of social conformity. "My problem with the label 'oppositional' is that no system is really ever satisfactory," insisted Borowski. "So
this is not so interesting to me as is my personal search for truths about people and their dreams and their nightmares."[48] The new work, *Sabbath*, dramatizes the persecution of witches during the Inquisition, and the 8th Day
ensemble takes the rising power of the Right in Germany and Poland as its
inspiration. "We are trying to defend these 'witches,' but in this way we are
defending all 'others' and the value of 'otherness,' " according to Kęszycki.
Meanwhile, teenagers have become the 8th Day's best audience, coming to
the theater with fewer assumptions and more complex questions than did

the generation that preceded them. "They don't come to the theater because it's a legend, blah-blah-blah, but because they are asking questions and believe we might help them," said Kęszycki emphatically. In one instance, more than one hundred young people came to the theater for a weekend symposium on "1968" and its counterculture. "We want to poison them," added Kęszycki, with a wink.[49]

As an "official institution," a concept with which it is not completely comfortable, the Theatre of the 8th Day is doubly challenged to maintain its creativity, morale, and purpose. The desire to add new performers has been frustrated not only by a lack of money for salaries but by the difficulty of bringing young new partners into an ensemble that has been working together exclusively for a generation. "We are afraid of dominating them and inhibiting their initiative, and we recognize that they will never quite be our equals, and yet we have to try," admits Kęszycki.[50] The search has even led to an unprecedented tryout for a young woman trained in an acting academy.

At a time when many Polish cultural institutions are confronting the possibility of oblivion, perhaps nothing will determine the ultimate vitality of the Theatre of the 8th Day as much as its ability to develop impressive new works and regenerate its artistic reputation. But this task, already hampered by the departure of Raczak and the proliferation of popular culture in contemporary Polish society, is also complicated by the multiple hats the 8th Day company now finds itself wearing. The group's dream come true of having a theatrical home has allowed it to create an alternative culture center in Poznan, hosting symposiums, art shows, workshops, films, and touring theatrical performances. But, as Borowski laments,

> It had always been our dream that we would have a lot of time—but it's not true. We have this place, and the doors are open, and various time demands impinge upon our creative process. . . . It is most important that we have time to really concentrate on a new creation—we are not a factory; we do not make productions.[51]

In promoting an expanded new identity as a cultural site, the Theatre of the 8th Day may be generating institutional goodwill within its community at the expense of new theatrical audiences.

But the efforts of the company to nurture other artists, younger audiences, and local culture are also clearly indicative of its own maturation. The core members now have families, and they frequently make reference to their "roots" and the new responsibilities that have come with freedom. For Ewa Wójciak, the return to Poznan has been ideal.

> I am very much connected to this reality in Poznan. . . . I find it strange when some people seem disappointed that we are not avant-garde enough or fitting their myth of the New Europe. I'm not interested in the word *nation* but rather my homeland.[52]

Borowski echoed her belief in the provincial: "You know, for many years Kantor did performances about small villages from his past, and he was doing the most universal theater in the world."[53] Still, they remain committed to performing as frequently and widely as possible, as though the cultural and artistic exchange of international touring has always mattered more than their domestic reputation. "A theater that is permanent, in one place, is dying," claimed Kęszycki, "like a ship that is always anchored."[54]

Perhaps the 8th Day Theatre can afford to be optimistic; it has already weathered so many crises that nothing on the horizon appears insurmountable. "I like to think that the present is not just a bad time for theater, but a time for the acid test," said Kęszycki. "Now, theater can exist for its own sake."[55] This ensemble may in fact prevail due to some ultimate combination of strengths: small size, self-reliance, moral scope, the cultural and artistic cross-pollination made possible by frequent touring, liberation from dramatic texts, eschewal of institutional hierarchies and other "monopolies of thought," provincialism, and the improvisational working mode that has always been the source of its artistically gripping mise en scène. *No Man's Land,* a work so abstractly conceived that it never even mentions the Berlin Wall or the political situation that framed it, has already demonstated that the Theatre of the 8th Day can address postmodern issues theatrically. But in its new situation the Polish alternative theater must now confront and acknowledge its ideological function, as well as its artistic progress, in order to demonstrate that theater cannot really exist for its own sake.

NOTES

1. Adam Borowski, interview with the author, May 11, 1993. Unless otherwise noted, all quotations of 8th Day company members are from personal interviews conducted on May 10 and May 11, 1993, in Poznan.

2. Tony Howard, "New Polish Maps of the Mind," *New Theatre Quarterly* 9, no. 35 (1993): 295.

3. Aldona Jawlowska, *Wiecej niz teatr* [More than theatre] (Warsaw: Panstwowy Instytut Wydawniczy, 1987), 8. Jawlowska claims that approximately two hundred student theater groups appeared during the 1970s in Poland.

4. Quoted in Tony Howard, "A Piece of Our Life: The Theatre of the 8th Day," *New Theatre Quarterly* 2, no. 8 (1986): 292.

5. The Orange Alternative, a Wroclaw-based group of young people under the leadership of Waldemar Frydych, began conducting carnivalesque happenings as well as other political pranks in the mid-1980s. In the spirit of *An Introduction To . . .* they created parodic celebrations of numerous holy days on the communist calendar such as May Day, Women's Day (March 8), and the anniversary of the October Revolution. (See Filipowicz, Malina, "Polish Theatre after Solidarity: A Challenging Text," *The Drama Review* 36, no. 1 [Spring 1992]).

6. As described in "Teatr Ósmego Dnia," anonymous pamphlet, ca. 1983.

7. Agnieszka Wojcik [pseud.], "Alternative Theatre," trans. Hubert Ross, *Index on Censorship* 1 (1985), 11.

8. The June 1976 strikes were prompted by the Politburo's decision to drastically raise retail food prices, including a 69 percent average increase for meat. The most violent outbreak was in the small city of Radom, where the party building was looted and set on fire. At least four lives were lost.

9. This impression was clear in my interviews with company members. Adam Borowski attempted to explain, "The people who go to actor's school have a vision of themselves." Lech Raczak, in an interview with Tony Howard (*New Theatre Quarterly* 2, no. 8 [1986]: 291), claimed that "any graduate of a Polish theatre school cannot act with his whole self."

10. Jawlowska, *Wiecej niz teatr,* 34–37. The primary thrust of Jawlowska's work is on the student theater as a reflection of a wider alternative culture movement in Poland. She likens this social movement generally to the "hippie" era in the West, although noting differences such as a lack of gay, women's, or ecology movements, ultraleftist groups, and housing for communal living experiments. It may be indicative of publishing in Poland—under the juristiction of communist censors—that Jawlowska downplays the idea of political revolt as a central motivation for student theater in favor of the notion that students were merely searching for simpler, existential values and new means of collective expression. At least, it seems suspicious that the author closes the period of her study immediately before the Solidarity strike of 1980 and the declaration of Martial Law at the end of the following year, events that profoundly affected the alternative theater movement in Poland.

11. Quoted in Kathleen Cioffi and Andrzej Ceynowa, "An Interview with Director Lech Raczak," *Drama Review* 30, no. 3 (Fall 1986): 83.

12. The chief beneficiaries were probably the universities with which the groups had been associated. They were relieved of responsibility for the actions of the theater ensembles at a time when political tensions were rising.

13. Quoted in Howard, "Piece of Our Life," 296–97.

14. Quoted (without documentation) in ibid, 296–97.

15. Wojcik, "Alternative Theatre," 11.

16. One actor, Roman Radomski, was imprisoned for a month for laying a wreath at the foot of a monument in honor of the workers who had been killed in the June 1956

revolt in Poznan. A year earlier, prior to Martial Law, Lech Raczak had "directed" the unveiling of the monument by Lech Walesa before hundreds of thousands of spectators. The Theatre of the 8th Day had habitually circumvented the theatrical censors by means that were familiar among alternative theater groups—inviting audiences to numerous "rehearsals" prior to an official performance, altering performances through improvisation, submitting "clean" scripts for review, or performing unannounced works. (I was shown one festival program that included the title and program text of one officially approved work along with production photos of an entirely different piece, which was actually performed.) The company was most inconvenienced by the last-minute bans of specific performances in other Polish cities where they were at the mercy (or whim) of local censors.

17. Janiszewski, quoted in Howard, "Piece of Our Life," 300.

18. Filipowicz, "Polish Theatre after Solidarity," 76.

19. Wojcik, "Alternative Theatre," 12.

20. Ibid., 14.

21. Quoted by Marc Robinson in "Notes from the Underground: Theatre of the 8th Day," *Drama Review* 30, no. 3 (1986): 78.

22. During their exile in Italy a Swedish documentary film, *Teater Attonde Dagen* [Theatre of the 8th Day], was made about their experiences and working methods by Joanna Helander and Bo Persson. For information, contact the producers: Swedish Film Institute, Box 27126, 102 52 Stockholm.

23. Quoted from *Kultur i zycie* [Culture and life], June 4, 1991 (translated by Janusz Marek).

24. In 1993, the three-man group Provisorium in Lublin was virtually the only other alternative theater of note in Poland (Provisorium was discussed along with Teatr Osmego Dnia in both of the articles on Polish alternative theater that appeared in the August 1993 issue of *New Theatre Quarterly*). Warsaw's Akademia Ruchu and the rural troupe at Gardzienice (east of Lublin) are still producing but function largely as research centers. Teatr STU and Teatr 77 have no resident actors—STU is most visible when hired to stage public spectacles, while 77 appears to be reduced to touring a one-person show. Since the death of Tadeusz Kantor in 1990, his Cricot 2 has operated only as a museum, performing infrequent revivals.

25. Piotr Gruszczyński and Tony Howard each published short reports on the general phenomenon of Polish alternative theater's uncertain place in the new Polish society in *New Theatre Quarterly* 9, no. 35 (1993).

26. An unpublished 1994 report, by Andrzej Ziebinski of the Polish Cultural Ministry, attributed this decline primarily to economics, despite figures indicating that ticket prices on average had not exceeded the ideal barrier of 1 percent of average monthly net income. He admits that the veracity of the statistics is questionable, however, because, while "previously there were more theatre-goers on paper than in reality for everything had to happen 'according to plan,' " the statistics today do not reflect free tickets given to "poor kids."

27. As in many parts of the world, American movies are extremely popular in Poland. But the *Jurassic Park* dinosaurs will not devour the fine arts in Poland without the assistance of their own booming VCR market and negligence toward copyrights. Pirated copies of recent American movies can be rented all over Poland for about fifty cents, and

despite the general poverty Poles are finding the means to purchase their first color TVs and VCRs, making home viewing the most popular entertainment form.

28. Filipowicz, "Polish Theatre after Solidarity," 85.

29. Marcin Kęszycki, interview, May 10, 1993.

30. Peter Brook, *The Empty Space* (New York: Atheneum, 1968), 98.

31. Quoted in Cioffi and Ceynowa, "Interview with Raczak," 90.

32. Piotr Gruszczyński, "No Alternative?" *New Theatre Quarterly* 9, no. 3 (August 1993): 292.

33. Ibid., 293.

34. Borowski, interview, May 11, 1993.

35. Quoted from "Teatr Ósmego Dnia," a self-published pamphlet written in part by Ewa Wójciak.

36. Lech Raczak, quoted in Howard, "Piece of Our Life," 305.

37. Wójciak, interview, May 11, 1993.

38. Borowski, interview, May 11, 1993.

39. Kęszycki, interview, May 10, 1993.

40. Quoted in Howard, "New Polish Maps," 295.

41. Marcin Kęszycki, telephone interview with the author, September 27, 1993.

42. Ibid.

43. Lech Raczak, personal correspondence, February 17, 1994. I wish to thank Dorota Słuharska for her assistance in translating this correspondence.

44. Ibid.

45. Kęszycki, interview, May 10, 1993.

46. Kęszycki, interview, May 10, 1993.

47. Ibid.

48. Borowski, interview, May 11, 1993.

49. Kęszycki, interview, May 10, 1993.

50. Ibid.

51. Borowski, interview, May 11, 1993. The creation of *Sabbath* was an improvisational process, as has long been the group's method, but it marked the first such project developed without the directoral supervision of Raczak.

52. Wojciak, interview, May 11, 1993.

53. Borowski, interview, May 11, 1993.

54. Kęszycki, interview, May 10, 1993.

55. Ibid.

10.

Diana Taylor

Theater and Terrorism: Griselda Gambaro's *Information for Foreigners*

Questions about the place of theater in a "well-run society," originally debated by Plato and Aristotle, take on a new meaning, as well as a special urgency, in criminal states in which theaters are bombed and spectacular acts of cruelty exceed the boundaries of the stage. In Argentina during the 1970s, both state and antistate terrorism competed to capture the public's attention and control its behavior by staging highly dramatic acts of violence.[1] Terrorism, with its scenes of torture and abduction, proved highly theatrical both on a practical and on a symbolic level. Terrorists dressed their parts and set the drama in motion. The victims, like actors, stood in (albeit unwillingly) for someone or something else. Antagonists appeared on the scene as if by magic; protagonists "disappeared" into thin air. The revelation of corpses at the appropriate moment was as typical of terrorism as it was of the Elizabethan stage. Crimes became "unreal," invisible in their theatricality. After all, doesn't theater allow us to deny what we see with our own eyes? Even with thirty thousand people missing in Argentina between 1976 and 1982, and continuing disappearances throughout Central and South America today, state authorities assure shattered populations that everything is under control.[2] The witnesses, like obedient spectators in a theater, were encouraged to suspend their disbelief. Terrorism draws on the theatrical propensity simultaneously to bind the audience and to paralyze it. Theatrical convention allows for mass splitting, enabling the audience to respond either emotionally or intellectually to the action it sees onstage without responding physically. Terrorism in Argentina pushed this convention further, both to atomize the victimized population and to preclude the possi-

bility of solidarity and mobilization. Everyone was vulnerable; the unexpected attack could come anytime, from anywhere. As the case of Argentina
illustrated, acts of terrorism could endow the national frame with a strange
spectacularity. An aura of tragedy enveloped the country. The suspense
mounted. The crisis seemed fated. The Mothers of the Plaza de Mayo, like
a Greek chorus, were a physical reminder of the personal and national dramas that violence conspired to erase from history.

All this is not to suggest that terrorism is essentially representational.[3]
Terrorism and the torture associated with it in Argentina during the 1970s
were not theater or magic, but they were designed to look that way.[4] They
were acts of deliberately orchestrated violence set in motion to destabilize
the Argentine society, to divert public attention from the urgent political
and economic contradictions facing the country.[5] Recognition of the performance qualities of terrorism and torture does not reduce them to performance acts; on the contrary, it allows for their demystification. Griselda
Gambaro, one of Argentina's most prominent playwrights, has undertaken
to make visible the obfuscating theatricality of Argentina's violent politics
through theater since she began writing plays in 1963. During the 1960s, her
plays focused on the increasingly fratricidal nature of Argentina's civil
conflict *(The Siamese Twins,* 1965), which culminated in the particularly
repressive Onganía coup of 1966. Criminal violence had become an
accepted part of political struggle: "A deadly toxin had entered the Argentine body politic."[6] In more than twenty plays written between 1963 and
the 1990s, Gambaro focuses on the themes of persecution and criminal violence resulting from Argentina's warring political factions, on the country's
ongoing fascination with fascism, on its misogyny, its anti-Semitism, and its
racism.[7] The important modulations in Gambaro's plays during these three
decades parallel Argentina's radical shifts in leadership: the struggle between
the military and the Peronists of the 1960s; Perón's second ascension to
power and the Peronismo of the 1970s (which did not end with Perón's
death in 1974 nor with the deposition of his wife "Isabelita" from the presidency in 1976); the military takeover and dictatorship, with its "Dirty
War," from 1976 to 1983; and the new democracy under Alfonsín in 1983.
During the 1970s, Gambaro received death threats. Although she is one of
Argentina's most respected and popular playwrights, at home and abroad,
whose plays are staged not only in the most prestigious theaters of Buenos
Aires but throughout the United States and Europe, her published plays
were censored and her new plays went unpublished, circulating only in
manuscript. She was forced into exile from 1980 to 1982. In 1981, during

the Open Theatre festival in which her play *Saying Yes* was staged, the Picadero Theater in downtown Buenos Aires was burned to the ground.

Information for Foreigners (1973), the most complex of her pieces, is a chronicle in twenty scenes presenting various forms of violence—from fragments of theatrical representations of violence like *Othello* and Lorca's *Blood Wedding,* to scientific experiments carried out on human bodies, to torture and abductions, to staged and "spontaneous" incidents of terrorist attacks. The spectators are warned before they enter: "The show is restricted, prohibited to those under thirty-five and those over thirty-six. . . . Everyone else can come in without difficulty. No obscenities or strong language. The piece responds to our way of life: Argentine, Western, Christian. We're in 1971. I ask you not to separate and to remain silent" *(Information,* 70).[8]

Information for Foreigners examines not only the theatricality of terrorism and the way it shapes our perception, or paralyzes us as bystanders, but also the way in which theater participates in ideological struggle. Theater is an unstable vehicle for expression, as capable of obscuring problems as it is of clarifying them, as instrumental in mythifying victimization as in working to end it. By staging violence, Gambaro draws attention to how theater's illusionist qualities can be manipulated to control not only what people see and how they see it but how they can deny the reality of what they see and know to be true, for example, the practice of torture and criminal politics. The population in and outside Argentina knew what was going on during the 1970s. Did anyone really not know that the Argentine military government systematically terrorized its people between 1976 and 1982? Did anyone really not know that the U.S. government supported the military with economic aid and training?[9] The question is, how can the public's attention be diverted so that it can dismiss that knowledge and claim innocence? How does theater participate in the campaign either to conceal or to expose information? Can theater help spectators recognize, and therefore respond to, their lethal predicament, as Augusto Boal would argue?[10] Or, on the contrary, does it offer them the consoling illusion that by attending theater they are doing something about it? By allowing spectators to sit passively and watch others engage in conflict, by enabling spectators to experience the thrills vicariously and benefit from cathartic release, spectacles might arguably diffuse the rage, frustration, and energy that, revolutionary advocates like Frantz Fanon maintain, might change the unlivable situation.[11] Does theater's aesthetics undermine its ethos by depicting violence seductively, or, as Susan Sontag would argue, pornographically, enabling the audience to enjoy acts it would otherwise "see with pain" (following the

FIG. I. A protestor being dragged away by members of the Armed Forces, 1982. (Photo by Daniel García.)

line of reasoning extending from Aristotle to Adorno)?[12] Or, rather, does the mere existence of outspoken theater like Gambaro's become a "speech act" that directly presents, rather than represents, a challenge to those who maintain their power by force? Is theater safe? Does "watching" somehow protect either the seer or the seen? The implications of these questions also exceed the boundaries of the stage. The issues raised in Gambaro's *Information* pertain not only to Argentina and not only to Latin American theater; they raise questions about "watching" violence everywhere.

Set explicitly in Argentina in 1971, Gambaro's *Information* not only thematizes but re-creates the climate of terror. The action takes place in a house. The audience is split into groups upon arrival, each led through the house by a Guide who introduces the different scenes with short excerpts about abductions and murders taken from contemporary newspapers, "information" for foreigners. This information is verifiable, accessible both to the audience in the house and to the reading public in and outside Argentina.[13] There are thus two audiences, the groups walking through the house and the reading audience outside Argentina, the "foreigners" of the title, that is, us. The audience follows the Guide down long, dark passage-

FIG. 2. Picadero Theater, where Argentina's antidictatorship's Open Theatre festival was held, burned to the ground in 1981. (Photo courtesy of
Julie Weisz.)

ways cluttered with corpses and prisoners, up and down steep, dangerous
staircases, and in and out of small rooms in which isolated acts of torture or
theatrical rehearsals are forever being played out. In one room, actors are
rehearsing the final moments of *Othello*. In another, a mother sings a lullaby
from *Blood Wedding* to her child. The highlight of the tour is the visit to the
catacombs in the basement, the tombs of martyred Christians. Although a
member of the group (actually an actor) is attacked and abducted by
unidentified men, the Guide encourages his group to overlook these violent
intrusions. He dispels the incessant, unexpected outbursts of violence as
marginal or accidental in relation to the audience's right to entertainment.
As screams and shouts echo through the halls, he clamors for amusement
and "a little gaiety, damnit!" and grumbles about the bad scripts and the
unsavory subject matter. Complaining that "modern theater is like that! No
respect" (107), he nonetheless points out to the spectators that now that
they have paid for their tickets they might as well enjoy the show.

  The house as theatrical space subverts the lines of demarcation between
public and private and emphasizes the corrosive and contagious nature of

FIG. 3. March for human rights, Argentina, 1986. (Photo by Rafael Woll-
mann.)

violence that blurs all physical, moral, and judicial frameworks. Scenes of
political violence are not limited to prisons and torture chambers but are
played out on public streets, in private houses, on human bodies. The
takeover of the house, which is concurrently a social structure, the family
home, and the body's protective shell indicates that the three spaces—body,
family, and society—are interconnected and mutually supportive. Terrorism in the home "gets us where we live," nullifying the existence of any safe
space. Staging political confrontation on the human body has shattered the
limits of personhood, gutted domesticity, and transformed society as a
whole into a terrifying theatrical set, giving new meaning to the term *environmental theater*. Like terrorism, which atomizes populations, *Information*
deracinates the audience. Gambaro's play as a whole has no plot, no logical
"conflict" in dramatic terminology, no climax, no resolution, no characters
in any psychological sense—simply fragmented scenes and a series of roles
such as Guide, Guard, Tortured Girl, Abducted Man, and, of course, Audience. As in terrorism, the audience plays a major, and highly disconcerting,
role. It makes its way through the dark passages, peering through half-open
doors. No one is safe, and the Guide reminds his charges to watch their steps

and their pocketbooks. The house reflects the invasive tactics of terrorism and torture. Terror deterritorializes; we are all foreigners in this house.

Throughout the tour, Gambaro calls attention to the way that the public's perception is directed and controled by those in authority. The Guide, for example, physically ushers his group from room to room. He tells his group where and when to look, and he censors what the viewers can see: "Sorry, but ladies can't see this. The men can, if they like . . ." Much of this "guidance" perhaps seems inoffensive, maybe even necessary. The Guide, after all, does this for a living. We have never been in the house before, and we do not know our way around. Who can we trust? While this may be hell, though, this Guide is no Virgil. He steers his group away from the atrocity but only to protect the perpetrators of the deeds. He himself participates in the violence, pushing the corpses out of sight with his foot, as he flashes "a wide, fake smile" at his group. He constantly reveals his hatred of women. He omits (the literal translation is "eats" [90]) the "ladies" of the "ladies and gentlemen," claiming that it takes too long to say the whole phrase ("me como las señoras"). He thrusts his hand under the Tortured Girl's skirt and he complains about the "ungrateful" girl, muttering "Who understands women? Difficult gender." However, as women are raped, tortured, and killed throughout the house, we realize that these seemingly trifling, "personal" sexist remarks and gestures in fact tie into a rampant national misogyny. As Gilles Deleuze and Felix Guattari point out in *Anti-Oedipus,* "desiring production is one and the same thing as social production. . . . Thus fantasy is never individual; it is group fantasy.[14]

The Guide's allusion to "eating," and thus omitting, the "ladies" is profoundly indicative of a group fantasy for the dehumanization and elimination of "subversive" women, the enemies of the state. When he fumbles under the Tortured Girl's skirt, he in fact signals that women's sexual organs are the target of most attacks on women.[15] However, *Information* also demonstrates that the distinction between "good women" and "bad women," at least tentatively upheld by the protofascists that Klaus Theweleit studied in *Male Fantasies,* has been subverted in Argentina. The scene in which the Mother is abducted in front of her children dispels all myths about differentiation between "bad" and "motherly" women, a distinction that has been particularly rigid in Latin America.[16] The Mother may remind her abductors that "no one would harm a mother!" and the police may cling to the fiction that no one is punished unjustly, but they order the Mother to strip, and it is clear that she will be raped just the same.

Respect for the authority of those in power, Gambaro illustrates, can be dangerous, indeed. It can lead innocent bystanders to be indirect, and even direct, participants in torture. As the spectators follow the Guide into another room, the Milgram experiment is under way, a restaging of an actual experiment carried out at the universities of Yale, Princeton, and Munich in the 1960s. The pseudoscientific trappings of the process veil the fact that it actually tests an individual's capacity for inflicting pain and death on a stranger on the orders of an "expert." The young man playing "pupil" is strapped to a chair and given electric shocks by the man playing "teacher." Although the pupil suffers from a bad heart, the Experimenter urges the teacher to increase the voltage. While the teacher knows that the shocks could cause the pupil's death, the Experimenter posits the traditional arguments that place obedience to authority over personal responsibility: the experiment is necessary; it is for the greater social good; the man dialing up the lethal voltage is not responsible for the victim's death. How can people deny a reality that they know to be true? They do it by listening to an expert telling them that the scene is really something else, by participating in a drama that inverts roles and changes names to create the illusion of innocence. The theatricality of the proceedings, on a practical level, admirably fulfills its real function. It makes people participate in an act they would otherwise find repellent. While most people probably disagree with the Massuist position that "torture is not merely permissible but morally mandatory," the Milgram experiment proved that the majority of the population can potentially be deformed into torturers—65 percent of the American participants tested; 85 percent of the German.[17] So torture and torturers are not quite the monstrous Other we like to imagine. And the audience obediently moves from room to room.

How can one distance oneself from the reality one sees with one's own eyes? By turning it into theater. Gambaro's scenarios of torture demonstrate that theatrical distancing and role playing are essential for the continued functioning of torture, even when these acts are not obscured by "professional" trappings. A young woman, totally despondent, dripping wet and shivering in a chair, has just been submitted to the "submarine." The visual image of the tortured woman is incongruent with the apparent benevolence of the scene, for the Guard acts as if he were a friend or lover trying to protect her. He complains about the "shitty service" (no towels) and lends her his coat. As he loads his pistol, he asks, "Why so sad? *(Signaling to the spectators)* Nothing will happen to you. Too many people. They're watching us. *(Puts his pistol away)*." Like the prototypical victimizer, the Guard inverts the roles and blames the victim for precipitating the violence. It is her fault; he is only trying to help. He generously leaves her his loaded pistol just in case she wants to end it all.

However, the theatricality of torture, even on a practical level, goes beyond these shams of goodwill. The theatricality of torture protects the victimizers from the repercussions of their actions by allowing for the split between appearance and reality, the split between action and emotion. A part of the torturer can carry on the gruesome work and split to protect the innocence and integrity of the whole personality, much like in Brecht's *Good Person of Setzuan,* in which the splitting of the bad Shui Ta supports the image of a good Shen Te. Studies on fascist and Nazi discourse, such as Lifton's *The Nazi Doctors,* Kaplan's *Reproductions of Banality,* and Friedlander's *Reflections on Nazism,* show that the psychic numbing and dissociation implicit in splitting also works through its opposite, through doubling.[18] Like the actor, the torturer is simultaneously a monstrous villain and an ordinary citizen, guilty of atrocious acts and guiltless of them. Within this theatrical frame, the room, with its props, its scripts for extracting information, and its professional terminology, the torturers can safely proceed with the annihilation of others. They can maim or kill their victims by convincing themselves that they are doing something else; they are defending themselves and the country from the dangerous enemy or they are carrying out a necessary scientific experiment. Even when, or perhaps *especially* when, the tormentors enjoy killing, as in the cases of fascist murderers described in *Male Fantasies,* they must place their actions within a frame that justifies and exonerates them. The theatricality inherent in constructing this other reality makes the action safe for the torturer.

The theatricality of torture remains central, though less clear, in respect to the audience's role in torture and terrorism. In *The Body in Pain,* Elaine Scarry proposes that the exercise of power, however abusive, lends credibility to the tottering regime. She observes that during periods of sociopolitical crisis "the sheer material factualness of the human body will be borrowed to lend that cultural construct the aura of 'realness' and 'certainty'" (14). Torture, that "grotesque piece of compensatory drama" (28), converts the reality of "absolute pain" into the "fiction of absolute power" (27). "Now, at least for the duration of this obscene and pathetic drama, it is not the pain but the regime that is total, not the pain but the regime that is able to eclipse all else, not the pain but the regime that is able to dissolve the world" (56).

As beautifully articulated and compelling as Scarry's argument is, one should recognize that she omits one vital player: the spectator. Torture works on several levels simultaneously. It annihilates the victim. It destroys the victim's family, sometimes into later generations, as when children are forced to watch the brutalization, rape, or murder of their parents (family torture). It undermines the immediate community that is involved, often threatened but unable to put an end to torture. It affects the larger international community that, even when it does not feel immediately threatened, still feels powerless to stop it. The public (national and international) assists in the conversion of pain to power. Terrorism and torture are not designed to prove to the victims that the regime has the power to exterminate them—such proof is manifested in the violent act itself. The aim of terrorism and torture is to prove to the population at large that the regime has the power to control it. Segments of the public, both the one walking through the house and the foreigners reading newspapers, are in different ways the intended audience of terror's "pathetic drama."

The amplification of torture, through which twenty victims can paralyze an entire community or country, functions by means of its theatricality. Confronted with the reality of torture, our tendency as an audience, as in the traditional theater, is to identify with the protagonist, in this case with the victim. We cannot identify with the torturer without acknowledging the sadistic tendencies that make up part of our (usually) unconscious fantasy world. We feel for the Tortured Girl, for the kidnapped Mother. But Gambaro, almost in a Brechtian fashion, does not allow us to identify too closely with them, for she demonstrates that our identification with the victim is both misleading and disempowering. We are not being victimized; we have a capacity for choice and for action that the victim does not. Torture and terrorism function most effectively when members of the population feel *as if* they were the victim, as if they were next on the list. The arbitrary choice of victims serves to strengthen the identification between public and victim by accentuating the random nature of this atrocity ("it could happen to us"); studies indicate that very few victims are actually politically active or have information to give their tormentors.[19] The aim of torture is, according to Edward Peters, to reduce the victim to "powerlessness" and "to transform forced cooperation and broken-willed assent to the principles of the party."[20] This aim, however, also holds for the spectator. Torture and terrorism, as those who orchestrated Argentina's Dirty War knew, destabilizes the population and makes it easier for the government to maintain power by creating "a climate of fear in which subversion would be impossible."[21] Scarry mentions that torture collapses the world of the victim (35). But torture also threatens to reduce the world of the public. People do not like to talk or think about real (unaestheticized, uneroticized) violence.

Hence, there is less and less that people can think, watch, read, and say. The equation established by Scarry, that "the prisoner's steadily shrinking ground . . . wins for the torturer his swelling sense of territory" (36), also holds true for innocent bystanders. They, too, make it possible for torture to continue by giving ground, by not daring to venture into that realm of knowledge. While we, the audience sitting in distant lands, may not fear the violent intrusion of victimizers into our homes, we fear giving up our peace of mind. If we understood that the practice of torture is tied to financial interest, that torturers are not monsters but people who are trained to do what they do, and that lack of public interest makes atrocious politics possible, the public might have to do something about it or else consider itself complicitous.[22] The very existence of torture is threatening but in fundamentally different ways. It threatens the lives of the victims, it paralyzes the immediate population, and it undermines the distant spectators' sense of well-being, our easy assumptions about human nature and the civilization in which we live.

Terrorism deconstructs reality, inverts it, transforms it into a grotesque fiction. Accounts of terrorism show that victimized populations write their own dramas; missing persons must have moved, they must be someplace, anyplace, other than that no-place in which people are brutalized and assassinated. In the *Blood Wedding* fragment of *Information,* the traditional theatrical plot flows imperceptibly into terrorism, a "modern" drama. The father tells his child a story, but the narration revises the events we see before us. Two men are attacked and abducted. But that's all right, the father explains, they were bad guys, dark, Bolivian, had lots of children, they deserve to be punished by the good guys. The unacceptable (the abduction) becomes not only acceptable but necessary. Torture and terrorism create their own looking-glass world, concrete even if it does not appear on city maps. Old maps no longer correspond to or guide us through this world. The tour through the house demonstrates that traditional concepts concerning one's home, one's family, one's body, have collapsed under the systematic assault inflicted upon them. The theatricality of torture and terrorism tempts us to rethink our world, to somehow accept or make room for these performative acts within our canon of the admissable, thus producing normative changes. As another scene shows, an abduction of innocent victims by the Police magically turns into a righteous extermination of "terrorists" before our very eyes. Labeling people as terrorists allows them to be erased without a trace. And the Police congratulate themselves that "justice always wins out" (111). The flagrant theatricality of the scenes, however, warns us against accepting theatrical or magical solutions to political conflict and cautions us against thinking of the nonvisible spaces as nonspaces. What happens to characters who leave the stage? What do magicians do with all those bunnies? Actors go backstage to their dressing rooms, bunnies go back to their cages, and abduction victims end up in torture chambers and unmarked graves.

The theatricality of terrorism exceeds the mechanics of staging atrocious acts. Terrorism, as the tour through this haunted house shows, functions like a social transformer. As the audience walks down the dark corridors, it becomes clear how terrorism manipulates social fears and inverts cultural symbols. The audience's reaction, as it stumbles in the dark, up and down stairs, signals that terrorism plays with potent images of the unknown, the pit, darkness. It capitalizes on infantile fantasies as the torturers exploit the fear of destruction, dismemberment, and suffocation. The screams resounding through the loudspeakers emphasize that this kind of destabilizing violence works through amplification; twenty victims can hold an entire society hostage. Phantoms loom over a cowering population. The hideous intrusion of children's songs and games into the play illustrates how terrorism pushes the population to regress to those early realms of experience that prove the most overwhelming and the hardest to decode. The spectators simply do not understand what is happening. One approaches as an adult and turns away as a frightened child incapable of action. Cultural norms enter and come out skewed. The innocent are called enemies. Theater becomes terror. Mothers are raped. And the transformation is real not illusory. It actually changes society. The general public does in fact become complicitous and guilty by participating in the transformation. The victims are found guilty; the torturers are acquitted.[23]

Torture turns bodies inside out through violence, but it also turns our moral and judicial systems upside-down. This, the house shows, is an unnatural universe; the lights go on and off throughout the play. Light becomes dark, the visible becomes invisible. Here I disagree with Anthony Kubiak's assertion that while antistate terrorism has performative qualities, "State terrorism (by far the more virulent of the two forms of terrorism) typically relies on the non-theatrical in-visible techniques of torture, clandestine operations, disappearances, and night-time bombing runs."[24] Aside from pointing out that "night-time bombings" are highly visible, it is important to realize that dealing in disappearance and making the visible invisible is also profoundly theatrical. Only in the theater can the audience believe that those who walk offstage vanish into limbo. So the theatricality of torture and terrorism, capable of inverting and fictionalizing the world, does not necessarily lie in its visibility but rather in its potential to transform, to re-create, to make the visible invisible, the real unreal. Perhaps the fact that we know what is going on but cannot see it makes the entire process more frightening, riveting, and resistant to eradication.[25]

Given that the theater's effectiveness can be used to incapacitate the population and preclude its constructive participation, how can Gambaro hope to communicate the atrocious reality of terrorism and torture through theater? One might ask if Gambaro's depictions of torture and terrorism in these and other plays are not themselves a variation of a form of torture called "showing the instruments." Does Gambaro want to further terrorize an already terrorized audience? Does she want to inflict violence on her actors? Or, are we, members of audience, victims who have stumbled into the wrong play? Is she accusing us of being complicitous with the atrocity? By stripping the spectators of their conventional invisibility and placing them in the (Lacanian) lethal field of Other, or as (Sartrian) objects of another's gaze in a situation in which danger and death are everywhere, is she not victimizing them?[26] And, by representing the violence through the theater, which is always involved on some level with the buying and selling of pleasure, is she not, inevitably, falling into the trap of rendering violence pleasurable, perhaps even pornographic? The theatrical act by definition skews the process of victimization—the actress playing the Tortured Girl in Gambaro's play is there of her own free will; real torture victims are not. Doesn't the theatrical event, then, necessarily add the element of *consent,* which differentiates theatrical violence or even sexual sadomasochistic violence, from torture?

The dangers of representing violence are manifold, and Gambaro, as *Information* demonstrates, is well aware of them. Clearly, she never inflicts actual pain on the actors or spectators; the actors do not have their heads submerged in water; the Tortured Girl sits soaking wet near the tub—the idea is that she has just emerged from the "submarine." Other actors "disappear" offstage rather than to their deaths. The audience members, she specifies in the stage directions, are never involved in the action against their will. This is theater not torture. We could not withstand the action if it were torture. Simply reproducing violence would not help elucidate the mechanism of social manipulation that Gambaro reveals through this most manipulative work. The other questions are more difficult to answer. Gambaro's ethical concern with the representation of violence differs, to a degree, from that voiced by Adorno or by playwrights depicting the horrors of the Holocaust who try to preserve the unaestheticized memory of an event in the past. The Gambaro of *Information* lived in a society that was becoming increasingly terrifying. The only way to survive in a criminalized society, she felt, was to challenge it, to challenge its myths, its distortions, its monsters. Faced with a life-threatening situation, Gambaro felt she had no choice but to respond to it. I would argue that her depictions of atrocity do not reproduce violence but demystify it; they are not life-threatening but potentially life-saving. The subject matter is unpleasant, and we, like the Guide, can complain about the unsavory scripts. Gambaro's intrusions into traditional realms of pleasure are as unwelcome as the mandatory review of emergency procedures that intrudes upon a pleasure cruise, as the Guide jokes. "Come in," he says to the group, "Watch your step. All that's missing is a 'fasten your seatbelts and refrain from smoking.'" However, with the waves of indiscriminate violence washing over Argentina, as well as other parts of the world, Gambaro warns that we must learn to see violence in its many guises; we must recognize our role and the role of people "just like us" in maintaining it. She is not demanding information from us but offering it: information for foreigners. As R. I. Moore points out in his preface to Edward Peters's *Torture,* "ignorance has many forms, and all of them are dangerous" (vii). This information empowers the audience, local and foreign alike.

The emphasis in *Information,* moreover, is not on the violent acts themselves but on the audience's role as spectators watching the violence, on the act of watching itself. There are many ways of watching, some empowering, some disempowering, some associated with wisdom (clairvoyance), some with perversity and criminality (voyeurism). To Michel Foucault, watching can be empowering; like the panopticon, surveillance functions "ceaselessly" and "the gaze is alert everywhere."[27] Watching is a powerful tool of the totalitarian state: Big Brother is watching. Gambaro, however, challenges the dangerous fiction that watching in itself can somehow empower the spectator or control violence. Although the Guard reassures the Tortured Girl that she is safe because people are watching, the audience will see the Girl's corpse before the end of the play. The myth that the public, local as well as international, can miraculously avert violence by watching it runs deep. The word *watch,* in the names of groups dedicated to ending political and racial violence such as Americas Watch and Klanwatch, indicates the quasi-magical power we attribute to watching. The play shows, however, that watching, in and by itself, never saved anyone. Americas Watch, Klanwatch, Amnesty International, and similar organizations do not simply watch. Another Girl in a different scene is singing sweetly when a man (supposedly an audience member) approaches and suffocates her in front of the group. Four hospital attendants are called to the scene: they zip the Girl's body into a plastic shroud and away they go. Did the audience save her? Watching, potentially empowering when it forms part of a broader network, can be extremely disempowering when it is reduced to the spectator's passive "just watching."

Is watching itself a form of violence? Is it a form of torture (known in Argentina as family torture) in which we must look on as someone we love is humiliated or destroyed before our eyes? Or is watching the unauthorized, or even criminal, scopophilia of voyeurism?[28] The Guide's flashlight accidentally falls on a prisoner, cowering in a corner, "who raises his head, surprised and terrified. He covers his sex with his hands" (71). The spectators, paying customers, are suddenly cast in the role of Peeping Toms. Worse still, having paid for tickets to a restricted play we might have anticipated the nudity and violence, indisputably the two major selling points of commercial theater. John Berger states it simply in *Ways of Seeing*: "[W]e want to *see* the other naked."[29] Here, however, we catch a glimpse of things we do not want to see, a body under a tarp, a naked man gagged and stuffed in a cage, a murder. Faced with this twisted version of what we have paid for, we are shocked into considering, perhaps for the first time, what our expectations were and what we thought we were buying. What are we doing in the theater? After paying for our tickets, do we merely feel an obligation to get our money's worth? Are we perverted? We are on dangerous ground.

The desire to *see* is nowhere so prominent as it is in the theater or cinema. We go to the theater to see, to hear. Christian Metz, in *The Imaginary Signifier,* writes that cinema "is only possible through the perceptual passions." Seeing and hearing are sexual drives, powerful but subliminal, different from other sexual drives in that they function through distance and absence. Christian Metz notes the importance of lack or absence in fueling this erotic desire: perceptual drives "always remain more or less unsatisfied . . . the lack is what it wishes to fill, and at the same time what it is always careful to leave gaping, in order to survive as desire."[30] Roland Barthes also links desire to absence and distance in describing an erotic photograph: "The erotic photograph [unlike the pornographic] does not make the sexual organs into a central object; it may very well not show them at all; it takes the spectator outside the frame, and it is there that I animate this picture and that it animates me—as if the image launched desire beyond what it permits us to see."[31] Lack, absence, distance, beyond . . .

Gambaro does not allow for the distancing of scopic pleasure, nor for the more vital distancing of voyeuristic pleasure. If, as Metz (following Freud) argues, "voyeurism, like sadism in this respect, always keeps apart the *object* (here the object looked at) from the *source* of the drive (the eye)," Gambaro abolishes that distance by having us stumble on what we do not want to see. We are in the same room. This naked body does not, as in cinema, exist in the realm of the imaginary, pure celluloid; it is materially present. And, unlike traditional theater, which still maintains distance even as the actors and audience coexist within the same four walls, here members of the audience actually bump into, or stumble against, a naked body. Unlike theater that eroticizes or aestheticizes nudity and violence by "covering" as much as it reveals, Gambaro's theater simultaneously exposes violence and draws us into it. The audience sees the raw nakedness of another human being without the erotic distance, the accompanying sympathy, love, or desire that renders the sight tolerable or titillating. Gambaro, moreover, calls attention to the fact that those perceptual desires, or "passions," have already been socialized and politicized in ways we do not recognize. Theories linking desire to a visual lack fail to account for what we feel standing in front of the half-open doors leading to torture chambers. Is the "beyond" here a visual lure? Is our reluctance to look a reluctance to satisfy our desire, a reluctance to see lest we satiate (terminate) desire itself? Is it not, rather, the horror of witnessing real absence, a case of political absenting, that is, disappearance? If we see it, we might have to do something about it. The lack, then, is of a fundamentally different nature when we move to the physical and political arena of abductions and atrocity. There is nothing safe, erotic, innocent, or gratifying about this vision, which inverts traditional theatrical perception, producing pain, perhaps even shame, but precluding pleasure. Intolerable sight, sight that traps both seen and seer, captures both the revolting sight and the viewer's revulsion, all in the same frame.

The same point also holds for the audience's feelings of transgression. Creeping through the halls, peeping into dark rooms, the spectators act like intrusive children stumbling on a primal scene. Originally, however, the prohibition against transgression, much in the manner of taboos, was conceived by populations to protect humanity. Theatrical representations and rituals originally mediated between the human and the divine, shielding humans from the awful (in the sense of holy). Examples as culturally diverse as Euripides' *The Bacchae* and pre-Columbian ritual stress the danger of transgression, of *seeing* that which exceeds human comprehension. The power of the superhuman, like Zeus in all his splendor, threatens to blind and destroy the human.

Gambaro, however, demystifies the notion of transgression and challenges its politics: what is behind those doors and why do we not have legitimate access to it? Fears of transgression obfuscate the mechanics of power, rather than protecting the sensibilities of humanity, whether the sanctum sanctorum is the pre-Hispanic *cue,* the parental bedroom, the masking societies of West Africa, the Pentagon, or Oz. The public is excluded from the production and reproduction of power: hence the masks, the hideous sculptures, the admonitions. The politics of the awesome have given way to the politics of the awful: political secrecy replaces taboo, the off-scene has become the obscene, and terrorism, like an ancient gargoyle, compels us and repels us with its horror. The hidden nature of torture, abductions, and other scenes of atrocity frighten us away from seeing and recognizing them by appealing to ways of seeing that we consciously or unconsciously associate with *bad* seeing, perversion, voyeurism, and transgression. We are socialized to avert our eyes from sexually charged sights. Binding the sexually charged image with annihilating violence tempts us to look away. We do not want to feel like children peeping at keyholes, like voyeurs, like perverts. We do not want to feel complicitous. Yet the identification with peeping children and perverts is a misleading one; although spectators have no place in the bedroom, the same does not hold for the political arena. There the public gives up its place and its right to participation at its peril: torturers can get away with murder.

In order to be empowered by seeing, to be able to look back at monstrous gargoyles without turning into lifeless stones, we must see beyond the theatrical frame and decode the fictions about violence, about torturers, about ourselves as audience, and about the role of theater in this "pathetic drama." Gambaro develops a dangerous theater, one that provokes audiences to resent and reject theatrical manipulation, one that shocks and disrupts and breaks the frames of theatrical tradition in order to make the invisible visible again. She pushes theater to the limits of representation and, some might argue, beyond. Almost like the guerrilla theater so popular in Latin America during the early 1970s, *Information* "raids" theatrical traditions: a little Shakespeare, a touch of Lorca. But spectators never witness a complete scene, and events fail to connect in any coherent or causal way. By introducing fragments of theatrical scenes with acts of criminal violence,

Gambaro indicates the degree to which theater in Latin America is the arena of intense and dangerous ideological conflict. As Desdemona lies dead, the police burst onstage to arrest Othello. This is more than the failure to accept theatrical convention, more than an ironic reminder that only in drama do the police protect the victims. The policing of theater, the censorship of scripts, and the harassment of theater practitioners illustrates that authorities regard theater as subversive. Radical practitioners, on the other hand, see theater as one more stage on which to play out oppression and cultural colonialism. Desdemona will continue to die on Latin American stages and Emilia will continue to defend the noble man's right to murder his wife. For others, theater is (or should be) merely entertainment.

In closing, I would like to comment on the broadest temporal frame in the play, the catacombs. They provide one more perspective from which to recognize not merely the violent reality that the historical frame highlights but the violent reality that it keeps out. The catacombs, as the site of historical scapegoating, sacrifice, and death, frame ongoing persecution. Enshrined as historical evidence of nobler times, the violence associated with the annihilation of those martyrs becomes almost invisible. By dwelling on the heroism of these deaths, the Guide and spectators can overlook the horrors of their context. They can ignore the irony that it was the military rulers, who prided themselves on being Christian, Western, and Argentine, who were in charge of the persecutions. So, while the catacombs provide a reference to a historical past in which death was perceived as meaningful, in another sense the observance of that past is ahistorical, a red herring, diverting attention from the atrocious present.

Framing is problematic in that it allows for issues to be kept artifically separate, and Gambaro combats its propensity for distortion by having the audience and actors move, having the sounds and screams resound throughout the house. *Information* is metapolitical theater in that by constantly pushing aesthetic forms to their limits it enables us to carry that inquiry into politics. One example must suffice. Robert Skloot's introduction to his anthology *The Theatre of the Holocaust* focuses on some of the issues I have raised here. He asks: "How could these horrifying events occur in one of the most civilized and advanced nations of the world? Why did most of the free world remain aloof to the plight of the Jews and other persecuted minorities. . . . Had we been involved in the events of this time, how would we have behaved?"[32] The point, *Information* makes clear, is that these questions are not hypothetical. This in no way suggests that the terrorism holding Latin America hostage today compares with or is "like" the Holocaust, although some scholars maintain that "what happened in Argentina in the years that followed 1976 was probably closer to what happened in Germany after 1933 than anything else in the Western world during the past four decades."[33] The Holocaust was a unique historical event. It ended, but atrocity and fascism live on. The tactics of terror, the bureaucratic and systematic extermination of countless victims, continues today in camps and torture chambers. By juxtaposing the catacombs with traditionally theatrical scenes, with torture, and with terrorist attacks, Gambaro forces us to relinquish our comforting assumptions about violence, our claims to deniability, innocence, and quietism, and instead urges us to understand what prompts it and how we participate, as either voyeurs, investors, bystanders, or victims. In a way, *Information* submits the audience to its own Milgram experiment. Will its members continue to follow the Guide and passively participate in the situation? Will we ask for our money back or walk out of the show? As the spectators move from room to room or turn the pages of the newspaper for "information," the question is being answered. The response is not hypothetical; the play will not allow us to split off. We are the spectators; we are involved. Whether we peep through those half-closed doors or glean our information from the newspapers, this is our show. Can we stop merely watching and end it? If not, as the Guide says, we might as well enjoy it: we're paying for it.

Epilogue

The problems of witnessing and seeing that Gambaro addresses in *Information for Foreigners* are as important now as they were when I wrote this essay. The Argentine military has not staged a coup since 1990, but the threat of violent politics remains constant in a country that has experienced more years of dictatorship than of constitutional rule during this century. As recently as April 1994, the police discovered an enormous cache of weapons, explosives, and even helicopters in the hands of the ultrarightist sector of the military known as the "carpintadas," or "painted faces." The constitutional government of Carlos Menem, which has made many concessions to the military, is struggling to keep the fascist factions among its ranks from taking over. Griselda Gambaro's recent work continues to stress the vital role a population plays in a system of terror. Unlike *Information for Foreigners,* her 1986 work *Antigona Furiosa* focuses on those who risk everything by recognizing political atrocity for what it is, calling it by its name, and fighting back. In that play she also explores the role traditionally assigned to women in civil conflict.[34]

NOTES

1. There was growing opposition to General Onganía's repressive policies, after the 1966 coup, which culminated in the *cordobazo*, the huge riot and strike in Cordoba in 1969 that for two days turned the city into "a theater for pitched battles between rioters and police" (David Rock, *Argentina: 1516–1987* [Berkeley: University of California Press, 1987], 349). Groups of rebels formed. Beginning in 1970, three new Peronist groups appeared—the Montoneros, the Fuerzas Armadas Peronistas (FAP), and the Fuerzas Armadas Revolucinarias (FAR). The Peronist groups allied with the Montoneros, headed by Mario Firmenich. There were non-Peronist parties, the People's Revolutionary Army (ERP, a small Trotskyite party), and the right-wing group Mano (*Hand*). It became clear that during the "Dirty War" the military itself was manipulating these groups in order to justify its own repressive measures. In "Dirty Secrets of the 'Dirty War,' " Martin Edwin Anderson notes that Mario Firmenich was in fact a double agent for the military (*Nation*, March 13, 1989, 340).

2. Abductions, kidnappings, torture, and death lists are a daily reality still in countries like Guatemala, El Salvador, and Colombia.

3. Barbara Ehrenreich, in her foreword to Klaus Theweleit's *Male Fantasies* (trans. Stephen Conway [Minneapolis: University of Minnesota Press, 1987]), warns against interpreting fascist violence as primarily performative: "The problem here is that, too often, fascism tends to become representational, symbolic. In the commonplace attenuated version of psychoanalytic theory that most of us have unthinkingly accepted, fascism is 'really' about something else—for example, repressed homosexuality. Fascist murder becomes a misdirected way of getting at that 'something else'—a symbolic act, if not a variety of performance art" (xi). As Klaus Theweleit himself suggests in *Male Fantasies*, violence is intimately linked to desire; torturing and destroying others is not a symbolic act but rather what the fascist *really* wants to do.

4. Terrorism, Herbert Blau notes in *Take Up the Bodies: Theater at the Vanishing Point* (Urbana: University of Illinois Press, 1982), "has always been designed theatrically. There is a plot, choreography, coup du théatre, and all the attendant apparatus of the staged performance" (272). Elaine Scarry, in *The Body in Pain* (New York: Oxford University Press, 1985), repeatedly refers to torture, metaphorically, as theater: the "mime of uncreating" (20), an "acting out" (27), an "obscene and pathetic drama" (56). The torturer, to Scarry, "dramatizes the disintegration of the world" (38). Subsequent page references to Scarry are included in the text.

5. In *Modern Latin America* (New York: Oxford University Press, 1984), Thomas E. Skidmore and Peter H. Smith write that "the 'disappeared' were victims in a tactic consciously designed to terrorize the country" (107). The attack by the government against its population went on throughout the 1970s, during Perón's term in 1973–74, escalating during Isabelita's term in 1974–76, and culminating in the "Dirty War."

6. Ibid., 103.

7. Griselda Gambaro (b. 1928) is not only one of Argentina's foremost playwrights, with almost thirty plays to her credit, but she is also an award-winning author of seven novels and numerous short stories. A few of her works have been published in English, most notably Marguerite Feitlowitz's translation of her plays in *Information for Foreigners: Three Plays by Griselda Gambaro* (Northwestern University Press, 1992) and translations included in William L. Oliver, ed., *Voices of Change in the Spanish-American Theater* (Austin: University of Texas Press, 1971). Her work has also been translated into French, German, Czech, and Polish. Her plays have been staged throughout the United States, Europe, and Latin America. She has lectured widely in the United States at Yale, Cornell, Dartmouth, Rice, and the University of Texas at Austin, among other academic institutions. She has won a number of awards and prizes for literature, including the Fondo Nacional de las Artes and a Guggenheim Fellowship. Gambaro is of a working-class family in Argentina, descended from Italian grandparents. The Argentine population is primarily made up of Spanish and Italian descendants since the indigenous population was almost completely exterminated in the mid-nineteenth century. Gambaro does not go into Argentine anti-Semitism in *Information,* although the persecution of Jews and the nazilike military is the subject of her play *The Camp* (1967), published in Oliver, *Voices of Change.* See Jacobo Timerman's *Prisoner without a Name, Cell without a Number* (trans. Toby Talbot [New York: Vintage, 1982]) for a more complete description of anti-Semitism during the Dirty War.

8. All translations of *Information for Foreigners* are my own. Marguerite Feitlowitz's translation, which is included in her edition, *Information for Foreigners: Three Plays by Griselda Gambaro,* had not appeared when I wrote this essay. While several of Gambaro's novels were published in Argentina during the 1970s, her plays were not published there during this period. The collection of Gambaro's plays published by Ediciones de la Flor appeared in 1984. *Information,* included in this collection, circulated in manuscript form before its publication and has never been performed in its entirety. This circumstance does not invalidate the work's attempts to reach different audiences, including the reading (foreign) audience of the title. The questions we could pose about its performance, such as what would happen if a member of the real audience offered the Tortured Girl some dry clothes or if someone walked out, are still valid. What would happen if someone responded? The question is not hypothetical. The answer is that it has not happened and that acts of repression (the censorship of this play included) keep happening in Argentina and elsewhere. The play's intent is to scrutinize the public's ability to deny facts that it knows to be true.

9. See Noam Chomsky and Edward S. Herman, *The Washington Connection and Third World Fascism: The Political Economy of Human Rights* (Montreal: Black Rose, 1979).

10. Augusto Boal argues that "theatre is a weapon" for changing society, "a very efficient weapon. For this reason one must fight for it" (*Theatre of the Oppressed,* trans. Charles A. McBride and Maria-Odilia Leal McBride [New York: Theatre Communications Group, 1985], ix).

11. Fanon's position on dance and possession in the colonial world also has implications for cathartic theater in colonized countries: "[A]ny study of the colonial world should take into consideration the phenomena of the dance and of possession. The

native's relaxation takes precisely the form of a muscular orgy in which the most acute aggressivity and the most impelling violence are canalized, transformed and conjured away" (*The Wretched of the Earth*, trans. Constance Farrington [New York: Grove Press, 1968], 57).

12. Susan Sontag, *Under the Sign of Saturn* (New York: Noonday, 1980). Aristotle, in *Poetics* (trans. Gerald F. Else [Ann Arbor: University of Michigan Press, 1973]), suggests that the pleasure afforded by mimetic representation is rooted in human nature, thereby making it difficult, if not impossible, to separate pleasure from imitation (20). Carried to its extreme, this argument leads to positions like the one advanced by Theodor Adorno that art denigrates suffering and victimization: "The aesthetic principle of stylization, and even the solemn prayer of the chorus, makes an unthinkable fate appear to have had some meaning; it is transfigured, something of its horror removed. This alone does an injustice to the victims" ("Commitment," in *Aesthetics and Politics* [London: Verso, 1986], 189).

13. These incidents are detailed in press reports published between April and December of 1970. See articles in *La Prensa, La Nación,* and *Clarín,* for example, as well as Rock, *Argentina: 1516–1987,* 441.

14. Gilles Deleuze and Felix Guattari, *Anti-Oedipus,* Robert Harley, Mark Seem, and Helen R. Lane, trans. (Minneapolis: University of Minnesota Press, 1983), 30.

15. See Ximena Bunster Burotto's "Surviving Beyond Fear: Women and Torture in Latin America," in June Nash and Helen Safa, *Women and Change in Latin America* (South Hadley, Mass.: Bergin and Garvey, 1986).

16. "In "Self-Destructing Heroines" (*Minnesota Review* 22 [1984]: 105–15) Jean Franco indicates that the "division of the traditional city into public (male) spaces and private space where women's power derives from motherhood or virginity has deeply affected both political life in Latin America and the imaginary repertoire on which literature draws . . . the allegorization of women characters in their virtually invariant positions of mother, prostitute or love object" (105). Ximena Bunster also notes that women in Latin America are "basically recognized and valued only as mothers, after the Blessed Virgin Mother" and documents how torture of women in Argentina often involved "icons of the Virgin Mary." Many victims were beaten until they lost consciousness "in front of the image of the Virgin Mary" (quoted in Nash and Safa, *Women and Change,* 299).

17. General Jacques Massu's memoirs of the Algerian war, *La Vraie Bataille d'Algers,* became a classic defense of torture, giving rise to expressions such as Massuism and Massuist. Michael Levin follows the Massuist line of argument in "The Case For Torture," in *The Norton Reader: An Anthology of Expository Prose,* 6th ed., A.M. Eastman, ed. (New York: W. W. Norton, 1984), 619. For a general study on torture, see Edward Peters, *Torture* (New York: Basil Blackwell, 1985).

18. Robert Jay Lifton, *The Nazi Doctors* (New York: Basic Books, 1986), 420. See also Alice Yaeger Kaplan, *Reproductions of Banality: Fascism, Literature, and French Intellectual Life* (Minneapolis: University of Minnesota Press, 1986); and Saul Friedlander, *Reflections on Nazism,* trans. Thomas Weyr (New York: Harper and Row, 1984).

19. See Scarry, *The Body in Pain,* 28; Edward Peter, *Torture;* and Jacobo Timerman, *Prisoner Without a Name.* The situation described in *Nunca Más* succinctly states a con-

clusion about the gratuitous nature of the interrogation, which coincides with the findings reported in the different studies: "They were tortured, almost without exception, methodically, sadistically, sexually, with electric shocks and neardrownings and constant beatings, in the most humiliating possible way, not to discover information— very few had information to give—but just to break them spiritually as well as physically, and to give pleasure to their torturers. Most of those who survived the torture were killed" (*Nunca Más: Report of the Argentine National Commission on the Disappeared* [New York: Farrar, Straus, Giroux, 1986], xvi).

    20. Peters, *Torture*, 164, 162.

    21. *Nunca Más*, xvii.

    22. In *Argentina: 1516–1987*, Rock notes that Martinez de Hoz's economic measures, which aimed to stabilize Argentina "through the aggressive pursuit of foreign investment," were inseparable from the military's repression of the population, specifically labor leaders and union workers: "The Army's war on subversion and Martinez de Hoz's program elicited opposite responses from outside observers, who detested the extreme brutalities of the former but generally praised the latter. In many respects, however, the two policies were complimentary and inseparable" (369). On public complicity, see Peters, *Torture*, 179–84.

    23. Argentine President Menem's decision to pardon the criminals of the Dirty War is only the most recent example of the inversion attested throughout the literature on torture. Jacobo Timerman's description of the torture inflicted on him in Argentina in *Prisoner Without a Name* was discredited by many reviewers who defended the regime and accused Timerman of bringing "his own troubles, including his own torture, on himself" (Peters, *Torture*, 160–61). *Torture in Brazil: A Report by the Archdiocese of Sao Paulo* (trans. Jaime Wright, ed. Joan Dassin [New York: Vintage, 1986]) also notes that torture victims and families who demanded that the torturers be punished were considered vengeful; they were encouraged to forget, to "let bygones be bygones" (xii). Peters reports that in 1973 UNESCO refused to allow Amnesty International to convene in its Paris center because an Amnesty report reflected unfavorably on sixty of UNESCO's member countries then practicing torture (160).

    24. Anthony Kubiak, "Disappearance as History: The Stages of Terror," *Theatre Journal* 39 (1987): 84.

    25. Gambaro, in a 1982 interview, insisted (with an anti-Aristotelian inversion) that the theater must enable the audience to see again, for the public has lost its capacity to see reality: "[T]he dead are numbers, statistics . . . we can read about the war in Lebanon and it means nothing to us. . . . The aesthetic act has to wake us up, we have to come round, out of the anesthetizing misinformation, the emotional deformation, and the ideas that are the very basis of our society" (Griselda Gambaro, *Teatro* [Ottawa: Girol Books, 1983], 31).

    26. For a discussion of the disappearance of self in the field of Other, see Jacques Lacan, *The Four Fundamental Concepts of Psycho-Analysis,* trans. Alan Sheridan (New York: Norton, 1981); and Jacques Lacan, *The Function of Language in Psychoanalysis,* trans. Anthony Wilden (Baltimore: Johns Hopkins University Press, 1968). The audience's situation in *Information* recalls Jean-Paul Sartre's example of the individual peering through the keyhole: "My consciousness sticks to my acts, it is my acts; and my acts are com-

manded only by the ends to be attained (the spectacle to be seen), a pure mode of losing myself in the world. . . . But all of a sudden I hear footsteps in the hall. Someone is looking at me! . . . the person is presented to consciousness *in so far as the person is an object for the Other.* This means that all of a sudden I am conscious of myself as escaping myself. Not in that I am the foundation of my own nothingness but in that I have my foundation outside of myself. I am for myself only as I am a pure reference to the Other" (*Being and Nothingness,* trans. Hazel E. Barnes [New York: Washington Square Press, 1969]).

27. Michel Foucault, *Discipline and Punish: The Birth of the Prison,* trans. Alan Sheridan (New York: Random House, 1979), 195.

28. Christian Metz, *The Imaginary Signifier: Psychoanalysis and the Cinema,* trans. Ben Brewster (Bloomington: Indiana University Press, 1977), 63.

29. John Berger, *Ways of Seeing* (New York: Penguin, 1977), 58, Berger's emphasis.

30. Metz, *Imaginary Signifier,* 58–59.

31. Roland Barthes, *Camera Lucida: Reflections on Photography,* trans. Richard Howard (New York: Hill and Wang, 1981), 59.

32. Robert Skloot, *The Theatre of the Holocaust: Four Plays* (Madison: University of Wisconsin Press, 1982), 10.

33. John Simpson and Jana Bennett, *The Disappeared and the Mothers of the Plaza* (New York: St. Martin's, 1985), 9.

34. A collection of three Gambaro plays, *Information for Foreigners: Three Plays by Griselda Gambaro* (which includes *Antigona Furiosa*), translated and edited by Marguerite Feitlowitz, was published by Northwestern University Press in 1992.

11.

Lynne Conner

"What the Modern Dance Should Be": Socialist Agendas in the Modern Dance, 1931–38

In a review of a Doris Humphrey recital presented in February 1935, a dance critic for the radical leftist publication *New Theatre* complained bitterly about the content of the program, pointing to the "effete" and "abstract" quality of the evening's dance titles: "Credo," "Ecstatic Themes," "Duo-Orama," and "Affirmations." "This is not what the modern dance should be," she charged, adding that "it was not for this that the ballet was discarded, nor for this that we struggle for acceptance of the dance on an equal footing with the other arts."[1] This critic's call for the production of dances that would move beyond the "limitations of abstraction" and toward a revolutionary form of social change was becoming, by the early months of 1935, a familiar one in New York City's modern dance community. It was familiar enough, in fact, to be heard by the form's most powerful and most resolutely apolitical practitioners: Doris Humphrey and Martha Graham. This essay is concerned with narrating the effect of the radical Left's mandate on these two signal artists by defining and illustrating two symbiotic lines of cultural development. The first and broader line argues that political involvement within the modern dance field in New York City paralleled the progress of American radicalism during the 1930s, changing from a sectarian to a popular movement by mid-decade. The second line argues that the success of the Popular Front significantly influenced Humphrey and Graham, causing them to turn away temporarily from their characteristic pure aestheticism toward the prevailing concern for social activism in contemporary art. The essay, then, attempts to illustrate how social change in the culture at large brought about a short-lived but significant reconfiguration of the modern dance.

During the "high twenties," cultural New York City reflected the adventurous personality of the era, when an influx of information about the European avant-garde—combined with the heady effects of an economy driven by new (and seemingly plentiful) money—created a ripe environment for the development of an American modernism in all of the theater arts. In response, the first American modern dancers began emerging around 1926. Rejecting the romantic impulses that had guided their solo dance predecessors (including Isadora Duncan and Ruth St. Denis), the pioneers of modernism in the dance insisted that their own work be representative of contemporary life.[2] They sought a method of articulating America (at least the America they knew—the intellectual and artistic subculture of 1920s Greenwich Village) with the body as speaker. In 1928, Doris Humphrey wrote that she and her students were "stimulated by our enthusiasm for some discoveries about movement, which had to do with ourselves as Americans—not Europeans or American Indians or East Indians . . . but as young people of the twentieth century living in the United States. All this was quite nebulous as yet, but already vistas of a more genuine dance form could be glimpsed ahead."[3] As a result of this new impulse, their early work was concerned with developing a structural and philosophical approach to the dance. Martha Graham, interested in the potential power of a pure aestheticism for the choreographic process, was influenced especially by the work of abstract painters like Wassily Kandinsky.[4] Doris Humphrey, in her own vision of a pure aesthetic, rejected the solo dance figure in favor of the ensemble, stating: "One cannot help but notice the personal characteristics of the solo dancers . . . but in looking at the ensemble one is conscious first of the movement and its quality, because the bodies all merge into one moving mass."[5] Humphrey's call for the impersonality of the ensemble was a desire for dance artists to reject the limitations of the personality by replacing the romantic ideal of the "dancing woman" with the modernist ideal of a "dancing space."

The advent of the American economic depression of the 1930s brought enormous changes to New York City's political and cultural landscape. The failure of unchecked capitalism created new opportunities for the leftist political organizations that already existed in the United States.[6] In particular, the American Communist Party gained considerable momentum, especially among artists, intellectuals, and workers' groups. Between 1930 and 1934, the party's formal membership increased from 7,000 to 26,000, though as many as 57,000 new members are estimated to have joined at one time or another during the period.[7] Perhaps more significant than is reflected in membership numbers, however, was the gradual shift in ideology among many working-class Americans during this period. The high rate of unemployment (an estimated 9 million people in 1931, doubling to 18 million by 1932),[8] combined with a vocal minority of professional agitators, worked to effect new expectations among American workers within and without the party. Those new expectations included increasingly radical assumptions about the basic rights of all American workers, resulting in the demand for major changes in the way private enterprise was regulated. As a result, the radical Left in the United States found itself, for the first time, in a position of influence.

Around 1930, a small segment of the modern dance community in New York City began to respond to the call of the Left. The first ensembles to adopt a Marxist agenda were officially affiliated under an umbrella organization, the Workers Dance League, in early 1931. The league was comprised of two types of ensembles: amateur troupes of factory workers (including the Nature Friends and the Red Dance Group) and pseudoprofessional troupes of young artists/intellectuals (including the New Dance Group and the Theatre Union Dance Group). The amateur ensembles were similar to and perhaps modeled on the workers' theater groups that surfaced among trade-unionist organizations in the late 1920s. By 1929, for example, The Workers Dramatic Council of New York City consisted of twelve companies made up of amateur factory workers.[9] Both theater and dance performances promoted radical changes in factory and government structure and were designed for an audience made up of other factory workers. In Workers Dance League productions, titles like "Eviction," "Hunger," "Homeless Girl," and "While Waiting for Relief" were indicative of the class struggle being waged, and they suggest, by their literal quality, the aesthetic stance (or lack thereof) of these groups. Journalistic accounts of their occasional concert appearances—which began around 1934—repeatedly mention the amateur groups' predilection for "simple presentation of political ideas . . . in agit-prop form,"[10] indicating the socially motivated orientation of their work.

The professional arm of the Workers Dance League was responsible for most of the public rhetoric surrounding the early years of radicalization in modern dance. The "Workers' Dance League Manifesto," first printed in *New Masses* in February 1931, for example, was issued by a spokesperson for the New Dance Group who argued that the organization's "sole purpose is to serve the revolutionary movement by using the dance as a medium to further inspire the workers to greater militancy in the class struggle."[11] The revolutionary language echoed the rhetoric of the emerging workers' art and literature movement, a movement that courted an active affiliation with the Soviet system. The term *communism* was readily employed, and politically charged distinctions were made between the concepts of communism and socialism, radicalism and progressivism, and revolutionary activism and democratic reform. The leading arts and cultural journals, including *New Masses* (1926) and *Workers Theatre* (1931), promoted identification with the Communist Party and revolutionary activism. An early *Workers Theatre* editorial stated, for example: "The committee is confident that the Workers' Theatre will spread the knowledge of the platform of the Communist Party, and their main demands: Unemployment and Social Insurance; Emergency Relief for poor farmers; Equal rights for negros; Against capitalist terror; Against imperialist war."[12]

The journal's artistic agenda further echoed this mandate. Reviews operated on a prescriptive evaluative system derived (though certainly "Americanized") from the fundamental principles of historical materialism. "Good art," accordingly, operated under the structural and ideological principles of the emerging doctrine of social realism. It was functional, contemporary, and capable of successfully communicating an appropriate social message to its audience of workers.[13] Its structural characteristics included the frank (and usually literal) introduction of social issues into plot, theme, and character, presented through the use of didactic presentational theatrical devices. In the theater, for example, dialogue was often taken verbatim from party platforms, and politically charged actor-audience intercourse was common. In the dance, pantomimic gesture replaced abstract movement, offering a kinetic style of gesture-for-word literality. Not surprisingly, in the early 1930s, *New Masses* praised the revolutionary efforts of workers' dance troupes by emphasizing the potential transformative relationship between art and propaganda. The mainstream press, on the other hand, remained largely suspicious of politically motivated art. John Martin, the dance critic of the *New York Times*, frequently castigated the various troupes working under the Workers Dance League umbrella, criticizing their use of a literal movement vocabulary (Martin often labeled the work "unchoreographic") and general disregard for the emerging aesthetic criteria being defined by Graham and Humphrey.[14]

By 1934, however, the concept of socially committed art seeking to change society had entered a significantly wider segment of New York

City's arts community, so much so, in fact, that even John Martin was willing to praise it. In a review of a Workers Dance League concert of that year, he wrote that the evening "was fairly bristling with revolutionary protest."[15] Martin (no Marxist himself and working for the politically conservative publisher of the *New York Times*, Adolph Ochs), based his praise on what he saw as the league's increasing ability to convey "the difference between militancy and blatancy, between the force of the accurately directed logic of art and that of the stuffed club bludgeoning the air."[16] His commentary points to what a *New Theatre* editorial labeled the "art-versus-propaganda bugaboo."[17] The debate centered around what was seen by the Left as the spiritual and cultural waste of a pure aestheticism versus what the cultural mainstream saw as a lack of artistic viability in propagandistic art. By mid-decade, workers' cultural leagues operating under the *New Theatre* banner were actively in pursuit of some definition of an acceptable middle ground, where, as one essayist from a leading dance journal put it, the product becomes "communicable vital experience from the socially committed artist."[18]

These changes in artistic strategy within the Workers Dance League point to a larger shift in ideology that began occurring around 1934. Characterized as "a general retreat from revolutionary activity,"[19] the shift was apparent in the nearly wholesale realignment in the rhetoric and jargon of the cultural Left. *Workers Theatre,* having ceased publication in the fall of 1933, returned in January under the banner *New Theatre.* The Workers Theatre and Dance Leagues became the New Theatre and Dance Leagues. The term *new,* in fact, became a beacon, both to established members of the radical Left and to the growing New Deal populist movement. Its warning was clear: the new Left was turning away from the class-war ideology of the Communist Party toward a looser, more inclusive, more accommodating stance. Now labeled the Popular Front, it sought a membership base that would include not only communists and socialists but progressive liberal democrats.

The change was probably precipitated by the increasing liberalization of significant portions of the American public under New Deal welfare programs, and the United Front policy instigated by the Soviet regime's Seventh Congress. The former introduced a limited notion of a social welfare system without advocating socialism as a guiding ideological construct, thus making some aspects of progressive politics more palatable to Middle America. The latter allowed American communists to implement "joint actions between the proletariat and the other toiling classes in the fight against fascism,"[20] thereby loosening restrictions on affiliations with other workers' groups. This united "fight against fascism" quickly became the rallying cry of the Popular Front, reflected in the following quote from a 1935 editorial page of *New Theatre*:

> All readers of *New Theatre* are directly concerned in the recent establishment of a means by which they can directly participate in the building of a strong new theatre of definite social basis and direction. If you have been thinking seriously about it, you know beyond the possibility of self-deception that in the United States, as well as in other parts of the world, fascist tendencies are growing. They threaten, here as elsewhere, not only the work of radical artists, but all the cultural achievements that humanity has so slowly and laboriously built up throughout the centuries."[21]

The editorial proceeded to offer an invitation to "all the constructive, socially conscious elements in the theatre . . . to rally the vast masses of audiences as yet unaware of the dangers which confront us."[22]

Following this mandate, the New Dance League issued the following statement in its report on the Annual Conference of the New Dance League, New York City, May 22, 1936: "The New Dance League is an organization for all dancers, whether soloists, teachers, members of groups, professionals or amateurs, willing to support its basic program: for a mass development of the American dancer to its highest artistic and social level; for a dance movement dedicated to the struggle against war, fascism, and censorship."[23] The league's emphasis on artistic achievement was a distinct departure from the workers' philosophy of the old league, implying a level of professionalism directly contradicting the former ideal of a cultural movement exclusively for workers. Indeed, the earliest formations of workers' cultural leagues were aggressively against the participation of bourgeois practitioners. According to Mike Gold, the editor of *New Masses* and a leading figure of the movement during the early 1930s, professional artists were "vague rootless people" out of touch with the "tongue of the working class."[24]

Also significant was the Popular Front's new emphasis on issues of world politics as opposed to the radical Left's former focus on the economic problems of the working class. Following the mandate of the Popular Front, *New Theatre* urged its cultural leagues to join forces in a "united theatrical front against censorship, against fascism, against all imperialist drives for war!"[25] This change in focus was clearly reflected in the subject matter of both New Dance League and New Theatre League programs. A February 1935 *New Theatre* review of a Workers Dance League recital, for example, mentioned several pieces on world fascism, including "Van der Lubbe's Head," which projected "the horror and viciousness of the Hitler regime"; "Kinder, Kirche, Kuche," which encouraged the women of Nazi Germany to fight "against their lot"; and the "Defiance" section of "Anti-War Trilogy" by the Theatre Union Dance Group (founded by Anna Sokolow, a former member of Graham's ensemble), which focused "the entire canvas of imperialist war" on the uprising in Spain.[26] *New Theatre*'s "Play Reviews" sections of 1935 and 1936 covered similar ground. The Brooklyn Progressive Players' production of *Blood on the Moon,* for instance, dramatized "the mystical-fanatic basis of Hitler's strength among German youth, the brutality to which it lends itself, and the complete intellectual confusion and isolation of its middle-class victims."[27] Other New Theatre League productions from the mid-1930s dealing with fascism and imperialism included Irwin Shaw's *Bury the Dead,* the Theatre Collective's *Private Hicks*, and the Chicago Repertory Group's satirical cabaret *If This Be Reason.*

By the end of 1935, the primary political values of the Popular Front, first articulated in the call for a united stance against the growing number of fascistic governments, were now being more broadly defined. Censorship, warmongering, racism, imperialism, and monopoly capitalism were all targets and potential thematic points of departure. In the dance community, the most popular subjects were the Spanish Civil War and the condition of "Negroes" in the United States. For example, the modern dancer and choreographer Helen Tamiris, whose political involvement included organizing the Works Progress Administration's Federal Dance Project, created a series of "Negro Spirituals" that attempted to stage the plight of African Americans in dance terms. Amateur dance troupes like the Red Dancers and the Nature Friends also took up the cause, performing "Black and White" and "Cause I'm a Nigger" in factory and concert settings. And the war in Spain generated a plethora of dances, ranging from generalized antiwar cycles like Tamiris's "Towards the Light" to the more specific (and literal-minded) protests of the amateur troupes. In the theater community, the condition of African Americans was being addressed by white-dominated amateur troupes like the Workers Laboratory Theatre, whose production of *Scottsboro* (about the notorious "Scottsboro Boys" case) was making the rounds by 1935. But the topic was also the central focus of the newly formed Negro Unit of the Federal Theatre Project, in which professional productions of activist plays like *Turpentine* encouraged audiences to "rebel against the barbarous conditions prevalent in remote industrial regions of America."[28] Other recurring themes in the theater field included censorship (at home and abroad) and fascism (particularly as it applied to the war in Spain).

Perhaps the most far-reaching and politically inclusive value of the Popular Front, however, was the broad theme of Americanism. Rediscovery of the American past was a widespread cultural phenomenon in the 1920s, especially in rural communities where patriotic pageants and outdoor theater spectacles were popular community-based entertainments. In the hands of the Popular Front, Americanism was retooled into a new brand of patriotism in which the heroic working-class ideology of socialism was reconceived as democracy, with democracy standing in direct opposition to the tyranny of nineteenth-century-style monopoly capitalism. Popular Front Americanism lauded the democratic tradition of the United States by offering images from the American Revolution, the signing of the Declaration of Independence, and the Civil War as proof of the country's history of fighting for the common man. But it carefully avoided any explicit association with communism by emphasizing the individual heroic figure as a metaphor for the American worker. In doing so, it managed to embrace the growing tide of approval for workers' rights without disrupting the established iconography associated with the merits of capitalism (as in, for example, the Horatio Alger figure). In its everyman representation of the working-class hero, Americanism proved so powerful, and so popular, that even the Communist Party got on the bandwagon, using "Communism is Twentieth-Century Americanism" as its official election slogan in 1936.[29]

Nevertheless, before 1935, and despite the active political agenda of the New Dance League and its affiliated amateur organizations, both Doris Humphrey and Martha Graham maintained an apolitical stance in their public lives and in their dancemaking. In her biography of Humphrey, Selma Jeanne Cohen details the choreographer's lack of political involvement, even after she joined the Dance Unit of the Works Progress Administration as a dance teacher in 1935. According to Cohen, Humphrey had no "particular feelings about the political significance of the project . . . apparently considering it just another dance job."[30] Writing about Graham's political agenda, Agnes de Mille claims that, despite "extravagant" pressure to join the Communist Party in the early 1930s, the choreographer refused to make any specific political ties and based her actions strictly on the dictates of her own conscience.[31] During these years, Graham and Humphrey were engaged in all-consuming battles to create an artistic field for their new art. In the process, they became extremely clannish, refusing to involve themselves in established artistic or cultural platforms—or with each other. While fellow modernists in other fields participated in the heady intellectual exchange that was centered in Greenwich Village, Graham and Humphrey kept to themselves.[32] In the early 1930s, then, individual aesthetic agendas and a concern for establishing the modern dance's place as a "high art" worthy of an important position in the cultural hierarchy took precedence over any concern for social content.

This is especially clear in the structural aspects of both choreographers' early work. Humphrey's dances before 1934 emphasized formal values, making her "ability to handle a group, to divide it into contrapuntal sections and to set a single figure against all the rest," according to John Martin, "a source of constant variety and vitality in her designs."[33] Early titles like "Air for the G String" (1928), "Etude No. 1" (1930), and "The Pleasures of Counterpoint" (1932) indicate a formal interest in the relationship between dance composition and musical composition. Graham was concerned, as well, with applying her movement theory and choreographic philosophy to an ideal of dance as pure movement in the early years of her career. The titles of her first group dances ("Four Insincerities: Petulance, Remorse, Politeness, Vivacity" [1929], and "Two Variations: Country Lane, City Street" [1929]) reflect her interest in abstracting contemporary life in order to uncover its "universality" in kinetic terms. This quest was also apparent in Graham's growing fascination with ritualistic patterns in a variety of cultures, as can be seen in "Primitive Mysteries: Hymn to the Virgin, Crucifuxus, Hosanna" (1931) and "American Provincials: Act of Piety, Act of Judgement" (1934). Even her early solos, despite bearing titles such as "Revolt" (1927) and "Poems of 1917" (1928), were less a function of social activism than an experiment in style. According to de Mille, "Revolt" did not advocate the party line. In fact, when confronted with that idea after a performance of the dance, Graham responded by insisting that "Communists . . . should be demolition workers. . . . Just give them a building to tear down, and they'll be quite happy to leave our government structures alone."[34]

Beginning around 1935, however, both Graham and Humphrey began loosely associating themselves with the Popular Front. Neither of their companies was ever a member of the New Dance League, nor did their leaders make any official statements regarding political affiliations. But during the first part of 1935 Graham was a featured speaker at a benefit dinner for *New Theatre*, taking the lectern with Clifford Odets and Archibald Macleish. In December 1935, the Graham and Humphrey companies joined the Dance Unit of the New Dance League in a "Dance For Spain" group concert sponsored by the International Labor Defense. In 1936, Graham publicly rejected an offer from the Nazi government to participate in the Berlin Olympics. And in 1938 both companies appeared at a benefit for Spain sponsored by the American Dance Association (the new umbrella organization for New York City's various dance leagues, officially amalgamated in April 1937). Humphrey and Graham's rhetorical involvement in Popular Front ideology is hardly surprising, despite their political aloofness during the early 1930s. The movement, with its inclusive policies regarding liberal to leftist political organizations and its ideological focus on the fight against world fascism, became extremely fashionable among New York City's intellectual and artistic subcultures between 1935 and 1940. Given the political climate, serious artists and intellectuals would have been hard pressed during the latter half of the 1930s to ignore the social mandate in their work.

What is surprising is the apparent willingness of both artists to enact that rhetoric in their dancemaking after 1934. A significant portion of Graham's dancemaking during the last half of the decade dealt in some fashion with themes related to Popular Front political values. In 1936 and 1937, for example, she made three dances directly sympathetic to the defense of Spain, including "Chronicle," an hour-long group dance, and the solos "Immediate Tragedy" and "Deep Song." Of the three, only "Chronicle" is characteristic of the Graham canon in its use of the principles of abstraction to realize the thematic material. Divided into three sections designed to chronicle a universal understanding of the "advent and consequences" of war, the piece never directly addressed the situation in Spain and carefully avoided any pantomimic or gestural vocabulary. Interestingly, even John Martin found it too abstract. The dance, in his words, was "guilty of dryness and overformalism," which obscured the passion and immediacy of the cause.[35] The solos, on the contrary, constitute some of the first examples of Graham's willingness to enter the conceptual realm of propagandistic art. Premiered six months apart during the 1937 season, both dances made (as the titles imply) immediate references to the war in Spain. "Deep Song," in particular, was a broadly emotional call for sympathy and anger. Like "Lamentation," its close relative in the Graham canon, the piece featured a grieving woman seated on a bench. But, unlike "Lamentation," the woman's background and cause for grief were not portrayed as general or universal but as specific to the women of contemporary Spain. This aesthetic departure suggests that Graham felt growing pressure in the cultural community to create works that were more politically accessible.

Of the range of political values associated with the Popular Front, Graham seemed most comfortable with the theme of Americanism. In 1935, she premiered "Panorama," an ambitious dance theater piece that, according to the concert program notes, "endeavors to present three themes of thought and action which are basically American," and "Frontier," a solo about a young pioneer woman's struggle to settle the wilderness. "Panorama" was an overview of American history divided into three sections: the era of the Puritans, the heyday of slavery, and the contemporary era of rising social consciousness. Not a success with its audience or with the mainstream press (Martin felt that it was hastily composed), Graham never repeated it. (It has been staged by her company since her death, however.) Operating from the vantage point of its own political agenda, "Panorama" was praised by *New Theatre* as marking "the first occasion when Miss Graham, outspokenly, through program notes as well as theme, joined forces with those artists in America who find social comment the basis of their work."[36] "Frontier," which opened in April of 1935, was more successful with its audiences and with Martin. Focusing on a solo figure (Graham) and a limited movement vocabulary (the range between the open-spaced arc surrounding the human figure and the close-spaced angles of the clenched torso), it was intended to evoke the possibilities and frustrations of an undiscovered terrain. In both works, as in her pieces on the Spanish Civil War, Graham's social activism and her willingness to move beyond (however slightly) her prior commitment to addressing only universal qualities were expressed within the realm of theme and content. The formal design of these dances was defined by the abstracted movement patterns and leitmotivs of her earlier work and was not in line with the structural elements of contemporary social-realist dances.

Only in "American Document," which had its New York premiere at a benefit performance for *New Masses* in October 1938, was Graham willing to experiment with some of the structural particulars of state-of-the-art social realism. Framed by an interlocutor figure borrowed from the minstrel tradition, "American Document" addressed in one evening the enormous canvas of Americanism as idealized by the Popular Front, with sections that explored, according to John Martin, the "taking of the land from the Indians . . . the emancipation of the Negro and the present economic situation, with a final tableau, so to speak, in celebration of democracy."[37] In keeping with Popular Front sentiment, it was both patriotic and critical of American history, careful to separate the achievements of individuals from the restrictions and abuses of the system.[38] The piece's use of a spoken text (recited by the actor Houseley Stevens Jr.)—a compilation borrowed from poetry, historical documents, treaties, sermons, and proclamations—was in line with current fashion among the cultural Left. Accessible and instantly intelligible it gave the audience a direct line to the work's meaning, thus endowing "American Document" with a literal framework that stripped it of the abstraction often associated with Graham's brand of modernism. Indeed, Gervaise Butler's review of the piece for the journal *Dance Observer* proclaimed, "There is no mystery in *American Document* between the dancer and her audience."[39]

Even the pure dance sequences were a departure for the artist. The major dances included Graham's solo "Indian Episode–Native Figure," the large ensemble pieces "Lament for the Land" and "Emancipation," and two duets for Graham and Erick Hawkins, "Puritan Episode" and "Duet." The choreography was more accessible and instantly intelligible than that found in her earlier works, tackling the underlying political messages with an unusual literality. The movement in Graham's Indian solo, for example, was based on a kinetic interpretation of Indian sign language, and was, by most critical accounts, heavy handed. The dance critic Edwin Denby labeled it "too constantly solemn, too unhumorous, too stiff" and said that it suffered from a "monotony of equal thrusts."[40] Graham made a significantly larger departure in the two duets. Working for the first time with a male partner, the choreography that emerged out of her relationship with Hawkins (who later became her husband) was sexually suggestive, overtly sensual, and unabashedly romantic, all qualities essentially unexplored in her earlier works. Audiences responded positively to the "new" Graham, enjoying "American Document" for its chronicling of the nation's history, its accessible theatricality, and its joyous celebration of democracy. Critics saw it as an important transition, a turn toward the more theatrical, emotional, and demonstrative aspects of Graham's sensibility and the first of her great dance-theater pieces. In any case, it was the most popular piece in the Graham repertoire during the late 1930s, and it helped introduce the artist to a larger segment of the theatergoing population.

Like Graham, Humphrey began investigating the themes of the new Left around 1935. Her "New Dance" and "Theatre Piece," according to the choreographer, showed "the world as it should be, where each person has a clear and harmonious relationship to his fellow beings."[41] The premiere of the full evening performance of both works was uniformly well received. Both John Martin and Margaret Lloyd, the influential dance critic of the *Christian Science Monitor,* specifically praised the way Humphrey used formal qualities of composition to deliver the social message. *New Theatre,* characteristically on the other end of the critical continuum, lauded the evening's "content rather than . . . form" and praised "Theatre Piece" for its "all-inclusive . . . condemnation of our present society."[42] Both dances were said to be "the first attempts of this concert dancer to tear down consciously the old barriers that have kept her aloof from the world, smug in a little circle of intellectuals and pseudo-sophistocates. They are the opening wedge that will lead her to her rightful audiences, the masses of people who are eager to know and learn. 'New Dance' and 'Theatre Piece' incorporate a revolutionary spirit that is rebellious toward the old order and courageous toward the new."[43] Despite *New Theatre'*s enthusiasm for the "revolutionary spirit" of the two works, however, they were not formulated according to the structural criteria of social realism, and they did not directly address new Left themes. Highly abstract, both "Theatre Piece" and "New Dance" were characteristic members of the Humphrey canon, carefully crafted to maintain an aesthetic distance from any literal meaning, in either form or content. John Martin compared "New Dance," for example, to a symphony, stating: "Here is a work which has the same power to stir the emotions, to kindle esthetic excitement, as is to be found in symphonic music."[44]

Humphrey's singular experiment with a direct creative engagment of Popular Front political values premiered in January 1938. "American Holiday" was originally designed to include three freestanding dances on the theme of heroism during the American Revolution. Anticipating Graham's "American Document" (which it preceded by six months), "American Holiday" was intended as a sprawling commentary on the American past—part homage, part criticism. According to Humphrey's program notes, the first two sections—"Death of the Hero" and "Dance for the Living"—celebrated "the death of the hero in the American struggle for independence and proclaims the causes of freedom and justice for which he died . . . and the spread of his influence among the people and their dedication to the same causes which inspired him."[45] Critical accounts from the period make it clear that Humphrey's plan was to present both the positive and negative results of American hero worship. In particular, the projected third part, "Fourth of July" (which was never staged), was to have brought the piece up to the present, questioning the effects of the heroic ideal on the living.

FIG. 1. "American Holiday" by Doris Humphrey. (Photo courtesy THE
DANCE COLLECTION, the New York Public Library for the Performing Arts, Astor, Lenox, and Tilden Foundations.)

Structurally, "American Holiday" took its cue from contemporary social-
realist works, incorporating a spoken text recited by an actress, a large offstage singing chorus, another speaking chorus (which included the twelve
company dancers), and some of Humphrey's most literal choreography.

The first two segments of "American Holiday" were poorly received.
The flaw, according to critics writing for publications ranging from the
New York dailies to *Dance Observer* and *American Dancer*, was the static quality of the finished work. Most of the critics pointed to Humphrey's inability to weld the various theatrical components into some kind of unified and
satisfying whole, noting, for example, that "too great concern and preoccu-
pation with the use of the spoken work and choral singing cause the dance
itself to be neglected."[46] The other major critical objection was Humphrey's
overly literal interpretation of the piece's themes. The *New York Herald Tribune*, for example, criticized it for its "childishly and tiresomely applied ideology."[47] Martin called Humphrey's literalness "admirable" in purpose,
lauding the attempt on her part to "break through the tendency of much
modern dancing to be unintelligible." Nevertheless, he found the effort
"largely ineffectual and inclined to be platitudinous."[48] Based on these
accounts, it appears that Humphrey was unable to find an aesthetic middle

ground between pure abstraction and plain literality. Not surprisingly, then, the first two sections of "American Holiday" represent the only examples of Humphrey's direct engagement of the ideology and structural approach of the Popular Front. She never again used didactic techniques in her dance theater works or addressed topical social issues in a literal or specific manner.

In 1939, the Soviet Union's signing of the nonaggression pact with Germany brought about the end of the Popular Front in the United States, stranding the American Left in the midst of an ideological crosscurrent that could no longer be successfully negotiated with calls for a united stand against world fascism. Concurrently, with a new world war erupting in Europe and a rapidly strengthening economy at home, political activism was no longer the central concern of New York City's artistic culture. The changing landscape of American realism, in the theater and in the dance, was more concerned with the idea of accurate representation of day-to-day life than with an ideal vision of how that life should (and could, it was believed, under the correct political construct) be lived. In response to the changing climate and to their own evolving aesthetics, both Graham and Humphrey turned in new directions. Neither abandoned contemporary themes or the quest to articulate America and American ideals. (Graham's 1944 "Appalachian Spring," for example, was the crystallization of her desire to dance the American frontier.)[49] Both choreographers did, however, reject the didactic, presentational techniques of social realism in constructing those themes, moving toward the realization of a new dance theater in which theatrical metamorphosis became the guiding vision.

The meeting between modernist tendencies and committed leftist politics in the work of Martha Graham and Doris Humphrey stands, in retrospect, as a brief and unlikely moment in the history of the art form. That such diverse and seemingly contradictory impulses—the urge for a pure aestheticism versus the mandate for didactic, ideologically motivated performance—could find even temporary simultaneous residence in their work is not necessarily evidence of individual weakening in the face of popular sentiment. It can be seen, instead, as a fascinating testament to the power of cultural intercourse and to the constant exchange of causes and reactions that define any "historical" moment.

NOTES

1. Elizabeth Skrip, "Dance Reviews," *New Theatre* 2, no. 2 (February 1935): 28.
2. The American concert dance tradition began in the 1890s with the work of the solo dance artists. Attempting to recall the cultural power of ancient civilizations, the

solo dancers sought, through the dancing body, an ideal of universal truth. Duncan called her movement "Greek dancing," insisting that the Greeks "in all their painting, sculpture, architecture, literature, dance and tragedy evolved their movements from the movement of nature" (*The Art of the Dance,* ed. Sheldon Cheney [New York: Theatre Arts, 1919], 58). St. Denis's solo dances were an attempt to re-create an array of exotic cultures. She labeled them "translations" and insisted that her dancing "express principles of life" ("The Dance as an Art Form," *Theatre Arts* 1, no. 1 [February 1916], 75–77).

3. Quoted in Selma Jeanne Cohen, *Doris Humphrey: An Artist First* (Middletown, Conn.: Weslyan University Press, 1972), 61.

4. According to Agnes de Mille, when Graham saw her first Kandinsky painting in Chicago in 1921 she told her companion and mentor, Louis Horst, that she would "dance like that" (*Martha: The Life and Works of Martha Graham* [New York: Random House, 1991], 84).

5. "Miss Humphrey Speaks," *New York Herald Tribune,* March 31, 1929, sec. 7, p. 9.

6. For more information on socialism in America before 1929, see David Harris, *Socialist Origins in the United States: American Forerunners of Marx, 1817–1832* (Assen: Van Gorcum, 1966); John Earl Haynes and Harvey Klehr, *The American Communist Movement: Storming Heaven Itself* (New York: Twayne, 1992); and Harvey Klehr, *The Heydey of American Communism: The Depression Decade* (New York: Basic Books, 1984).

7. Klehr, *The Heydey of American Communism,* 153.

8. Klehr and Haynes, *The American Communist Movement,* 60.

9. Malcolm Goldstein, *The Political Stage: American Drama and Theatre of the Great Depression* (New York: Oxford University Press, 1974), 28–29.

10. Edna Ocko, "Dance League Recital," *New Theatre* 2, no. 2 (February 1935): 25.

11. "Workers' Dance League Manifesto," *New Masses* 6, no. 2 (February 1931): 20. The league's official title did not include an apostrophe after *Workers.* However, contemporary accounts in newspapers and magazines often inserted one.

12. "Workers' Theatre," *Workers Theatre* 2, no. 3 (June-July 1932): 3.

13. For American theories on Marxist art from the period (both pro and con), see Milton W. Brown, "The Marxist Approach to Art," *Dialectics* 2 (1937): 23–31; James Burnham, "Marxism and Esthetics," *Symposium* 4, no. 1 (January 1933): 3–30; and Dane Rudhyar, "Art and Propaganda," *Dance Observer* 3, no. 10 (December 1936): 109–13.

14. John Martin was especially sensitive on this issue, probably because he was the first critic-scholar to define the aesthetic components and rules of engagement in his book *The Modern Dance* (New York: A. S. Barnes and Co., Inc., 1933).

15. John Martin, "The Dance: Radical Art," *New York Times,* January 21, 1934, sec. 10, p. 8. Though the Workers Dance League was comprised of a number of troupes, Martin frequently referred to league concerts in the singular, not bothering to distinguish one member group's efforts from another.

16. John Martin, "The Dance: Young Talent," *New York Times,* December 2, 1934, sec. 9, p. 8.

17. "The W.P.A. Theatres and Censorship," *New Theatre* 3, no. 2 (February 1936): 26.

18. Rudhyar, "Art and Propaganda," 109–13.

19. Klehr, *The Heydey of American Communism*, 207.

20. Ibid., 170.

21. "February 1935," *New Theatre* 2, no. 2 (February 1935), 4.

22. Ibid.

23. This unpublished report is housed in the dance collection of the New York Public Library for the Performing Arts at Lincoln Center.

24. Michael Gold, "Reviews," *New Masses* 6, no. 1 (January 1931): 21.

25. "February 1935," 4.

26. Ocko, "Dance League Recital," 25.

27. "Play Reviews," *New Theatre* 3, no. 7 (July 1936): 24.

28. "Play Reviews," *New Theatre* 3, no. 8 (August 1936): 18.

29. Goldstein, *The Political Stage*, 152–53.

30. Cohen, *Doris Humphrey*, 140.

31. De Mille, *Martha*, 160, 192–93.

32. The resulting rivalry between the two choreographers is well chronicled in Deborah Jowitt, *Time and the Dancing Image* (New York: William Morrow, 1988), 187; and de Mille, *Martha*, 160–63.

33. John Martin, "Dance Theatre Opens Second Season," *New York Times*, February 2, 1931, 12.

34. De Mille, *Martha*, 87.

35. John Martin, "Martha Graham in Dance Recital," *New York Times*, December 21, 1936, 18.

36. Edna Ocko, "Martha Graham's 'Panorama,' " *New Theatre* 2. no. 9 (September 1935): 27.

37. John Martin, "Martha Graham Offers New Dance," *New York Times*, October 10, 1938, 14.

38. According to Edwin Denby, this careful balance was lost in subsequent stagings, especially during the war years. In a review for the *New York Herald Tribune* in 1944 he wrote: "Originally it seemed at least to conceal some sting of protest and to present our history as much for its disgraces as for its strength. At present it seems intended merely as smug glorification" (*Edwin Denby: Dance Writings*, ed. Robert Cornfield and William Mackay [New York: Knopf, 1986], 230).

39. Gervaise Butler, review of "American Document," *Dance Observer* 5, no. 9 (November 1938): 129.

40. Denby, *Edwin Denby: Dance Writings*, 56.

41. Quoted in Cohen, *Doris Humphrey*, 137.

42. Elizabeth Ruskay, "Dance Reviews," *New Theatre* 3, no. 3 (March 1936): 27.

43. Ibid.

44. John Martin, "The Dance: A New Work," *New York Times*, August 11, 1935, sec. 10, p. 5.

45. Quoted in Mary P. O'Donnell, "Doris Humphrey—Charles Weidman," *Dance Observer* 5, no. 3 (March 1938): 38.

46. Ibid.

47. Quoted in Marcia B. Siegel, *Days on Earth: The Dance of Doris Humphrey* (New Haven, Conn.: Yale University Press, 1987), 174.

48. John Martin, "New Work Seen in Dance Recital," *New York Times,* January 10, 1938, 12.

49. Nevertheless, and for all its external Americanism, "Appalachian Spring" was (and remains) a distinctly different kind of dance than "American Document." A study of character and culture achieved purely in movement terms, the focus of the piece is the relationship between, and the kinetic and visual quality of, public and private space. There is nothing remotely political about its content. And its structure, framed by the elegant Noguchi set and Copland's majestic score, points to a theatrical vision more in line with Aristotle than with Marx.

Contributors

Lynne Conner recently completed her Ph.D. in Theater History and Performance Studies at the University of Pittsburgh, where she is now teaching courses in drama and theory. She has written and broadcast dance criticism for *High Performance, The Pittsburgh Press, In Pittsburgh,* and WQED-FM.

Gregg Dion is a doctoral candidate at the University of Pittsburgh currently serving as adjunct faculty in the Department of American Literature at the University of Łódź, Poland. He received his M.A. from the University of Georgia.

Harry Elam, Jr., is Associate Professor of Drama at Stanford University. He has published essays in *Theatre Journal* and *Text and Performance Quarterly.* He has two books-in-progress, *The Ritual Process of Social Protest Theatre,* and *The Past as Present in Contemporary African American Drama.*

Loren Kruger teaches at the University of Chicago and is the author of *The National Stage* (University of Chicago Press), translator of *The Institutions of Art* by Christa and Peter Bürger (University of Nebraska Press), and editor of *The Autobiography of Leontine Sagan* (Witwatersrand University Press, forthcoming). She is also co-editor of *Theatre Journal.* The essay published here is part of a book-in-progress with the provisional title *Drama of Modernity: South African Plays, Pageants and Publics in Intercultural Context.*

Anthony O'Brien teaches English and World Studies at Queens College, the City University of New York, and has lectured at universities in Senegal and South Africa. His work has appeared in *Callaloo* and *diacritics,* and his book on South African literature and politics in the 1980s is forthcoming from Duke University Press.

Janelle Reinelt is the Chair of Dramatic Art and Dance at the University of California, Davis. Her books include *After Brecht: British Epic Theater* and *Critical Theory and Performance,* edited with Joseph Roach (University of Michigan Press), and *The Performance of Power: Politics and Theatrical Representation,* edited with Sue-Ellen Case (University of Iowa Press). She is the former editor of *Theatre Journal.*

Patricia R. Schroeder is Professor of English at Ursinus College where she teaches American literature, modern drama, and women in theater. Her publications include *The Presence of the Past in Modern American Drama* as well as essays on Marsha Norman, Wendy Kesselman, Emily Mann, and Alice Childress. Her latest book, *The Feminist Possibilities of Dramatic Realism*, is forthcoming from Fairleigh Dickinson University Press.

Katrin Sieg is Assistant Professor of German at Indiana University. She is the author of *Exiles, Eccentrics, Activists: Women in Contemporary German Theater*, and has published articles on German theater, as well as on feminist and queer performance theory.

Diana Taylor is Professor of Spanish and Chair of Comparative Literature at Dartmouth College. She is the author of *Theatre of Crisis: Drama and Politics in Latin America*, which won the Best Book Award given by the New England Council on Latin American Studies, and of *Disappearing Acts: Spectacles of Gender and Nationalism in Argentina's "Dirty War"* (Duke University Press). She co-edited *Negotiating Performance in Latin/o America: Gender, Sexuality and Theatricality* (Duke University Press) and *Radical Mothers: Politics and Social Change in the 20th Century*) (University Press of New England).

Mary Trotter is a doctoral candidate in the Interdisciplinary Ph.D. in Theater and Drama at Northwestern University. She received her M.A. in English at the University of Texas at Austin. She is currently writing a dissertation on the influence of political performance on national identity in turn-of-the-century Ireland.

Adam Versényi is Associate Professor of Dramaturgy at the University of North Carolina at Chapel Hill and Dramaturg for PlayMakers Repertory Company. He has written widely on Latin American theater including his book, *Theatre in Latin America: Religion, Politics, and Culture from Cortés to the 1980s* (Cambridge University Press). He is currently working on a book, *Theater Under Dictatorship: Argentina, Chile, and Uruguay.*

W. B. Worthen is Professor of English and Theater at Northwestern University, and Director of the Interdisciplinary Ph.D. program in Theater and Drama. He is the author of *The Idea of the Actor* (Princeton University Press), *Modern Drama and the Rhetoric of Theatre* (University of California Press), and of articles on Shakespeare, modern drama, and performance theory. He is past editor of *Theatre Journal* and has recently edited *The HBJ Anthology of Drama* and *Modern Drama: Plays, Criticism, Theory.* He is currently writing a book on Shakespeare, authorship, and twentieth-century performance.